CRIME
& Immigrant Youth

Books Under the General Editorship of
DANIEL CURRAN

CRIME AS STRUCTURED ACTION
by James W. Messerschmidt

EMERGING CRIMINAL JUSTICE
Three Pillars for a Proactive Justice System
by Paul H. Hahn

CRIME CONTROL AND WOMEN
Implications of Criminal Justice Policy
edited by Susan L. Miller

HOW TO RECOGNIZE GOOD POLICING
Problems and Issues
edited by Jean-Paul Brodeur

CRIME AND IMMIGRANT YOUTH
by Tony Waters

CRIME
& Immigrant Youth

Tony Waters

SAGE Publications
International Educational and Professional Publisher
Thousand Oaks London New Delhi

For information:

 SAGE Publications, Inc.
2455 Teller Road
Thousand Oaks, California 91320
E-mail: order@sagepub.com

SAGE Publications Ltd.
6 Bonhill Street
London EC2A 4PU
United Kingdom

SAGE Publications India Pvt. Ltd.
M-32 Market
Greater Kailash I
New Delhi 110 048 India

Printed in the United States of America

Library of Congress Cataloging-in-Publication Data

Waters, Tony
    Crime and immigrant youth / by Tony Waters.
      p. cm.
    Includes bibliographical references and index.
    ISBN 0-7619-1684-9 (cloth: acid-free paper)
    ISBN 0-7619-1685-7 (pbk.: acid-free paper)
    1. Juvenile delinquents—United States. 2. Teenage immigrants—United States. I. Title.
    HV9104 .W423 1998
    364.36'0973—ddc21   98-19775

This book is printed on acid-free paper.

99 00 01 02 03 04 05 7 6 5 4 3 2 1

Acquiring Editor:	C. Terry Hendrix
Production Editor:	Denise Santoyo
Production Assistant:	Nevair Kabakian
Typesetter/Designer:	Lynn Miyata
Cover Designer:	Candice Harman

Contents

Part II. Answering the Question Why: Community and Structure

Part III. Answering the Question How

Part IV. Conclusions

Preface

*I*n the 1990 U.S. Census, Southeast Asians made up 1.5% of California's population. Logically, then, Southeast Asians should make up 1.5% of the prison inmates in California, 1.5% of the college graduates, 1.5% of the engineers, 1.5% of the retirees, and so forth. But they do not. Just how far off this magic 1.5% mark Southeast Asians are was illustrated for me when I reviewed the statistics of the California Youth Authority in 1991. I found that 4.5% of California's most incorrigible youth were Southeast Asian. Of the roughly 9,000 wards of the CYA, 4.5% were Southeast Asians, mostly perpetrators and victims of California's gang wars.

The idea of the Southeast Asian gangster does not fit well, however, with another common stereotype of Southeast Asian youth, the common observation that Vietnamese immigrants are the state's latest "model minority." Here again, a random statistic backs up the point of how well Southeast Asian youth are doing: 8.5% of the 1991 incoming freshman class at the University of California, Davis, were Southeast Asians.

What causes this unusual distribution of Southeast Asian youth in California's juvenile justice system and in its universities? Does this mean that Southeast Asian youth are more delinquent than other youth? Does it meant that they are smarter or more diligent? Is this an issue that is specific to Southeast Asians, or is it the consequence of a more general social process?

The answer this book provides is that "waves" of juvenile delinquency are part of the migration process itself. Analysis of other

migrant groups shows that deviant youthful subcultures (i.e., gangs)
occur among second-generation immigrant youth in a predictable
and systematic fashion. The wealth of data available from the past
100 years of immigration, to California in particular and the United
States in general, points to this consequence. This book is about how
this conclusion was reached.

Why hasn't this conclusion been reached before? The answer to
this question is that migration has rarely been studied as a process.
Rather, single migrations are studied, or social issues associated with
ethnic groups are analyzed. Migration as a process that human groups
undergo is missed in such specific formulations.

Analyses of the Southeast Asians in California illustrate these
problems well. Thus Southeast Asian success is attributed to Confucian
ethics or Vietnamese concepts of filial piety. Crime is explained as a
response to inner-city residence, habits learned during the Vietnam War,
or the inadequacy of school programs. Such explanations are overly
convenient, however, because they ignore the fact that other Asian
immigrant societies, including Asian Indians, Koreans, and Chinese,
are also sending large numbers of students to America's universities
without sharing the legacy of gang activity. Likewise, other immigrant
groups that have not had the legacy of a cruel war have had gang
activity. Mexican, Molokan Russian, Irish, and Polish immigrants all
come to mind.

Anecdotal evidence supporting my hypothesis was unexpectedly
offered to me in the summer of 1993, when I gave an introductory
sociology lecture about social psychologist Erving Goffman's concept
of family or tribal stigma. To illustrate the point that family members
share the stigma of an errant family member, I related stories my
mother had recently told me about the youthful escapades of her Uncle
Charles, some 50 years previously. Uncle Charles had been involved
in gunfights with his neighbors in rural Colorado, ostensibly over
"water rights." My mother was embarrassed about her favorite uncle's
delinquencies and, as a result, was somewhat hesitant when relating
the incidents to me. To illustrate my point about Goffman's concept
of family stigma, I pointed out that the families of today's gang
members have much the same attitude of embarrassment about the
delinquencies of their cousins, nephews, sons, and brothers.

What happened next was somewhat surprising. The class I was
addressing was 15% Southeast Asian, and virtually every one of those

students looked like they wanted to crawl under their desks. Later, one of the Lao students whom I knew better than the others, Kathy, came up to me and explained their reaction. She said, "I thought that you were talking about my 13-year-old brother who has been arrested so many times, and that the whole class would find out. I was sure that you were talking about me." The more I talked with her, and the more I have reflected about her experience and that of my grandfather's family, the more I have come to believe that both family stories illustrate the incongruity that arises when college kids and delinquents come from the same family. These two family histories are, I think, a good way to introduce the central thesis presented here: that immigrant populations have an idiosyncratic relationship with the host society that is best understood as a patterned process. The reason immigrant populations are unusual has more to do with relationships emerging out of the structural circumstances in the host country than with an "Asian work ethic" or "gangland mentality" imported from the home country. There are social structural reasons that both college kids and delinquents emerge from America's immigrant families in such unusual proportions.[1] The following stories about two immigrant families illustrate my point.

KATHY AND SAK

Kathy left Laos for Thailand in the late 1970s as a 5-year-old. In Thailand, she lived in refugee camps with her family until approximately 1982, when she emigrated to the United States. She eventually ended up in North Highlands, one of the poorer areas of Sacramento.

I came to know Kathy better than I know most of my students because a friend of mine, Grant Denney, came to give a guest lecture to my introductory sociology class. I had invited Grant because he has an unusual history of working with Laotian refugees in Sacramento as a result of his two jobs: one as a Sacramento County sheriff's deputy assigned to the county jail, where he is the jail's Asian gang expert, and the other as a fifth- and sixth-grade teacher in the poorer areas of Sacramento. This odd combination of jobs gives Grant an unusual perspective on Sacramento's immigrant communities. The day before Grant was to speak, Kathy introduced herself to me and asked whether the speaker was the same man who had been her fifth-grade teacher and soccer coach. He was. As a result of conversations with Kathy and Grant, I have been able to piece together the story of Kathy's background as a Laotian immigrant in Sacramento.

When Kathy was in Grant's class in 1984, his school district had been recently confronted with an influx of refugee Hmong, Mien, and Laotian students who did not speak English. In an attempt to control the unusual situation, they established special "English as a second language" programs in one of the area junior high schools. Grant, however, picked out Kathy and one other student for "mainstreaming" into a regular English-speaking classroom, even though her language skills were inadequate at the time. As a result, she was sent to the local junior high school. Several years later, concerned with the upsurge in gang activity in the area, Kathy and her family moved into another area of Sacramento, where she attended another of the inner-city high schools. By this time, her mainstreaming was taken for granted, and she took a college-preparation course.

At high school, Kathy had little trouble making good grades. It was at this high school that, relative to the other Lao students who formed her peer group, she emerged as a "college girl." She remembers resisting the pressures from her boyfriend, family, peers, and her own impulses to get married, have children, and reproduce the working-class life—a course that would have been easily available to her. Instead, she somehow managed to find her way to the University of California, Davis, as a freshman in 1990. She did well as a dietetics major and had hopes of going to nursing school after graduation in June 1994. Her social life at college focused on other Lao students and a boyfriend who was half Thai and half Caucasian, but otherwise her focus was directed homeward. She very much felt the weight of responsibility for her younger siblings, her parents, and a 1-year-old nephew who lived with Kathy's parents in Sacramento.[2]

As do many of the immigrant students in my classes, Kathy moved back and forth between the modern college student life and that of her immigrant home. In particular, she has always been concerned about fulfilling her duties as a good daughter to her monolingual Laotian parents, a characteristic that the mass media might attribute to the "Confucian ethic," or to the idea of Asians as a "model minority." In fulfilling this role, she relied on the very different values that her family brought from rural Laos and those she found in the United States. For example, Kathy was particularly pleased that a younger sister had had the character to resist the temptations presented by the "gangsters" at her high school, and had begun classes at San Jose State University in the fall of 1993. Kathy complained to me that this had not always been so; her sister had, as a sophomore and junior, given in to baser impulses and run with a "wild" group, with whom she partied at the expense of studying. Kathy felt so protective of her sister that in early September 1993, she requested time off from my class to accompany her sister to San Jose, a situation made necessary, she explained, by the fact that her monolingual parents would not be able to read the road signs necessary to complete the trip.

Kathy's major familial concern, however, is her 13-year-old brother, Sak, who, far from being the "model minority," has been detained regularly by police since the age of 11. Typically, he has been arrested for violations involving cars and weapons, and has been released fairly quickly due to his age. She says that he is 6 feet tall, which is unusual in the Lao community, and matured physically at a young age. Kathy reports that he is always arrested when he is in association with his "gang" because of his inability to make good judgments in the presence of his friends—a situation that criminologists regard as typical. As a result, he has been arrested a number of times for theft and possession of weapons. Kathy is angry with the American legal system, which she says never scared Sak sufficiently to make him choose better friends.

Kathy thinks that a long period in juvenile detention would at least keep Sak safe from vengeful gangs, even if it does not reform him. A recent gang-related shooting in which one of Sak's friends was paralyzed drove home this point to Kathy, if not Sak. She points out that when Sak is in detention, he always promises to straighten up. Nevertheless, he always ends up hanging around his old friends again, with arrest the inevitable result. Sak's most recent arrest (January 1994) is perhaps illustrative of how Kathy's family has tried to come to grips with what is happening to their family in the United States. Kathy related the story to me after ruefully admitting, with a tip of her head, that once again her brother was "in." My notes of how she described the incident illustrate the paradoxes that are part of the immigrant situation. These include an emphasis on sibling and peer relations (as opposed to parent-child relations); a concern for the concept of "shame," which may have roots in a cultural perspective brought from Asia; and inconsistent beliefs about how the police should behave. Thus at one point Kathy is critical of the police for behaving aggressively, and at another she points out that juvenile detention will be of benefit to her brother. My notes of what Kathy had to say follow:

Ten policemen came with all of their lights on to arrest my brother because they suspected him in a recent shooting. They made everyone in the house come out, but my brother then locked himself in his room. They made him come out and lie on the pavement while they searched his room, but they didn't find any weapons or anything else. They didn't have anything on him! They shouldn't have done it like that, it wasn't right. It shamed my parents so much to have the police come in like that. Then they took [Sak] in on a warrant because he had not been going to school [i.e., violating a judge's probation order that he attend school]. Why should not going to school result in such an extreme response? . . . I am the only member of our family to whom [Sak] still talks. I visited him in detention recently, and we both cried. He promises that when he gets out he will go to school and do the right thing. I know he would try, but I'm not sure that he can. Maybe the detention will shake him up. But I don't know. Each time they keep him only for a week or two and release him, I guess because the jails are too crowded. I wish they would keep him longer. At least when he is in they cannot kill him. Maybe it is better. This helps my mother too since she is afraid all the time for him.

Much of Kathy's concern for Sak focuses on the effects that his troubles have had on her mother. In particular, she believes that her mother has steadily lost weight worrying about whether or not Sak will return home. Nevertheless, Kathy has hopes for her brother. She thinks that he is quite clever in his own way, and recalls with amusement how, 2 years previously, at age 11, he taught his then 19-year-old college-girl sister to drive a manual transmission car.

GRANDPA AND UNCLE CHARLES

The story of Kathy and Sak is ultimately just an individual anecdote. It is an interesting story, but is it illustrative of a wider problem of youthful crime in immigrant communities? A first step toward an affirmative answer is to examine yet another anecdote, this one from a group and location far removed from today's inner-city Sacramento. The story is from my own family, part of which migrated from rural

Sweden to the Rocky Mountains of Colorado in the 1890s. Although the cultures and places are very different, this story and that of Kathy and Sak illustrate very well the dynamics between immigrant parents and their children, as well as between second-generation siblings.

I have always known that my grandfather was the son of Swedish immigrants, but until recently I never identified him or his siblings with the issues of delinquency. Recent recollections by my mother and hindsight provided by this project, however, have begun to make me believe that they are as typical of the immigrant experience as Kathy and her brother Sak.

My great-grandparents came to the United States in the 1890s and settled in a Colorado gold-mining town. My great-grandfather managed to find at least some gold, and was able to buy a 640-acre ranch high in the Rocky Mountains. His first son, my grandfather, was born there in 1904. Seven more children, six boys and a girl, followed. Six of the eight children, all boys, survived to maturity. Uncle Charles was the second son, born in 1908.

My grandfather was the "college boy" of the family, and to this day presents himself as the straight arrow. In a journal he recently gave me, he proudly quotes his first-grade teacher, who wrote in 1911: "You were a very good and industrious boy. I remember that I walked down with you at recess one time and we could roll rocks down the hill into the Lake Fork River. You said, in a short while 'Let's go back and do some more readin' writin' and arithmetic.' " My grandfather left the ranch at an early age, and although always conscientious about his family duties, he fulfilled them from a distance. By 1930 he had a college degree, was married, and was living in Los Angeles, where my mother was born in 1931.

My information about Uncle Charles comes from my mother, who visited the ranch as a girl. He was her favorite uncle. Unlike my grandfather, he never bothered to finish college, and by the time my mother came to know him in the 1930s, he had acquired an eccentric image, letting his hair and beard grow. He was a doting uncle, which was important for a city girl in the wilds of Colorado. In particular she recalls his efforts to teach her to ride a horse, a pregnant mare by the name of Flicka.

On the other hand, my mother acquired in the city her father's college-boy repulsion for Uncle Charles's other exploits. Two sets of incidents remain in her mind. First, he obtained a commission as a forest ranger, which he then used as a license to shoot deer out of season; and second, there were legends about the gunfights he had had with a neighboring family, ostensibly over rights to ditch water for cattle, but as likely over issues of youthful honor.

Uncle Charles has, of course, stopped his poaching and gunslinging. After the ranch was sold in the 1940s, he had an itinerant career staking out his own diamond and gold mines in Arizona, Colorado, and Arkansas with his mother, for whom he cared until her death in 1973, a service highly appreciated by his more conventional older brother. In the 1960s, because he did not want to become identified with the hippie movement, he cut his hair. He has, however, kept his beard. Obviously, he has not led a conventional middle-class life, as his brother sought. Currently, he lives in a trailer in a small Colorado town and is known as a quiet eccentric.

Do the two sets of life histories described above—that of a Sacramento Lao college girl and her delinquent brother, and that of my grandfather and his brother in turn-of-the-century rural Colorado—have anything to do with each other? Might Sak simply become a quiet "aged-out" eccentric like Uncle Charles? In 50 or 60 years, will Kathy recollect the time she spent with her brother in juvenile hall, or will that simply become an unmentioned part of the autobiography she relates to her grandchildren? More important for this study, do the experiences of Kathy's family and my family have anything to do with the statistics that show that Southeast Asian youth are incarcerated in the California Youth Authority and attend UC Davis in disproportionately large numbers?

There is no definitive answer with respect to these individuals. However, it is my belief that these examples illustrate a common social process rooted in migration. Both cases illustrate a process in which children from immigrant communities grow up with unusual relationships with their parents and peers. Kathy's unusual relationship with her brother, and her insistence that she is needed "to read the signs on the road to San Jose," is an unusual reversal in the normal child-parent dependency relationship, to say the least—as does the case of Uncle Charles. Another consequence is that the younger generations of immigrant families create subcultures independent of the control of their elders. This results in their unusually strong dependence on peer relationships.

NOTES

1. This is a reference to criminologist Albert Cohen's (1955) description of working-class society in the United States in the 1950s. In developing strain theory to explain juvenile delinquency, Cohen said that working-class youth responded to the blocked opportunities created by poverty by conforming, by overcompensating and becoming "college-boy" overachievers, or by inverting middle-class values and becoming delinquents.

2. This nephew is the son of an older sister who lives in Texas.

Acknowledgments

*I*n reviewing this volume, I am impressed at how much my central theoretical thrust emerges out of conversations with Frank Hirtz. He first pointed out to me the centrality of the "process of migration," and that this idea leads to a conclusion that youthful crime waves will not be particularly sensitive to policy prescriptions. He also developed my interest in the sociology of law, forming one of the two legs on which the work stands.

Jack Goldstone encouraged me to pursue studies of comparative historical techniques for this work, as well as a number of other papers. Jim Cramer pointed me toward the demographic works that are the basis of the demography portion of this book. In his statistics classes he also taught me to think of many social problems in terms of dependent and independent variables.

Norman Skonovd, through his applied work at the California Youth Authority and his experience teaching at the University of California, Davis, bridged many of the gaps between academia and field research. Because of this he was able to offer incisive comments. I am also grateful for the access that his introductions gave me to the law enforcement community.

Lyn Lofland and Diane Felmlee both taught me about the social psychological perspective, which greatly informs Chapter 7 as well as much of my other sociological work. Discussions with Debora Paterniti helped develop the "definition of the situation," a concept that underlies Chapter 7.

The initial research for this project and my doctoral dissertation (Waters, 1995a) was funded by a 1991 California Policy Seminar grant; my thanks go to the California Policy Seminar for permission to use here some of the material from the working paper that grew out of that project, *Laotians in the Criminal Justice System* (Waters & Cohen, 1993). Likewise, the criminological background presented in Chapter 2 owes much to Professor Cohen's advice.

Many others have wittingly and unwittingly contributed to my thinking about immigrant and/or juvenile delinquency. These include Kouei Cho Saeteurn, Trang Duong, Fred Goraieb, Pearl Del Rosario, Ed Lemert, Meng Chiew Saeteurn, Dario Melossi, Alan Kobayashi, Grant Denney, Somkhit Khounamany, Laura Leonelli, Kao Vang, Saeng Saechao, Bill Waroff, Vince Macias, Joe Astin, Manh Cho Saeteurn, Bob Shadley, Roy Ropp, Randy Yen, Kathy Negri, Roberto Sarabia, Ray Rodriguez, Susan Hardwick, Nou Vang, La Khamphilanavoung, Maria Anguiano, and Jason Taylor. Candy Priano and Laura Sederberg assisted with the conversion of the figures into camera-ready Pagemaker documents.

At California State University, Chico, the collegiality of the Department of Sociology and Social Work has provided an excellent working environment for me to complete my work on this volume.

Part I

Framing the Problem

CHAPTER 1

Explaining Youthful Crime in Immigrant Communities

*T*his book is about crime in immigrant communities. This is an old subject in discussions of immigration to the United States and elsewhere. Host groups everywhere use new immigrant groups as scapegoats for social problems that may or may not have anything to do with immigration. Such scapegoating is only a small part of the issue of immigration and crime, however. Discussion of scapegoating cannot get to the heart of the matter, which in fact involves specific criminal acts typically committed within immigrant communities themselves. Irrespective of ambiguities of definition, there are outbreaks of youthful crime in immigrant communities, and there are gangs of immigrant youth that commit crimes. Sometimes these groups may be bigger or smaller, and the acts they commit may be more or less common. These outbreaks of crime may or may not coincide with scapegoating.

My thesis is that the formation of youthful gangs outside the norms of either the home culture or the host culture is a product of the process of migration. To explain how I have reached this conclusion, I discuss below what migration is as a process. I then put this together with a view of crime in immigrant communities, and ask what it is in migration that leads at times to waves of criminal activity.[1]

CONVENTIONAL WISDOM?

Excluded from my thesis are traditional explanations for crime, gang activity, and juvenile delinquency in immigrant communities. First, my thesis is contrary to the idea that crime is inherent to any particular cultural group and not others. Standard criminological wisdom reasons that because youthful "subcultures" and ethnic "subcultures" are involved with outbreaks of youthful crime in immigrant communities, there is an inherent relationship between the two, meaning that violence, theft, and gang activities are part of the values of some cultures and not others (Cohen, 1955; Jankowski, 1991; Long, 1996; Padilla, 1992). But despite the use of the common term *subculture*, youth subcultures and immigrant subcultures are two very different things. Youth subcultures are found in any modern society, whereas immigrant subcultures (which may also have youth subcultures) are generated only by groups that migrate. After all, if youth and immigrant subcultures were the same, there would be immigrant groups from some cultural areas that have never had youthful crime, and others that have always have had youthful crime, but outbreaks of youthful crime have been found in immigrant communities from areas as diverse as rural Laos, urban Kiev, Ireland, and Mexico.

Nevertheless, the argument that crime is inherent to particular groups (e.g., you can't understand Chinese gangs without reference to tongs, or Mexican gangs without focusing on machismo) continues to be common. Ironically, similar reasoning is used to explain the outstanding success of some immigrant groups. For example, it is often asserted that the "Confucian ethic" brought from Asia leads to unusually high respect for education among Asian immigrants, and therefore (by extension) a youthful subculture focused on achievement.

Second, my thesis is inconsistent with the idea that youthful crime results from "brutalization" learned as part of a specific historic circumstance. For example, it is often asserted that violence among Southeast Asian youth is the inheritance of practices legitimated during the Vietnam War (California State Attorney General, 1989; Long, 1996; Smith & Tarallo, 1993). My contention is that although this experience may be used to provide after-the-fact explanations of specific acts for some groups—familiarity with particular types of weapons, for instance—it has little to do with the actual causes of outbreaks of youthful crime.

As will become apparent in Chapter 2, neither of the theories noted above explains what is a basic empirical fact: A single immigrant group will at times have high rates of gang formation and at other times low rates. It is my contention that this is due the very nature of immigrant groups, and how immigrant groups socialize the second-generation children—that is, those born to the immigrants themselves.

WHY IMMIGRANT GROUPS ARE DIFFERENT

Immigration has been central to the historical and social development of the modern United States. The process began with the large-scale European influx that started about 1840 and continues today with the arrival of Asians, Latin Americans, and Eastern Europeans. How successive groups of immigrants have been integrated into U.S. society has often been evaluated, generally from a perspective focusing on a specific social phenomenon in a particular group at a particular time, such as street-corner "gangs" among Italians (Whyte, 1943, 1993), Korean entrepreneurs (Light & Bonacich, 1988), unemployed aerospace workers (Beers, 1993), academic success among Vietnamese (Caplan, Whitmore, & Choy, 1989), gangs among Vietnamese (Long, 1996), political success among Cubans (Portes & Rumbaut, 1990), and language acquisition among Mexicans (Cummins, 1981; Espinosa & Massey, 1997). Typically, such research has been undertaken from a cross-sectional ethnographic perspective focused on one interesting social issue relevant to one particular group at one particular time. Lost in this type of analysis is the sense that migration is a process that continues through time, involving shifts in relationships and social locations. In other words, the context of the problem is lost. For example, a study of academic success among impoverished first-generation Vietnamese immigrant boat people (Caplan et al., 1989) does not have much to say about the gang activity of American-born children of Vietnamese in 1993 (compare Long, 1996). The problems presented are radically different, even though the issues involve the same young people from the same immigrant group.

MIGRATION AS A SOCIAL PROCESS

From a logical perspective, at least three postmigration generations are needed for a complete birth-to-grave pattern of social interaction to become "encoded" into any kind of "tradition." This process can be followed logically: The immigrants themselves by definition have not been socialized into the host-country values as children. As a result, they cannot directly socialize their own children (i.e., the second generation) into the norms of the host society. Rather, the children are socialized into host-country values through an unusual dependence on peer group interactions, schools, mass media, and perhaps nonparental host-country adults.[2] Following this ideal-typical model, these children of immigrants are then able to socialize their own children (i.e., the third generation) in a "normal" fashion. As a result, only the third-generation children are socialized in the "normal" or typical fashion found in the "stable" population. This process may be interrupted, but nevertheless it is the ideal in an immigrant society like the United States, where social norms emphasize the desirability of acculturation and assimilation.

It is important to consider the logical sequence, or what natural scientists call the *progression toward equilibrium*, if one is to understand migration as a process that explains how the grandchild of an immigrant has a cultural orientation different from that of his or her grandparents from Asia, Europe, Africa, or Latin America. The ideal-typical result of this process of migration is that today, the third-generation American grandchild of a Polish peasant is as much a foreigner in the natal village of his or her own grandparents as in a Latin American, Asian, European, or African village. And more important, the American grandchild perceives the world differently than did his or her immigrant grandparents. The question, then, is: What are the sociological processes that so inevitably lead to this result?

Two generalizations are relevant to answering this questions, both of which are rooted in the logical interactive sequence. One emerges out of the social psychological changes that take place during migration, and the second involves the structural context in which the migration event takes place. The social psychological shifts occur as the reference group from which identity emerges changes radically. This occurs in a social structural context, which, as in any social group, determines with whom an individual is likely to associate. This social structural circumstance also varies with the immigrant group. In the modern United States, it has been structured by—among other things—education, income, availability of capital resources, racial attitudes, and social class (Pedraza & Rumbaut, 1996; Portes, 1995).

As will become apparent in the discussion below, a particularly important social structural feature of immigrant populations is the age and gender structure of the arriving immigrant population. This is because the emigrating population is never a random sample from the sending population. There is always self-selection for age, and often for gender. This self-selection in turn affects who the young can model when acting out the social code in the new environment.

Thus the two most important generalizations that can be made about the process of migration can be summarized as follows:

1. Migration causes a process of identity transformation, which emerges as the patterns of past relationships change and new ones develop in a new social environment. Logically, the major discontinuity in this process is expected to be between the immigrants, who have personal memories of the home country, and their children, who are socialized by the social institutions found in the new country.

2. This process of identity transformation occurs in the context of the social structure in which immigrants find themselves. This social structure includes many of the traditional correlates of sociology, such as education, income, availability of capital resources, racial attitudes, and social class. This context is shaped by the unusual sex and/or age structures inherent to immigrant groups, as well as the inevitable status loss that occurs during relocation and resettlement.[3]

MIGRATION AS A PROCESS AND THE CONCEPT OF BECOMING

Describing how these generational changes affect the process of integration into American society has been difficult. In large part this is because the actual mechanics of the integration process are embarrassing or "discreditable" to the successive reference groups toward which immigrants orient their behavior (see Goffman, 1963/1986, pp. 41-48). Ewa Morawska (1985, p. 4) describes this as the adaptation or "becoming" of an immigrant group faced with the "structurally induced" uncertainty inherent to the existence of immigrant laborers and their families in early-20th-century America. This process, Morawska writes, is

> about the coping and adaptive strategies used by [immigrants] and their children to solve problems and realize cultural goals and expectations in a restricted and uncertain environment. The process of coping or "appropriating" any space available under constrained circumstances generates new purposes and dilemmas. They are dealt with as people cooperate and invent ways to bring the environment into closer conformity with their purposes. (p. 3)

Because the purposes and dilemmas Morawska describes inherently do not have precedent, the solutions are often arrived at in a halting and uncertain fashion that does not meet the ideals of the old culture or of the new. In her discussion of Polish Americans in Johnstown, Pennsylvania, Morawska (1985, p. 7) describes this process as the becoming of an urban industrial society. Morawska notes that this means that immigrant and native create varying blends of culture, which may or may not "make sense" to either the immigrant or observers.

How does the process of "becoming" work in immigrant communities? How did the children of the Polish peasant villages of the 1890s become the grandparents of college students protesting American involvement in the Vietnam War in the 1960s? Or, to use a fictional example, how did it become possible for *All in the Family*'s Michael Stivic, the liberal grandson of Polish immigrants, to end up marrying Archie Bunker's daughter?

What is clear is that, as in any form of social reproduction, culture continues to emerge out of individual action. And it is clear that as with all social action, this reproduction is grounded in past experiences. In the case of the East Central Europeans described by Morawska (1985), for the parents these experiences were in Polish peasant villages, whereas for their children they took place in American grammar schools. For immigrant parents, this means that decisions about socializing children are rooted in the experiences of their own childhoods, which they lived in a different country and using standards that may not have relevance to the social environment of the urban industrial United States. In the case of groups that migrated from peasant societies to urban industrial neighborhoods, the contrast is extreme. This change presents a dilemma that can be thought of as a dichotomy requiring a shift from "traditional" forms of social organization to those of a modern industrial society.[4] On the other hand, migration does not induce change only when the move has been between "traditional" forms of social organization and modern industrial society; change occurs also between modern industrial societies.

BECOMING AND DISBECOMING:
A NEW SOCIETY EMERGES

If parents had the sole responsibility for transmitting values to their children, their having memories rooted in peasant societies would not be a problem. But socialization in a mass national society is a shared responsibility. The process begins with a heavy reliance on parents, but by the time a child reaches the age of 2, mass society begin to play a role. This happens in a variety of ways, including through exposure to the mass media, peer group interactions, and, ultimately, the process of mass education. Under ideal circumstances, the cultural messages conveyed by all these sources are closely linked. In practical terms, this means that some consistency of message can be expected among PBS's Mr. Rogers, Captain Kangaroo, Saturday-morning cartoons, peer group interactions, public education, toddler dance classes, and what parents model. Indeed, even a cursory examination of such socializing agents reveals similar messages about the nature of the individual and his or her role in society.

For the immigrant family, however, this consistency is, to borrow Morawska's term, "uneven." At the simplest level, it is a common-sense observation that immigrant parents who themselves were not exposed to the socialization opportunities offered by Mr. Rogers, Captain Kangaroo, and Saturday-morning cartoons are unlikely to use such tools strategically in the context of either home society norms or those of the host society. The same principle applies to other social control mechanisms of mass society, such as mass education, mass media, law, and government. Furthermore, the opposite is true: The tools that immigrant parents do have an intuitive grasp of—that is, those they have brought from their home countries—are likely to be ineffective. The point is that the norms are different, and therefore a discontinuity exists between the immigrant household and the social world in which the child lives.

THE STRUCTURAL UNCERTAINTY OF
IMMIGRANT CHILDREN: AN EXAMPLE

The following quotations—one from a social scientist, one from the child of an immigrant, and a third from an immigrant elder—illustrate the process of migration. These statements show clearly the intergenerational conflict inherent to the transmission of cultural norms across immigrant generations:

> *The social scientist:* Almost any attitude, any routine of life may precipitate the battle between the old and the new. The equilibrium disturbed, the young generation find, however, few adequate adaptive adjustments [in the norms passed on to them by elders] with which to meet the new conditions of life. Tensions and unrest arise. Life in its very essentials is in an upheaval. The road from the old to the new is uncharted and dangerous at every step. . . . The younger generation [builds] up its own society relatively independent of the influence of its elders.

> *The child of an immigrant:* Father still lives in the past and thinks himself very important. But really he does not understand very much here. He makes life very hard for us, and we cannot get any fun with him. He gets terrible angry if we have some fun on our own.

> *The immigrant elder:* The young ones won't pay attention to our traditional councils anymore, because the . . . government doesn't permit them to have any authority over our own. We can't enforce our will. [At home] they would have had to listen

to their elders [or they would have been subject to very severe corporal punishment]. Here the government won't let us enforce our decisions, though. So the kids run wild. They are good students in elementary school and junior high school, and even do better than the American kids. But then in high school everything goes wrong, and suddenly the American kids are doing better than ours. Please explain to the government that if we were permitted to handle our own problems, everything would be much better, and our young people would be good citizens and students.

These speakers could all be describing the same migration event. The youth's claim that his father "still lives in the past . . . but really he does not understand very much here" is consistent with the father's explanation that unaccustomed government interference in child rearing is what permits children to run wild. The summing up by the social scientist presents a plausible explanation for how the discordant views of the youth and immigrant father coexist. It is almost as if the three accounts represent conflicting versions of the same event. In fact, however, they are descriptions of different events from very different times and places. The first observation is a combination of the writing of sociologist Pauline Young(1932, p. 160), who studied the Molokan Russians living in the Boyle Heights neighborhood of Los Angeles in the mid-1920s, and the work of William Foote Whyte (1943, 1993), who studied street-corner culture in an Italian slum of Boston in the 1930s. The second is from sociologist Shmuel Eisenstadt's (1959) description of an interview he did with an immigrant Jewish boy in the late 1940s in British Palestine. The final comment was made to me in 1991 by a Laotian Mien elder in Sacramento, California.[5]

The reason these views of very different events match so well is that they describe the same process of intergenerational conflict. Both the youth and the elder make unspoken assumptions about what an ideal society would be like. But in doing this, they rely on very different standards for judging legitimate social behavior, despite the close kinship relations to which they refer. My point is that this discontinuity, although not desirable, is "normal" to immigrant families; it is what is known in shorthand as the "second-generation problem." Embedded in each statement are different assumptions about the nature of age and authority, relationships between the government and its citizens, and the role of individuals within the family.

As I have noted, these three statements about intergenerational relations fit together well despite the fact that they come from completely different times, spaces, and cultures. This makes sense only if we assume that the observers are talking about a common social process. This common process is the socialization of second-generation immigrant youth.[6]

But what does such "becoming" mean for the integration of the immigrant group into the new society? What does it mean for how studies of such groups are undertaken? Can a predictive model of how a particular social problem of immigrant groups emerges in the process of migration be developed out of the assumptions of such a description?

The process illustrated by the three statements above is what Morawska calls the becoming of American culture; it is a problem of identity that many youth face in both immigrant and nonimmigrant communities. But it is also inevitably the *disbecoming* of the home culture. This process is apparent in what a student of mine wrote about Lynelyn Long's (1993) book about Laotian society in Thai refugee camps:

> It was intriguing to hear stories of how life was in refugee camps since I was too young to remember my own experiences [as a 5-year-old]. The book is very informative of the different lives and cultures of families in the refugee camps. . . . Perhaps it may be too painful for some of the older generations to recall that time in their lives. I don't remember my parents talking about it in great detail, but they did mention how awful it was. The book reminded me of how little I knew about my refugee experience or about the history of my country [Laos]. I don't even recall the name of the camp [we lived in]. It was also funny to know that even though I am Laotian, I couldn't pronounce some of the cities or words in Lao. A visit and a talk with my parents is in need.

PEER GROUP CULTURE IN IMMIGRANT GROUPS

One effective way to study how norms are transmitted in immigrant groups is to look at peer group culture, because peer group socialization is very important in immigrant groups undergoing a cross-generational process of becoming and disbecoming. Certainly, my Laotian student Kathy (discussed in the preface) had an unusual relationship with her younger brother and sister. The street-corner groups in Boston's Little Italy in the 1930s that Whyte (1943, 1993) describes and Thrasher's (1927, 1963) descriptions of "the gang" deal with similar issues.

Other unusual relationships are found in more private spheres. In particular, the relationships between immigrant teenage women and their peers are interesting. Indeed, Kathy's descriptions of the pressures she resisted to "party" and have children are probably an indication of such unusual relationships. Of these social categories, however, the youthful gang is the only social grouping that has been systematically assessed by the social sciences across time. This is because crime is an emotional issue and criminal behavior has an impact on the wider society, which is willing to fund the research needed to find "solutions" to this social problem. As it has for many other researchers, this interest helped point me toward the subject as well.

A HYPOTHESIS: YOUTHFUL CRIME IN IMMIGRANT COMMUNITIES AND THE PROCESS OF MIGRATION

The conclusion that follows from the above discussion is that migrant groups are "at risk" for the formation of delinquent subcultures during the critical second generation of the migration process. Immigrant populations are at risk for youthful crime when they have a large cohort of young second-generation males who are socialized into host-country norms faster than their parents. Thus two variables in particular are relevant. First, there must be a large cohort of young males. This may be due to the immigration of large numbers of young boys in the immigrant stream, or to the birth of a large number of children in the host country. Not every immigrant population contains a large cohort of young males. However, for those that do, the rate and way young boys are socialized into host-country society become important. Second, there must be strong pressure for these boys to be integrated into the host society.

Thus it is hypothesized that there will be an upsurge in gang activity when two conditions are met:

1. A large cohort of young immigrant boys reaches the at-risk age for gang activity (i.e., 15-25), and

2. this group of young boys is rapidly integrated into host-country institutions (e.g., schools), creating a process of becoming and unbecoming.

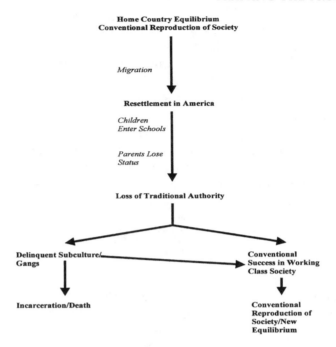

Figure 1.1. Path Model Describing How High Incidence of Youthful Crime
Emerges in Immigrant Communities

When these conditions are met, an outbreak in youthful crime
emerges coincident with the becoming and unbecoming inherent to the
process of migration. Figure 1.1 illustrates how this works. The top of
the figure shows how low rates of youthful crime would be expected
immediately after immigration. This is the period during which young
males (and young females) adapt to U.S. society. At the same time, in
some immigrant populations, large numbers of children are being born.
In these cases, neither prerequisite of the emergence of youthful subcultures exists. However, the roots of the problem have begun, as the status
of the parents drops following immigration. As a consequence, the
parents slowly lose control over their sons as adolescence approaches.
Likewise, it is during this period, when crime rates may be particularly
low, that young males begin to find the subculture of the youthful peer
group particularly attractive. After the family's drop in social status
becomes apparent to parent and youth alike, and peer culture is strengthened as a consequence, the incidence of youthful crime rates is likely to
increase.

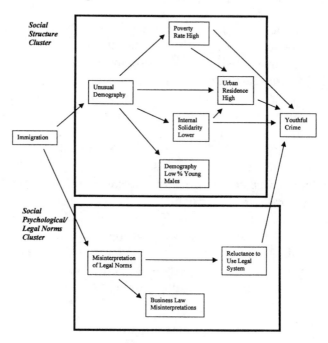

Figure 1.2. Path Model Showing the Prerequisites of the Emergence of Youthful Crime in Immigrant Communities

Although the path diagram in Figure 1.1 explains how the adjustments in relationships that emerge out of the process of migration work, it does not explain why some groups have waves of youthful crime and others do not. This, I contend, is because for the process described above to take place, there must also be a structural context. The empirical data discussed below indicate that this context emerges in some groups and not in others. The investigation of what separates immigrant communities that have major youthful crime waves from those that do not is the subject of this book.

Most important are the structural prerequisites of a high incidence of youthful crime. As for any group, the most important prerequisite is a large proportion of young males in a population. For example, it is common sense that populations that do not have large cohorts of young males will not have major waves of youthful crime. Figure 1.2 presents a path model that shows how the process of migration develops with respect to other social structural and social psychological variables. Likewise, social status, including social class and residence in

urban areas, should also influence rates of youthful crime. All such
factors affect the rates of youthful crime that emerge in immigrant
groups, and all are related to the process of immigration. As I will show,
particularly in the case of immigrant groups, variables such as demographics, residence, and poverty can vary a great deal as the groups
and individuals adjust. For example, immigrant groups can have
group-specific "baby booms" when large groups of fertile immigrants
are resettled (Gordon, 1990). Likewise, some groups tend to settle in
urban inner cities, whereas others settle in rural or suburban areas.
Some groups have disproportionately large numbers of upper-middle-
class professionals in the arriving cohorts, whereas others are dominated by working-class peasants. The ways these characteristics vary
across time help to explain the "why" of youthful crime in immigrant
groups. I will address these issues in Chapters 4 through 6, where I
conclude that the primary underlying structural factor is the age and
gender structure of the arriving population.

A THEORY OF YOUTHFUL CRIME AND
THE PROCESS OF MIGRATION

The central thesis of this book is that the formation of youthful gangs
outside the norms of either the home or the host culture is inherent
to the process of migration. Before showing how this process works in
actual cases, however, I would like to specify the conditions that are
part of the robust process out of which such youthful subcultures
emerge. Most (but not all) immigrant groups eventually face the
dilemma of raising children in the new culture.[7] When and how this
process occurs depends on the circumstances in which each immigrant
group finds itself. Consistent with how the following chapters are
organized, the relevant variables are divided into social structural
clusters. Chapters 4 through 6 discuss the relative importance of sex
and age structures, social cohesiveness, and socioeconomic status in
predicting the incidence of youthful crime. Chapter 7 provides an
analysis of the social psychology involved in the way outbreaks of
youthful crime are perceived by immigrant and host communities.
Together, Chapters 4 through 7 make up the meat of my argument,
explaining how and why youthful crime emerges in immigrant communities. More complete summaries of all the chapters are presented below.

In Chapter 2, I describe past approaches to youthful crime in immigrant communities, and in the process place the conclusions that I draw into the context of past discussions. I test the empirical record against the proposed model and show that the model cannot be validated because of specific shortcomings in how previous authors have assessed the data. I then use the conclusions reached to speculate about how data could be developed to reach a more definitive conclusion.

Chapter 3 is a statement of the methods needed to deal with the limitations of criminological data, and how existing data can be reorganized to develop a dependent variable that reflects the variations among immigrant groups and across time. In this chapter I identify five immigrant groups that are appropriate for the study of youthful crime in immigrant communities and describe the variations among them. The result of this chapter is an ordinal-level dependent variable called *youthful crime*. I construct this dependent variable by developing a detailed description of how youthful crime has varied in different migrant groups.

In Chapter 4, I present age and gender demographics of various migrant groups and analyze the points at which particular cohorts of children (mainly boys) enter the at-risk age for criminal activity, arrest, and incarceration. These points are calculated relative to the migration events themselves. Related to these points are the sex ratios of the arriving populations, because these can affect exogamy and the level of involvement of host-country nationals in the raising of the youth. I conclude Chapter 4 by noting that age structure is the single most important prerequisite of a high incidence of youthful crime in an immigrant community.

In Chapter 5, I discuss the degree of cohesiveness within immigrant communities. More cohesive groups are able to pool the available information about how the youthful environment is to be interpreted, and as a result have more effective social control. I conclude that if social cohesion is internally generated, it can be important in certain circumstances in suppressing the rate of youthful crime. However, it is not as important as the age structure of the youthful population.

In Chapter 6, I consider various socioeconomic conditions among immigrant populations. This is an important variable, because the poverty and discrimination suffered by many immigrant groups are often cited as important explanatory factors in discussions of youthful crime. Likewise, most (but not all) immigrants are likely to have poorer educational backgrounds than host-country natives. Both of these elements are known to have direct correlations with rates of youthful crime independent of migration status, and for this reason need to be accounted for. I conclude Chapter 6 with the observation that, despite a theoretical expectation to the contrary, in the case of immigrant groups, poor socioeconomic conditions do not necessarily correlate well with a high incidence of youthful crime. Certainly, as a variable, low socioeconomic status does not have the explanatory value of fluctuations in the gender and age structure of immigrant group populations.

Criminal law, and how it is perceived and applied, has a great deal of variability across space, time, and migrant groups. This variable has a great deal to do with how members of immigrant groups come to be perceived by social control agencies, as well as how immigrants themselves perceive the law and the relationship of the individual to the state. I discuss these issues in Chapter 7, where I conclude that this social psychology of migration is in fact a "constant" that is "normal" to the process of becoming and disbecoming. As a cause of youthful crime, this constant can be trivial when there is a small proportion of young males in a population. However, when the proportion of young males in a population rises, this constant serves as an "accelerator" that causes the incidence of youthful crime to rise beyond what would be expected in a nonimmigrant population.

The key to the theory of youthful crime in immigrant groups is the interaction among the four factors covered in this volume: demographics, social cohesion, socioeconomics, and social psychological variables. When used with the caution inherent to such techniques, these factors can allow us to make predictions about the processes that particular groups of immigrant children are likely to go through. In Chapter 8, I summarize the significance of this argument for the migration, criminology, gang, and policy literature, emphasizing again the important role of age and gender demographics. I also discuss the theoretical implications of this study of migration processes, and reach the logical conclusion that as long as the United States remains a free society with a continuing demand for cheap immigrant labor, the second-generation issue of youthful crime and gangs in immigrant communities will persist, despite the efforts (few of which will be successful) of social service agencies to prevent and control the spread of youthful crime in immigrant communities.

NOTES

1. Note the causal direction. Migration processes lead to crime, not the other way around. Crime does not lead to migration by the perpetrator, except in the most trivial of circumstances. That is, a child's getting a criminal record would only in the most unusual circumstances cause mass international migration.

2. William Foote Whyte's (1943, 1993) ethnography of an Italian American slum in Boston, *Street Corner Society*, provides perhaps the best example of the unusual nature of second-generation socialization (see particularly Whyte, 1993, pp. xviii-xix).

3. Notably, this emphasis on the second generation differs from the arguments made by many current analysts of migration, who claim that there are fundamental differences between the immigrants in the post-1965 wave of immigration to the urban industrial United States and those in earlier waves. Portes (1995, pp. 248-275), based on an analysis of second-generation immigrants, claims that the cultural adaptation of their offspring (i.e., the third generation) will be different from that of past immigrants to the United States. My view is notably different, and emphasizes the common process of intergenerational adjustment that occurred during both migrations to urban industrial America.

4. I am aware of the attacks on the concept of linear-polar conceptions of tradition and modernity. I agree with Morawska (1985) that the two concepts should not be thought of as extremes on a continuum. Particularly problematic is the fact that such concepts do not take account of cultural variation. However, the use of these concepts as opposites is, I think, still useful. Modern concepts of the individual, the family, bureaucratic organization, capitalism, mass communication, and equality form a cluster that can be contrasted with "traditional" conceptions.

5. The letters quoted in Thomas and Znaniecki's *The Polish Peasant in Europe and America* (1920/1995) contain passages remarkably similar to the three statements provided here. Thrasher's book *The Gang* (1927, 1963) also contains similar accounts.

6. The Mien elder went on to complain about how Mien children, using information they had obtained in American schools, threatened their parents with arrest for child abuse should the parents use any type of corporal punishment. Mien parents, unaware of the nuances of California law, responded with the frustration described above. This is a stark reminder of what Morawska's (1985) uneven becoming can mean in a concrete immigration situation.

7. In some countries and in some periods, immigration policies have done away with the need of immigrant groups to raise their children in the new culture. Czarist Russia (Waters, 1995b) and mid-20th-century Thailand (Hamilton & Waters, 1995, 1997), two disparate examples, legally excluded immigrants from interactions with host-country institutions. In both cases, schools

were established for home-country instruction in the country of settlement. In the United States, of course, there have also been cases of legal exclusion that meant that immigrant groups established separate social institutions and, as a consequence, never were socialized into the mainstream society. Obvious examples include the Chinese in 19th-century California and African slaves and freemen in the antebellum United States.

CHAPTER 2

Youthful Crime and Migration
The View From Criminology

Youthful crime in immigrant groups has typically been addressed from the perspective of criminology. During the past 100 years or so, many criminologists have applied to this problem various theories developed to explain crime in inner cities. As the following review shows, however, they have by and large been unable to develop a predictive model of when, where, and how youthful crime will emerge in immigrant groups. Thus they continue to be confused when crime waves occur (and do not occur) in immigrant communities.

As will become apparent below, the problem of crime among immigrant youth remains unsolved because it is rooted in the challenges associated with the cross-generational transmission of culture in immigrant groups, and not in such issues as "social disorganization," "strain," "subcultures," "social control," and "labeling." In large part, the failure of criminologists to understand the problem stems from the fact that past studies have, in effect, "sampled on the dependent variable." That is, groups that have had high rates of crime have been studied because of those high crime rates. Groups that have not had high crime rates—the negative examples—have been ignored, because, after all, there has been no problem to study. But the development of a theory of crime that will have predictive power requires the study not only of where crime occurs, but where it does not occur.

Sampling on the dependent variable is a particular problem in the gang literature. "Gangs" are studied, and then theories about why gangs are present in particular groups are developed, without reference to groups (or even the same group) in which they are absent. As a consequence, even groups that have had high rates of crime in the past but are no longer so troubled are excluded from analysis. Also relevant is the fact that declines in youthful crime have never been analyzed. Two of the better-known theories developed to explain youthful crime in immigrant communities, social disorganization theory and strain theory, consistently make this error.

SPECIFYING THE PROBLEM

Social Disorganization: An Early Attempt at Theory and Generalization

In the first half of the 20th century in the United States, youthful crime and immigration were systematically associated by sociologists working at the University of Chicago. Thrasher (1927, 1963) and Shaw and McKay (1942) took advantage of this situation and were among the "Chicago school's" more prolific authors. These sociologists associated high rates of juvenile delinquency with the poor neighborhoods in which immigrants settled. The theory of social disorganization, which describes the causes of youthful crime, was developed from their work.

Shaw and McKay (1942) provide perhaps the most systematic description of this position; they associate high rates of youthful crime with the "ecology" of the city. They point out that where there are high rates of economic dependence, ethnic heterogeneity, and residential mobility, there are high rates of crime. These are the conditions that they describe as leading to "disorganized" neighborhoods. In such areas, there appears to be a breakdown in the ability of immigrant parents to control their American-born children. Shaw and McKay point out that this weakening of control is associated with a variety of circumstances inherent to the integration of immigrants' children into the urban United States.

Shaw and McKay's argument is not a simple one; they include a variety of conditions in their description of social disorganization. Among these are (a) the conflict between the values brought from European peasant societies and those found in urban America; (b) the allegiance that a boy may develop to a youthful group as opposed to his "old-fashioned" parents; (c) the confusion caused by a variety of cultures in ethnically heterogeneous neighborhoods of first settlement; (d) the lack of interest in developing the inner cities among immigrants, whose main interest is in moving to the suburbs; and (e) the lack of precedents in the peasant immigrant family for meeting the problems encountered in urban America.

In many respects, what I am proposing is consistent with what Shaw and McKay concluded in the 1940s. Indeed, I am arguing that there has been a resurgence of the problems Shaw and McKay describe; it is my intent to outline the mechanism through which what they describe occurs. Unlike Shaw and McKay, however, I (a) limit the use of such models to immigrant groups and (b) emphasize the impact that differential age and gender structure has on this process in immigrant communities.

Strain Theory: The Role of Social Class and Blocked Opportunities

Social disorganization theory is based on research into immigrant communities. But, by the time this theory became popular, widespread mass immigration into the United States ceased, and along with it sociological interest in youthful crime in immigrant communities. Indeed, in the ninth edition of their classic text *Criminology*, Sutherland and Cressey (1974, p. 142) claim that the assimilation of large numbers of immigrants is no longer a serious social problem in the United States; they assert that the relationship between immigration and crime is of only historical interest.

In the 1950s, the focus of American sociology shifted from the problems of immigration and social integration to those of racial conflict, ethnic identity, and class stratification among Americans.[1] Albert Cohen's book *Delinquent Boys* (1955) reflects this shift from "disorganized" immigrant neighborhoods to issues of ethnicity, race, and class. Cohen helped to focus concern on the deprivations of the class system (poor schools, lack of employment opportunities, and the like) rather than relations between parents and youth. Thus, instead

of emphasizing the "disorganization" seemingly inherent to the immigration process, Cohen evaluated delinquent behavior in the context of a class system. In the class system, working-class boys are
socialized into norms that make the acquisition of middle-class lin-
guistic, academic, and "social" skills difficult. The consequence, according to Cohen, is a "corner-boy" culture in which conformity
to middle-class values interferes with the values of the corner-boy
working class. Most corner boys, Cohen notes, respond by acquiring
conventional working-class occupations. This is consistent with the
norms of society and does not lead to delinquency (pp. 128-131).
However, as a result of these circumstances, some of these corner boys
respond by forming delinquent subcultures in which values are in
actual opposition to those of the mainstream middle class. For such
boys, Cohen writes, the only way to "win" the status game is to become
part of a subculture in which nonconformity to middle-class values
sets them above conventional society. From this situation emerge the
comparatively high delinquency rates associated with poor urban
neighborhoods.

   Thus the study of youthful crime during the last half of the 20th
century focused not on the consequences of the immigration process,
but on crime rates among working-class ethnic minorities who only
incidentally are immigrants (see Chin, 1990; Gross, 1989; Jankowski,
1991; Launer & Palenski, 1989; Moore, 1975; Padilla, 1992; Sung,
1977; Vigil, 1989). However, unlike in the earlier literature, the
focus has not been on issues of assimilation or social integration,
but on the conflict between conventional cultures and "subcultures."
Thus, in emphasizing such issues, a basic question is missed: Are the
processes that Shaw and McKay (1942) and their colleagues in the
Chicago school described among the immigrants of the early 20th
century the same as those that exist among immigrants of the late
20th century?[2]

   There is no definitive answer to this question in the theoretical
literature, because recent studies have not systematically compared
earlier waves of immigrants with later waves. Likewise, because the
more current subcultural approaches emphasize that working-class
ethnic communities have inherently cohesive sets of social values,
they do not ask the same questions about the relationships between
youth and their parents that the social disorganization theorists ask.[3]

THE EMPIRICAL RECORD: ANALYZING GROUPS

The theories discussed above are ultimately only interpretations of actual data. Such theoretical views aside, how does the empirical record— that is, what has actually been observed—correlate with the theories?

When we examine the issue of youthful crime in immigrant communities, it becomes clear that it does not necessarily correlate with the theories very well. Examination of the available empirical evidence in fact presents an ambiguous picture. Studies comparing aggregated arrest or incarceration rates of foreign- and native-born persons generally indicate that the rates are roughly the same or are lower for the foreign-born (see Francis, 1981, pp. 27-32; Savitz, 1975; Tönnies, 1929/1971, pp. 241-247; Van Vechten, 1942; Wickersham Commission, 1931). This unexpected observation becomes even more confusing when individual immigrant populations are disaggregated. This is because, although there is no evidence that as a group the foreign-born are more likely to be arrested than are the native-born, there is a great deal of variation among immigrant groups in arrest and incarceration rates. In other words, the arrest and incarceration rates of some immigrant groups, relative to the general population, are exceedingly high, whereas those of other immigrant groups are exceedingly low. Examples of groups with high incarceration rates include New Zealander immigrants in Australia in the 1970s, Chinese immigrants during the 1920s in San Francisco, Greeks during the 1920s in New York and Chicago, and Irish in 1870s Detroit.[4] Examples of immigrant groups with low rates of arrest or incarceration include Chinese youth in Vancouver in the 1930s, Mexicans in Los Angeles during the 1920s, and Italians and Greeks in Australia during the 1970s (see Francis, 1981, p. 193; MacGill, 1938; Wickersham Commission, 1931, p. 100).

But when populations are disaggregated by age structure, anomalies emerge. For example, Taft's (1936) study of arrests in 1930-1933 illustrates this well. Taft found that Austrians, Greeks, and Italians over age 15 in the United States had incarceration rates twice that of native-born Americans. He attributed this difference almost entirely to the different proportions of 15- to 24-year-olds in those populations (p. 733). Another disaggregation for age was done by Van Vechten

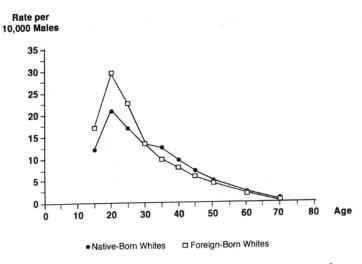

Figure 2.1. Incarceration Rate per 10,000 Males for Foreign-Born and Native-Born Whites, 1940
SOURCE: Van Vechten (1942, p. 142).

(1942), who looked at the incarcerated foreign-born population in the United States at the time of the 1940 census (see Figure 2.1). When he compared the "native white" population with the "foreign-born white" population, he found that the commitment rates of the foreign-born were higher for those under age 30, but lower for those over age 30.

What does an empirical record such as this indicate about youthful crime in immigrant communities? The answer, I think, is that no conclusion can be drawn about the validity of subcultural or social disorganization theories for immigrant groups. What is apparent, however, is that arrest and incarceration rates in immigrant communities do not always approximate those of the native-born, as the aggregated statistics imply. Second, it is apparent that the patterns of youthful crime may differ among different age groups of the foreign-born, as Taft (1936) and Van Vechten (1942) have described. In other words, the current examination has confirmed the confusion that Shaw and McKay observed in 1942:

> Comparisons indicate that the white as well as the negro, the native as well as the foreign born, and the older immigrant nationalities as well as the recent arrivals range in their rates of delinquents from the very highest to the lowest. While each

population group at a given moment shows a concentration in certain types of social areas, and hence a characteristic magnitude in rate of delinquents, adequate samples of each may be found also in areas which for them, are at the time atypical. (pp. 152-153)

Why then did social disorganization theorists of the early part of the 20th century so consistently conclude that migration is associated with youthful crime? And finally, why have criminologists failed to comment on the presence or absence of similar problems during the post-1965 immigration?

EUROPEAN IMMIGRANTS: THE 19TH AND EARLY 20TH CENTURIES

Crime has been a persistent feature of the analyses of authors who have critiqued immigration. For example, Sanderson (1856, pp. 32-38) wrote immediately after the first major wave of 19th-century immigration arrived in the United States, between 1844 and 1855, when most immigrants were from Ireland and Germany. According to a survey done in 1850, the rate of incarceration for the foreign-born was 1/165; for the native-born the rate was 1/1,580. Arrest statistics that Sanderson cites from Philadelphia indicate also that a disproportionately large number of Irish were being arrested in 1856, whereas arrests of other foreign-born persons (especially Germans) were relatively small.

Sanderson does not speculate about why the rates are so high. He does indicate, however, that about 60% of the arriving population was male, and that they by and large settled in urban areas. Both factors could influence the incarceration rates cited above. Sanderson also notes that the population of New York City in 1850 was 46% foreign-born or of foreign parentage. Of these, 52% were Irish by birth or parentage, and 43% were German (p. 19). At the time, some 19% of the U.S. population was of "white non-Anglo-Saxon background," primarily Irish and German.

Another critique of the earlier period of immigration from Europe is found in Schneider's (1980) study of social order in early Detroit. Schneider found that during the 1870s, arrests of Irish immigrants in Detroit were higher than those of German immigrants. He describes the different patterns of offenses among German and Irish in the 1870s:

The native-born and the Germans were under-arrested, and the Irish over-arrested for public order offenses, given what seemed to be their propensities for criminal activity. The Irish, though conspicuous and disorderly in their drinking habits, were not disproportionately represented among more serious offenders; the Germans, though rarely drunk, disorderly, or vagrant were more commonly guilty of serious offenses; and the native-born, though often drunk or vagrant, were even more often burglars or assaulters. (pp. 113, 115)

This information is interesting because, at least in a very general way, it indicates that a great deal of variation in arrest rates among different groups is not strictly a 20th-century phenomenon. However, it is far too general for use in drawing any conclusions about my specific hypothesis regarding youthful crime and migration.

YOUTHFUL CRIME IN IMMIGRANT GROUPS: THE EARLY 20TH CENTURY

Shaw and McKay (1942, pp. 149-159) analyzed ethnic succession in immigrant neighborhoods of 19th- and 20th-century Chicago, and correlated this with delinquency rates. They did this for white ethnic groups such as Germans, Irish, Italians, and Poles. They found that high rates of delinquency correlated with residence of the foreign-born in the poorer neighborhoods of first immigrant settlement. Furthermore, they point out that as groups moved out of poor areas and into areas where crime rates were lower, those groups' arrest rates also fell. In other words, Shaw and McKay argue that a group's official delinquency is a function of the poorer neighborhoods in which it lives. They go on to note that Chinese are an exception to this rule, but by and large make the argument that proximity to criminal activity due to residence in poor neighborhoods of first settlement, and not immigrant status, results in high rates of delinquency.

Shaw and McKay's study still stands as the most systematic attempt to answer the question of whether immigration itself leads to high rates of youthful crime. Their answer seems to be that it does not. Rather, they claim that what causes high rates of delinquency is residence in poor and disorganized immigrant neighborhoods, where the subcultural norms of delinquency become attractive when old and new values conflict.

Shaw and McKay make the important argument that it is contact with antisocial values in the poor neighborhoods of first settlement that causes youthful crime. They go on to point out that as ethnic groups succeed each other in the poor, "disorganized" neighborhoods, young males in each group acquire the antisocial values that are present. They also point out that the incidence of delinquency increases because of the conflicts among parental norms rooted in the home country, peasant values, and the American homes of the new industrial society into which their children are born. In this respect, Shaw and McKay's argument is similar to Eisenstadt's (1959) concerning youth in Palestine. And like Eisenstadt, Shaw and McKay present good circumstantial life-history evidence to illustrate this point. However, they do not correlate this evidence with the contradictions described by their more ambiguous arrest statistics. In other words, they do not explain why most groups at one time or another have both high and low juvenile arrest rates.

Finally, there is also a tautology in Shaw and McKay's argument: They seem to conclude that immigration does not cause high crime rates, but residence in poor immigrant neighborhoods does. In part, this is an artifact of the time and place in which they studied. In early-20th-century Chicago, most poor urban neighborhoods were occupied by immigrants. Thus, although their argument that it is contact with antisocial values that leads to youthful crime may be accurate, they are never able to isolate the effects of the immigration process itself. In other words, Shaw and McKay do not answer the question of whether the immigrant situation is inherently disorganized or whether it emerges out of the structural circumstances of the surrounding neighborhood, such as the presence of antisocial values, the age structure of the immigrant population, selective movement to suburban areas, processes of social integration, and the poverty seemingly inherent to the immigration experience of the Europeans they studied. For these reasons, it is difficult to conclude whether or not a "wave effect" occurs in communities of immigrant youth.

Chinese

Chinese immigrants to the United States have had both high and low crime rates reported. The following historical overview describes the circumstances implied by these successively high and low rates.

In the 19th century, Chinese immigrant communities were known for controlling much of the vice that occurred along the West Coast

(Light, 1974, 1977).[5] Arrest rates sometimes reflected this: The Wickersham Commission in 1931 reported that foreign-born Chinese had
the highest arrest rate of any ethnic group in San Francisco (p. 100).
Unfortunately, the commission's report does not indicate the age
distribution of the arrestees, or how long after immigration the arrests
occurred. What is clear is that gambling (numbers running) in particular led to unusually high arrest rate of Chinese in San Francisco and
in other major cities, except Los Angeles (see also Beach, 1932).

At about the same time the Wickersham Commission's report was
published, Judge Helen MacGill (1938) of the juvenile court in Vancouver,
British Columbia, remarked on the unusually low rate of incarceration
among the immigrant Asian juveniles found there (see also Hayner,
1942, pp. 373-377).[6] She concluded this after examining the ratio of
official delinquents to total population for the period 1928-1936. She
found that the delinquency rate for non-Asians was 15.6 times that of
Japanese and Chinese.[7] This she believed was due to the presence of
unusually strong family ties in the Asian communities of her city. She
went on to observe that these low rates persisted despite the presence
of the Chinese in the least desirable areas of Vancouver and a pronounced poverty that, in other groups, was correlated with high rates
of juvenile arrest. This was also presumably despite the presence of a
112% increase in the Chinese population of Vancouver between 1922
and 1940 (Hayner, 1942, p. 376). Unfortunately, comparative data
about the age and gender demographics for both San Francisco and
Vancouver are not available.

Renewed interest in criminality (or lack thereof) in immigrant
Chinese communities has emerged since the new wave of immigration
to the United States began in 1966. Again, the reports reflect a contrast
between groups that are perceived as being "model minority immigrants" (Caplan, Whitmore, & Choy, 1989; Chin, 1990, pp. 1, 94;
Sung, 1977, p. 137) and those seen as the breeding ground for brutal
gang activity among disaffected immigrant youth.[8] As with the earlier
descriptions, these reports tend to reflect short-term cross-sectional
analyses lasting from 1 to 10 years. A minor exception to this is Delbert
and Joe's (1989) effort to put their qualitative study of Vancouver's
Chinese gangs into a longer-term perspective. They note that the
youthful gangs that they observed in the late 1970s were disappearing,
and did not expect them to last past the time when there was a ready
supply of newly arrived immigrant youth.

Chin's (1990, 1996) studies of the "Chinese Mafia" in New York are more thorough in description than many other studies. Using a subculturally based description, Chin claims that the Chinese criminality he observed in New York is highly influenced by the presence of Asia-based organized crime. He asserts that Asian syndicates use as "soldiers" disaffected immigrant youth from Hong Kong who have tried to integrate into American society but lack the necessary skills to do so. In turn, he correlates this lack of skills with poor American social skills (especially English-language skills) among those who arrive as teenagers, which in turn blocks their access to conventional opportunities. He goes on to point out that recruitment by organized crime is found among the same group of youth who, in the absence of organized crime, would be susceptible to the formation of a gang-oriented youth subculture (Chin, 1990, pp. 93-102; see also Long, 1996; Toy, 1991).

However, concerning the role that immigration itself might play in the emergence of such youthful crime among Chinese immigrants, Chin's studies leave several questions unaddressed. First, although Chin shows that youth immigrating from Taiwan do not have similar problems with delinquency, he does not indicate why. Second, he makes no precise comparisons between the Chinese youth he studied and youth from other immigrant groups who find themselves in similar situations of poverty. In addition, although he indicates that there are unusually large numbers of males in their teenage years in the Hong Kong Chinese population (p. 94), Chin makes no attempt to correct for this factor when making generalizations about criminality in the Chinese community. Finally, Chin's main concern is extortion rackets—indeed, in his 1996 study, his focus is on this criminal activity alone.

In sum, the data about youthful crime in Chinese immigrant communities are ambiguous regarding the subject of immigration itself. On the other hand, there is adequate evidence to indicate that Chinese immigrant communities can be affected by waves of youthful crime. In other words, there is nothing inherent to Chinese culture that guarantees that youthful crime will not become a problem in an immigrant population. This situation fails to support what Shaw and McKay (1942) assert on the basis of MacGill's study—that is, that unusually strong norms regarding filial piety control Asian youth in ways not found in non-Asian immigrant groups.

Mexicans

Much of the literature about crime among Mexican immigrant communities in the United States has focused on gang activity (see Jankowski, 1991; Moore, 1975; Padilla, 1992; Shelden, Tracy, & Brown, 1997, pp. 75-77; Vigil, 1989). As a result, much of the emphasis has been on how the unique norms and mores of such youthful subcultures are maintained. Not addressed have been issues of why gang activity is found in some cases but not others. As a result, it is difficult to make comparisons of Mexicans with other immigrant groups. Nevertheless, some conclusions about how the problem has emerged can be drawn from an examination of this literature.

There have been two major waves of Mexican immigration into the United States, the first after the Mexican Revolution (i.e., from about 1918 to 1930), and the second beginning at the time of World War II. Studies of arrest and incarceration have been made primarily of the earlier wave, whereas later studies have attempted to show how a cultural tradition of gang formation began among the children of the earlier wave and continues today. Moore's (1975, 1991) work provides something of a bridge between these two periods.

The Wickersham Commission's (1931) report represents the earliest systematic work on "crime and the foreign-born." Commissioned by Congress just after wide-scale migration from Europe had stopped, it focused on Mexicans, among other groups. Thus this report is a good source of descriptions of criminal activity among Mexican populations in the 1920s; it also includes three essays about the nature of criminal activity among Mexicans in Texas, Illinois, and California. The arrest rate that the Wickersham Commission found for Mexicans tended to be a bit higher than that for the general population, with the statistics showing that a disproportionately large number of these arrests were for such misdemeanors as vagrancy, possession of marijuana, and violations of Prohibition-era laws against public drunkenness. The commission also found that the numbers of Mexican prisoners in the state prisons at San Quentin and Folsom were disproportionately *lower* than their presence in the general population (pp. 199-332). Notably, these statistics were generated from an immigrant Mexican population that was disproportionately found in poor urban neighborhoods, such as Maravilla in Los Angeles.

Bogardus (1934) investigated the problems that Mexican immigrants had in urban areas of Los Angeles in the early 1930s. The crime statistics that he presents are consistent with the generalizations of the Wickersham Commission and indicate that although Mexicans constituted about 10% of Los Angeles County's population, they accounted for 14.5% of the arrests for the fiscal year ending June 30, 1933.[9] Again, these arrests included a disproportionately large number of violations of the Prohibition-era state poison act for the use of both alcohol and marijuana. Bogardus found that these problems were greatest among the "middle ages," a group that excludes the youth focused on here (pp. 52-58).[10]

Bogardus also notes that arrests for juvenile activity are different from those of adults, and focused on petty theft, auto theft, morality offenses, and truancy (p. 55). By 1934, the juvenile probation department in Los Angeles had a caseload in which 13.5% of the total was Mexican, or of Mexican parentage.[11] This was a rate not that different from Bogardus's estimate that Mexicans (presumably including parents and offspring) were 10% of the total population of Los Angeles County. This would seem to indicate that, despite residence in low-income areas and high reliance on public relief (Morgan, 1990, p. 242), the total incarceration rates were about the same for juveniles who were immigrants and those who were not. Put bluntly, when poverty is controlled for in the Mexican population of the early 1930s, there is probably a negative correlation between immigration status and youthful arrest and incarceration. That is, the period from about 1920 to 1935 was a period of low youthful crime in the Mexican immigrant community.

Mexican Immigrant Communities and Gangs

Notably, neither Bogardus (1934) nor the Wickersham Commission (1931) mentions the presence of gang subcultures, a topic that dominates later discussions of youthful crime in Mexican American communities. According to Moore (1975), this is because Chicano youth gangs emerged out of legitimate youth groups that had their origins in the churches and community organizations of the 1930s and 1940s. These groups, Moore writes, evolved into the turf-oriented gangs of the 1960s-1990s that are the focus of the current literature about youthful criminality in Mexican immigrant communities.

McWilliams (1948) and Griffiths (1948) offer the earliest systematic descriptions of the "zoot suiters" or pachuco youth subculture that emerged in the Maravilla barrio of Los Angeles in the early 1940s. These authors both note that the pachuco subculture flourished among the Mexican American juveniles, a majority of whom were the sons and daughters of parents who had arrived in California during the 1920s (McWilliams, 1948, p. 235). Using journalistic accounts, McWilliams claims that the emergence of the pachuco subculture was caused by the systematic exclusion of Mexican American youth from mainstream society. Such exclusion, he notes, included limited access to public recreation facilities, concentration in public housing, and harassment by the police. This harassment resulted in the "zoot suit riots" of mid-1942, when U.S. sailors invaded the barrio in order to attack pachucos. This activity resulted in the arrests of large numbers of Mexican youth. McWilliams also asserts that "in Los Angeles, twenty years ago gangs [similar to the Mexican pachucos of the 1940s] were made up of the sons of Russian Molokan immigrants" (p. 240).

Citing anecdote, McWilliams goes on to describe why he thinks gang formation was so common in the Los Angeles barrios of the 1940s:

> Discovering that his status approximates the second-rate school, has the effect of instilling in the Mexican boy a resentment directed against the school, and all it stands for. At the same time, it robs him of a desire to turn back to his home. For the home which he knew prior to entering school no longer exists. All of the attitudes he has learned at school now poison his attitude toward the home. Turning away from home and school, the Mexican boy has only one place where he can find security and status. This is the gang made up of boys exactly like himself, who live in the same neighborhood, and who are going through precisely the same distressing process at precisely the same time. (p. 240)

Moore (1975) provides a more systematic discussion of how Chicano gangs emerged in Los Angeles in the 1940s-1970s. She indicates that the first large gangs emerged in the late 1930s and early 1940s. They became involved with narcotics in the late 1940s and 1950s, and have since become a permanent subcultural institution in L.A. barrios.

In her more recent book *Going Down to the Barrio: Homeboys and Homegirls in Change*, about two East Los Angeles gangs, Moore (1990)

TABLE 2.1 Population Growth in Los Angeles: Total Population and
Mexican Foreign-Born, 1900-1970

Year	Total Population	Mexican	% of Total
1900	102,479	817	0.8
1910	319,198	5,632	1.8
1920	576,763	1,653	0.3
1930	1,238,048	53,573	4.3
1940	1,504,277	36,840	2.4
1950	1,970,358	39,742	2.0
1960	2,481,456	53,338	2.1
1970	2,915,998	104,045	3.8

SOURCE: Moore (1975, p. 6).

correlates the youthful crime waves of East Los Angeles with "moral panics." These include the response to the zoot suit riots of the 1940s and the "War on Drugs" of the 1980s (pp. 1-2). In making this correlation, Moore makes the important point that poor and racially distinctive young men are the targets of such panics.

Moore (1975) is less specific, however, about the relationship between immigration itself and the perpetuation of the gang subculture. Nevertheless, two of her observations are particularly relevant here. First, she notes that although the barrios where the gangs persist are areas of first settlement for immigrants, the population turnover is also very high: "So it happened that within a comparatively short period the Chicano barrios experienced a circulation of population through 'unchanging' Mexican neighborhoods" (p. 6). If this is correct, she seems to be describing a process of "ethnic succession" analogous to what Shaw and McKay (1942) observed in the primary settlement neighborhoods of Chicago and other cities (see below).[12] The only difference is that the groups that succeed each other in Los Angeles are of the same ethnic origin, and therefore not as easily analyzed as distinct immigrant groups. This can be inferred from an examination of Table 2.1.

This table shows that shortly before the emergence of gang activity in the 1940s, there was a decline in the total Mexico-born population of Los Angeles. This could be consistent with what McWilliams (1948) observed about the pachucos being the children of immigrants from the 1920s, although it is not clear. However, this raises an interesting question about what the demographic structure of the Mexican immigrant population looked like in the 1920s, when there was little if any youthful gang activity, compared with the 1940s, when there apparently was an upsurge. The answer is that, at least for 1940, the "foreign-born" Mexican population declined due to mortality, deportation, and return migration, and the American-born population actually increased (Truesdell, 1943, p. 94).

Unlike Chicago in 1900 to 1930, immigration to Los Angeles has been persistently from one country, and as a result the barrios have had a culture that has been persistently Mexican and Spanish speaking, and that includes gangs, even though the population itself may not be stable. This leads to a third observation: Although the gangs themselves have well-defined identities, the boys who successively join are not necessarily from the same families.[13] Unfortunately, however, Moore (1990) does not specify exactly how this continual population turnover affects actual gang membership. Indeed, she is critical of films, such as *American Me*, that imply that gang activity is a generational process; she does not believe that there is any such thing as a generational "gang tradition." Indeed, she calls accounts of "hereditary" membership passed from father to son a "myth" of police and the media (p. 114).

Vigil (1989), in an ethnography of Chicano gangs in Los Angeles, offers even less toward an understanding of whether immigration and youthful crime are related. His book, although rich in ethnographic description, is not useful for an analysis of the relationship between youthful gang activity and immigration. Vigil proposes a theory of "multiple marginalization," meaning that the more marginalizing factors (e.g., poverty, racism, abusive parents, parental criminality, broken home) a youth is subject to, the more likely that youth is to join a gang. Such an idea is interesting, but it provides no precise means by which comparisons can be made with other immigrant groups.

Finally, Jankowski (1991) addresses the issue of youthful Chicano gangs in particular and ethnic gangs in general. He compares the Chicano and African American gangs of Los Angeles to the Puerto Rican, Irish, Jamaican, Dominican, and African American gangs of New York and Boston, and does much to identify the similarities that such youthful gangs have, particularly with respect to subcultural norms. He claims that what these groups have in common is "defiant individualism" created by exclusion from mainstream society. Unfortunately, although he indicates that the gangs he studied are ethnically based, it is not clear whether the individual members immigrated or for that matter whether there is a relationship between immigration and youthful gang formation. Likewise, despite the comparative nature of Jankowski's work, it also lacks any systematic assessment of the data generated by Shaw and McKay or others from the Chicago school. In large part, this failure to make such an obvious comparison stems from Jankowski's inaccurate equation of social disorganization theory with "poverty" and thus his dismissal of the value of any comparison. This is unfortunate, because Jankowski's book is potentially a rich source of comparative data for assessing whether immigration as a process results in patterns of youthful crime.

In sum, an examination of the rich literature available about youthful crime in immigrant Mexican communities provides no conclusive indication of whether or not migration itself has an effect on youthful crime. Conclusions cannot be reached for several reasons, including the absence of longitudinal data, a general failure to separate immigrants from subsequent American-born generations, lack of precise demographics, and the absence of systematic controls for poverty, low education, and other correlates of the Mexican immigrant experience.

One interesting fact that does emerge, however, is that from 1920 to 1935, arrest and incarceration rates for Mexican immigrants were either comparable to those of the native-born or, when poverty was controlled for, lower. This is what would be expected if youthful crime emerges in response to factors other than poverty. As with the Chinese, the one thing that is apparent about the Mexican population is that patterns of youthful crime across time are different from those of native-born whites.

Pauline Young's View and the Molokan Russians

A more specific view of how a high incidence of youthful crime might emerge is found in the work of Pauline Young (1932), who conducted an ethnographic study of the Molokan Russians in Los Angeles. The Molokan Russians were an ascetic religious sect of the Russian Orthodox Church that settled in the Boyle Heights neighborhood of Los Angeles in 1904-1906. Their religious ideals included pacifism; indeed, the demands of the Russian draft for the Russian-Japanese War were cited as the cause of their flight from Russia in the first place. Pacifism and draft resistance also became galvanizing forces in the Boyle Heights community during World War I.

**Number of
Delinquents**

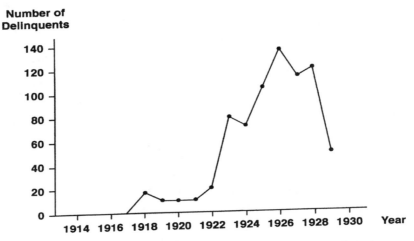

Figure 2.2. Official Delinquencies Recorded for Molokan Russian Boys in East Los Angeles
SOURCE: Based on data in Young (1932).
NOTE: This figure shows the number of official delinquencies recorded for 181 boys in 108 Molokan families. The Molokans arrived in Los Angeles as a group in 1905, but delinquency data were generally not available until 1915. At that time, delinquency rates were low. Unfortunately, Young (1932) does not specify the size of the at-risk cohort for each year.

There has been little follow-up of Young's study, although Sutherland and Cressey (1974, pp. 147-148) comment on it briefly in their influential textbook, as have later ethnographers of the Molokan Church writing in recent years (Dunn & Dunn, 1978; Hardwick, 1993). Young's study, however, is particularly interesting because she followed a small immigrant group for a full generation and used juvenile delinquency as a focus in examining the socialization of immigrant youth.

Before 1920, there were very few official delinquencies among the 181 boys from 18 families that Young analyzed (see Figure 2.2). A wave of delinquencies began about 1923. According to Young, this was because Molokan elders were able to maintain authority throughout the early period due to a "reactive solidarity" in the religion-focused ascetic society.[14] She notes that the delinquency problem emerged with improving economic conditions; that is, as community members began to get permanent working-class jobs in the Los Angeles industrial economy, delinquency rates increased, because this lifestyle was inconsistent with the maintenance of the ascetically based religious authority.

Unfortunately, Young does not specify the size of the at-risk cohort for each year, or discuss the incarceration of large numbers of at-risk Molokan youth (p. 205). Nor is there any indication of what role demographics played as youth moved beyond the age where reports to the juvenile authorities were legally possible. Young did indicate in a personal communication to Donald Cressey in the 1970s that by the 1940s the Molokans had dispersed to the suburbs, and that by the 1970s, the image of the Molokans as delinquents had completely vanished from law enforcement agencies (Hardwick, 1993; Sutherland & Cressey, 1974, p. 148).

Hardwick (1993) conducted an ethnographic study among the Molokan Russians in the 1980s, but by that time, memories of both the large colony that had been in Boyle Heights in general and juvenile delinquency had faded. Dunn and Dunn (1978) comment on delinquency among the Molokan Russians only briefly. They note that among the problems they observed in the small San Francisco Molokan community, "drugs and crime seem a problem only for second-generation Molokans . . . [and a] comparatively minor one except in the eyes of community elders" (p. 356). Indeed, the Molokan identity that Dunn and Dunn and Hardwick investigated was one of religious purists wrestling with the use of Russian and English in church, rather than the problems of youthful integration that were the central theme of Young's book written in the 1920s.

As in other immigrant groups, the nature of the offenses in the Molokan community had a pattern. The bulk of the 708 offenses Young counted involved petty larceny; only 2 cases involved assault. Unlike the arrests of Mexicans in Los Angeles during the same period (who were primarily "middle-aged"), there were few arrests for drunkenness. Although she does not provide statistics, Young does indicate that the bulk of the delinquencies were committed by predacious youth gangs, what she calls a "fortuitous grouping"; she cites Thrasher's (1927) work on gangs as a model.

Unlike the other authors surveyed here, Young offers a plausible model to explain how and why the "crime wave" began and peaked in the Molokan community. Notably, she connects her model to the process of migration by breaking the immigrant youth into three groups in order to explain how the "delinquency wave" emerged in the Molokan community as a result of culture conflict between elders and the different cohorts of youth (pp. 207-209).

The group that Young designates as Group C was 25-29 years old at the time of her study in 1929. She notes that members of this group were born in Russia, but went to school until the fifth or sixth grade in the United States, and then began to work for their parents. This occurred between 1910 and 1917. They spoke both English and Russian, though Russian might be dominant. They had a very low incidence of delinquency, and at the time of Young's study had embarked on traditional Russian lives, were under the control of the elders, and held steady jobs as auto mechanics, master workmen, foundry workers, and the like.

Group B was 20-24 years old in 1929. Members of this group stayed in school longer than their older brothers because they did not need to work to help support their families. They were born in the first few years after arrival in the United States. As a result, they had more free time and, unlike their older brothers, mingled with other cultural groups. Their behavior diverged widely from that of their parents, and the community began to experience delinquencies. This corresponded to the period from about 1916 to 1923. However, Young's examination of the life histories of the Group B youth showed that once they took industrial jobs, they married other Molokans and reidentified with Molokan society—or, to put it in criminologist Albert Cohen's terms, they became corner boys.

Group A was 9-19 years old in 1929. Members of this group were also American-born, but they were born into a home situation where parental control had begun to deteriorate. The delinquencies of this group are reflected in the data for approximately 1922 to 1929 in Figure 2.2. Cultural conflict was at its height with these boys. No conclusion about their life histories can be reached base on Young's work, however, because her study ended in 1929.

Young's study provides clues about how the process of both high and low rates of youthful crime might emerge in an immigrant group. What her study suggests is that in immigrant populations, the causal factor for a delinquency wave is not economic status, poverty, adolescence, or nationality, but the intergenerational conflict seemingly inherent to the process of social integration. This is an intriguing model, and one that Sutherland and Cressey (1974) believe is adequate to propose a general model for early-20th-century immigration (p. 147). Unfortunately, comparable data are not available for other immigrant groups, nor, for that matter, are complete data available for the Molokans. Three things are lacking in Young's study of Molokan Russians. First is the context of other immigrant groups. If what Young writes is true, similar patterns should be identifiable in other immigrant groups also living in Los Angeles at that time (e.g., Mexican).

Second, although Young does say that the Molokans had large families in the United States, she does not provide the demographics of the group at different points in time in any systematic way. Finally, there has been no test of Young's model against other immigrant groups from either the early or the late 20th century.

YOUTHFUL CRIME IN OTHER IMMIGRANT GROUPS: THE LATE 20TH CENTURY

Leonard Savitz (1975) examined the arrest records of Philadelphia's urban African Americans in the late 1950s. In order to test whether migration caused higher rates of delinquency, he obtained the records of black students in Philadelphia public schools in 1957 (i.e., children born in 1939-1945), and compared the juvenile court records of those born in the South to those born in Philadelphia. He found that the migrant children had lower arrest rates than those who were born in Philadelphia when age and "years at risk" were controlled for. This, he notes, is consistent with the report of the Wickersham Commission (1931), but inconsistent with social disorganization theory, which implies that rates among migrants should be higher than for the native-born. Notably, however, Savitz did not test his hypothesis in the context of Young's (1932) information developed from the Molokan example.

Savitz's study is useful because, like several other studies, it indicates that high delinquency rates are not inevitable in immigrant communities. However, although much of Savitz's work is carefully done, it is also cross-sectional and looks at a cohort of youth born during a relatively brief period (7 years). Finally, it is not clear whether the differences in conditions for blacks between the southern United States and Philadelphia would make the experience of an individual traveling from one to the other equivalent to immigration.[15]

Robison (1958) compared the rates of Jewish delinquency in New York between 1930 and 1952 and found that there was a marked decline in four boroughs of New York as measured by juvenile court referrals. Indeed, during these years, the referrals declined from a point where Jewish boys had juvenile court referrals at approximately the rates that would be expected of the under-15 population to a point where the rates were one-tenth of what would have been expected (pp. 536-538). Robison notes that this change coincided with a dramatic shift in the offenses for which there were reports. In 1930, peddling or begging without a license was the leading cause for referral, whereas in 1952, when offense rates were minuscule, the leading cause was violent or aggressive behavior. Unfortunately, in her short article, Robison reports controlling only for the under-15 population, and not for older age cohorts. Comparison to other groups, as well as the context of the different legal systems, is also lacking.

Vietnamese

A large group of Vietnamese first arrived in the United States in 1975, and a second group arrived in the 1980s. Like the Chinese, the Vietnamese are an anomalous group that has a reputation for both being a "model minority" (e.g., producing large numbers of ambitious students; see Caplan et al., 1992) and having unusually high rates of youthful gang activity characterized by extremely violent extortion attempts (California State Attorney General, 1990; English, 1996; Long, 1996; Shelden et al., 1997; Smith & Tarallo, 1993; Waters & Cohen, 1993).

Youthful crime among Vietnamese immigrants emerged out of the cohort that first arrived in 1980; there is no evidence of the children from the 1975 arrivals being involved. Rather, the focus is on the alienated youth who arrived in the United States in the 1980s.

Accounts from the Vietnamese community about gang activity emphasize the lack of control that parents have over youth who acquire American cultural skills—conventional or criminal—more quickly than their parents. Much like the Molokan Russians described above, the result is a generation cut off from the cultural norms of their parents.[16] If this is the case, then the process that the Vietnamese community is undergoing, including the wave of delinquencies, could be explained by the same mechanism that Young describes for the Molokan community. However, precise information about the Vietnamese community needs to be available before it can be tested against the model suggested by the Molokan data.

Laotians

In earlier work, I have described the problems with youthful crime associated with the Laotian community in California in general and

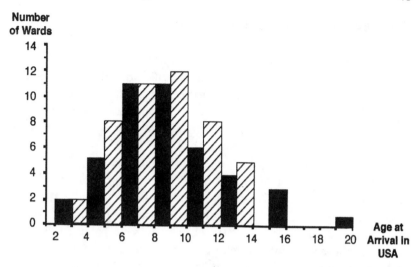

Figure 2.3. Ages at Arrival in the United States for 95 Laotian CYA Wards, 1991
NOTE: More than half of the wards in this sample arrived in the United States between the ages of 6 and 9. More than 90% were arrested for gang or ganglike activity. However, all 4 of the wards in this sample who entered the United States after the age of 13 were not arrested for gang-type crimes.

Sacramento in particular (Waters & Cohen, 1993). A wave of youthful crime began among Laotians in about 1989, at least in Sacramento. This wave emerged some 7-8 years after the first substantial populations of Laotians moved into Sacramento. Judging from California Youth Authority (CYA) records as well as newspaper reports, that wave continues today. Police accounts and newspaper reports indicate that this activity is associated with "gangs."

The development of data from the CYA has shown that at least in 1991, Laotians assigned to the CYA had come to the United States between the ages of 5 and 9 (see Figure 2.3). Very few arrived as 12- to 17-year-olds. The absence of arrests for youths who arrived between the ages of 2 and 5 is explicable given the relatively recent arrival of Laotians and the consequent absence of such a group in the at-risk ages for youthful crime. However, the absence of 12- to 17-year-olds in the arrest statistics is less understandable.

In Sacramento, the earlier arrests included large numbers of car theft, burglary, and weapons charges. In 1993-1994 there were also a large number of home invasion robberies reported (Magagnini, 1994b, 1994c).

Three Examples From Other Countries

So far in this review, we have looked only at the effects of immigration on youthful crime in the United States. However, the assumptions of the model are not specific to the United States, and it seems reasonable to ask whether data from other countries can contribute to the discussion. Three studies are available that analyze youthful criminal activity in countries other than the United States: Tönnies's (1929/1971) examination of pre-World War I Prussia, Eisenstadt's (1959) investigation of delinquency in Jewish Palestine, and Francis's (1981) study of modern Australia. These works cover a diverse set of circumstances; their differences and similarities are highlighted below.

Ferdinand Tönnies (1929/1971), who was probably the earliest sociologist to ask about the relationship between incarceration rates and immigration, studied prison records in the Schleswig-Holstein Region of Prussia from 1874 to 1914. He found that prisoners who had been born outside of Schleswig-Holstein were more likely to be incarcerated for crimes committed as a result of deliberation (e.g., robbery, burglary) rather than passion (e.g., rape, fighting, and murder).[17] He also found that the ages of the foreign-born prisoners were different from those of the native prisoners, but he does not indicate which group was older or younger.

Eisenstadt (1959) was interested in Jewish immigrants to British Palestine. He started with the assumption that migration is the type of situation that "necessarily transforms both the internal structure of the family . . . and the shrinkage in the field of effective social participation" (p. 202). By this he meant that the very process of migration changes with whom individual family members will interact and, therefore, how status works. He concludes that out of such situations, two types of youth groups could emerge to compensate—the first conventional and the second delinquent. The youth who join the delinquent groups are more likely to have parents who insist on their maintaining old traditions brought from Europe. In this respect, Eisenstadt's descriptions are similar to those of Shaw and McKay (1942) and Young (1932).

Francis (1981) conducted a study of immigration in Australia. Like the Wickersham Commission (1931), Francis found that in the aggregate, there was little difference between the rates of incarceration for native- and foreign-born persons. On the other hand, during the

1970s, Greeks and Italians in Australia had particularly low incarceration rates (when controlled for age) and New Zealanders had particularly high rates (also controlled for age). Those in Francis's category "U.K./Eire" had a rate slightly lower than that of the general Australian population.

In his discussion, Francis does not offer a theoretical conclusion about why these variations exist. Rather, he simply points out that a number of anomalies persist in the data, and that existing theory is inadequate as an explanation.

So what do all these data really tell us about the occurrence of youthful crime in immigrant communities? Obviously, youthful crime waves do occur, but when and where are they more pronounced? Is there any pattern to the types of groups that are effected?

CONCLUSIONS:
THE PATTERNS IN THE EXISTING DATA

The apparent relationship between youthful crime and migration has been persistent enough to attract the interest of sociologists for more than 100 years. Much of the discussion has been colored by the political passions of the times, but five conclusions can be reached.

First Conclusion: A Halo for the Foreign-Born

The foreign-born, when the data are aggregated, do not have higher arrest or incarceration rates than the native-born, despite the theoretical expectations of both variants of criminological theory that they should. This has been found in both the United States and Australia, and is an empirical observation that the early social disorganization theorists systematically ignored in their analyses. Any theory that explains youthful crime in immigrant communities needs to take account of this empirical observation.

Second Conclusion: The Limitations of the Existing Data

The conclusions described above suggest a patterned process of arrest emerging out of processes of immigration and subsequent integration. However, they are only suggestive; no systematic study has employed adequate controls for age structure of a population, rates of assimilation or social integration, number of generations since migration, or poverty and degree of urban settlement. Even using comparative techniques, we cannot draw conclusions about the relationship between youthful crime and immigration; the empirical data are too inconclusive. Just how spotty the data are is evident from a review of the cases described above.

First, in the case of the Chinese in North America, there are widely divergent conclusions; both high and low rates of youthful arrest are found. Likewise, in only a few of the smaller case studies have there been controls for youthful crime as opposed to adult crime, and in these cases there is a time series of only 10-15 years (e.g., Chin, 1996; Delbert & Joe, 1989; MacGill, 1938). Light (1974, 1977), on the other hand, used a longer time frame in his study of early-20th-century Chinatowns. However, although his time series is long enough to control for the birth of a cohort in the United States, he does not indicate whether he is dealing with immigrants or their children, nor, for that matter, does he specify what ages the arrestees were. Judging from Light's descriptions of the aging Chinese population in the 1920s, it might be surmised that the Chinese population was primarily an older group of immigrants, and certainly disproportionately male. However, this is only an assumption.

Different problems are presented by the Mexican data. Again, there is the fact that there are no controls for birthplace, although there are hints that high rates of youthful crime are associated primarily with the problems of socializing children into the new society. The first generation of youthful immigrants, at least in the 1930s, seems to have fairly low incidence of arrest when poverty and age are controlled for. Presumably, the later Mexican data are also affected by the repeated "circular migration" pattern that is a feature of some Mexican American communities.

The difficulty of separating issues of social integration and migration within the Mexican immigrant population is complicated by the persistent movement of Mexicans into California during the latter part of the 20th century. Unfortunately, the studies of gangs conducted in this era have not systematically assessed whether the gang participants are recent immigrants or the children or grandchildren of immigrant parents (e.g., Jankowski, 1991; Moore, 1975; Vigil, 1989). This question is largely unexamined despite the fact that the connection between the American-born children of immigrants and gang-type activity was noted by criminologists studying the issue in the 1930s and 1940s.

To a certain extent, Shaw and McKay (1942) control for this factor when they note that as groups move out of the poorer inner-city neighborhoods of primary immigrant settlement, delinquency rates within the groups start to drop. They also integrate well the social disorganization and subcultural approaches in what is probably the most theoretically complex treatment of the subject. There are, however, two problems with Shaw and McKay's approach. The first is an issue that they themselves acknowledge: that every group has periods when delinquency rates are high and periods when they are low. They imply that this is because older groups have moved out of neighborhoods of first settlement after they have enough money. This is a clean solution; however, Shaw and McKay do not present any empirical data to back it up. It also does not explain groups such as the Molokans, who, immediately after arrival and for 10-15 years thereafter, had unusually low rates of delinquency, despite residence in poor inner-city neighborhoods. The second problem with Shaw and McKay's approach is a chicken-and-egg type of question that remains unanswered: Did the immigrants move out of the neighborhood in which they initially settled because they had integrated with the general population, or did they assimilate because they moved out? Unless the two processes are analytically separated, it is not possible to answer this question.

The Molokan case is particularly interesting because it is the only one in which first- and second-generation immigrants were studied systematically. Young (1932) also proposes a plausible model of how a "wave" of delinquency emerged in the Molokan community. There are three problems with this approach, however. The first is that there has been no systematic test of the model among other immigrant groups. Second, although the model proposed is plausible, the empirical data backing it up are incomplete. Despite the fact that Young's work includes both the immigrant generation and their children, it is still inadequate for answering the question of what happened after the apparent peak in arrests was reached in 1925-1928. Finally, it is not clear how big the actual cohort of at-risk males was.

The cases of the Vietnamese and Chinese in the 1970s and 1980s indicate that youthful crime in immigrant communities is not solely a product of the U.S.-born children of immigrants. But it also does not answer the question of whether or not youthful gangs in Vietnamese communities are a product of a disjuncture between the values of immigrant youth and their parents. Finally, it does not explain the anomaly of the outstanding success of many youth from these communities.

Third Conclusion: Age Structure

Although several studies have controlled for age, or youth versus adult arrest and incarceration, there has been no control for the proportion of second-generation youth in immigrant populations. This is critical for evaluation of any hypothesis of youthful crime and gang activity, for two reasons. First, as I have noted, immigrant groups themselves often have very unusual distributions of both sex and age. This means that there could be an interaction effect in the evaluation of youthful crime in immigrant populations that should be considered. Second, economically active groups (e.g., males aged 16-30) are often overrepresented in migrant groups, whereas children are underrepresented. Refugee groups can be the opposite—that is, children and young women can often be overrepresented. Likewise, the immigrants themselves can have unusually high birthrates after arrival in a new country, or very low rates. Given that arrest and incarceration are so strongly correlated with the number of young males in a population, it would seem that these are factors that should be controlled for. However, in none of the studies described here were questions raised about the issue of age structure.

Fourth Conclusion: The Contextuality of Criminal Law

As in many comparative studies, comparisons have been made across wide sweeps of history here. Although the robustness of comparative historical technique does permit such comparisons, they can be made only in the context of what is defined as criminal. This is particularly true if comparisons of youthful crime rates—that is, infractions of criminal law—are to be made across time and space. What is considered criminal, as well as the policing mechanisms leading to arrest or other forms of official report, varies a great deal across time and among jurisdictions. An obvious example is the

Prohibition years (1920-1933), when the manufacture, sale, and consumption of alcohol were federal crimes, a factor that inflated the arrests of Mexicans, but not Russians. Likewise, at the same time, laws against marijuana use were by and large unenforced (Morgan, 1990, pp. 244-246). More subtle are variations in police practices across time and place. The elimination of the beat officer in favor of the vehicle patrol is one way in which community relations shifted over time. Another example might be the disappearance of street peddlers from New York, with a consequent decline in arrests for peddling without a license.

This contextuality is only part of the problem, however. Related are the interactions through which the law and law enforcement become "real" for the immigrant population and police. This in effect is the process of becoming and disbecoming described in Chapter 1.

Fifth Conclusion: Searching for an Appropriate Methodology

In sum, a wealth of data indicate that immigrant groups do have unusual patterns of youthful crime. It is also clear that this probably happens in patterned outbursts specific to particular immigrant groups. Exactly what these patterns are, however, has yet to be specified in the literature. In large part, this is due to the irregularities in how the data have been collected. The slow, time-dependent nature of youthful crime waves means that standard methods of sociological analysis, employing standard cross-sectional data sets, cannot be used to describe this process. This does not, however, mean that the issue should be ignored. Rather, it means that we must use techniques that are suited to the situation. How this can be done is the topic of the next chapter.

NOTES

1. This emphasis on issues of class and ethnicity in assessing gangs and delinquency continues to the present. The consequence is that the new wave of post-1966 immigration is framed as an ethnic issue, and not one of immigration. The new immigration has been substantial enough to cause a notable shift in the ethnic composition of many U.S. inner cities that is, in outward appearances, similar to that in the earlier part of this century. However,

the return of immigration as an issue has yet to receive the widespread attention of criminologists.

Immigration from Latin America and Asia to the United States became more probable with the liberalization of the U.S. Immigration Act of 1965. Passage of this act in turn coincided with specific economic and political conditions in a number of sending countries, including Mexico, Cuba, Vietnam, Korea, Taiwan, and Hong Kong, that precipitated the "new immigration."

2. On the basis of data collected in Los Angeles in the early 1960s, Klein (1971) asked himself whether the gangs he observed were similar to those that Thrasher (1927) observed in Chicago. He answered his own question with a qualified affirmative, but also noted that although conditions had changed, there were virtually no empirical studies done of gangs between about 1940 and 1965 (pp. 20-21). This may have been due to the fact that during this period there were few gangs, and as a consequence they did not represent the social problem they had in the past. A plausible explanation is that this was due to a cessation in immigration. Equally likely to have contributed to this absence, however, was the impact that World War II and the military draft had on redirecting the attention of at-risk youth (see Shelden et al., 1997, pp. 75-77).

3. Indeed, a look at the indexes of a number of recent criminology textbooks indicates that the new immigration is not routinely associated with youthful crime, even though ideas derived from the social disorganization perspective continue to play a prominent role in any general discussion of delinquency (see Empey, 1982; Gottfredson & Hirschi, 1990; Nettler, 1984; Vold & Bernard, 1986).

4. See Francis (1981, pp. 174, 188) for information about Australia, the Wickersham Commission (1931, p. 100) on the Chinese in San Francisco and Greeks in Chicago and New York, and Schneider (1980, p. 113) for a description of the Irish in Detroit.

5. Light (1974) also goes on to note that the bulk of the Chinese population in the United States between 1870 and 1940 was male, due to the 19th-century arrival of gold miners and agricultural laborers. Wives for these men were prevented from following due to the Chinese Exclusion Act of 1882, which restricted entry of Chinese into the United States. As a result, the Chinese population by the 1920s was disproportionately male and older. It is not known, however, how the arrest statistics may be related to such demographic facts.

6. Hayner (1942) indicates that the rates of juvenile arrest in Seattle and Portland were also low for immigrant Chinese youth.

7. MacGill (1938) used a ratio of school enrollment to cases brought before the juvenile court. The bulk of the Asian at-risk population was Chinese and Japanese. There were very few "Hindus" in Vancouver at the time Judge MacGill was writing.

8. For descriptions of San Francisco, see Toy (1991); for descriptions of New York, see Chin (1990); for a description of gangs in Vancouver, see Delbert and Joe (1989).

9. Population estimates were derived from public school enrollments. Because natives were not subject to arrest for violation of immigration laws, these numbers have been removed from Bogardus's (1934) original calculation.

10. See also Morgan (1990, pp. 233-350) for a discussion of marijuana use among Mexicans during the 1920s and 1930s.

11. Of all boys' cases, 14.9% were Mexican; 9.8% of all girls' cases were Mexican (Bogardus, 1934, p. 55).

12. McWilliams (1948, p. 240) notes that the Mexican pachuco gangs of the 1940s succeeded the Molokan Russian gangs of 20 years earlier.

13. The recent film *American Me* implies that gang activity is a generational process. However, I see little evidence that this is so in anything except the most general sense. A recent *Los Angeles Times* series titled "Orion Avenue: A Life Apart" emphasized that in the Mexican immigrant neighborhood observed, there is a continually high turnover of the immigrant population (Johnson, 1997a, 1997b; Johnson & Cardenas, 1997; Johnson & Cole, 1997).

14. Such a description is reminiscent of Judge MacGill's (1938) analysis of Asian youth in Vancouver in the 1930s. MacGill emphasizes "Asian values," whereas Young (1932) emphasizes "ascetic values." Later writers have tended to emphasize "Confucian values" in assessing Vietnamese and Chinese immigrant societies.

15. E. Franklin Frazier's (1966, pp. 484-486) description of prewar migration from the rural South to urban cities in the North indicates that this migration was every bit as "long distance" and dislocating as the migration of European peasants to the same cities.

16. Long (1996) includes a rich compilation of accounts from the Vietnamese wards he counseled in California's juvenile halls.

17. Tönnies (1929/1971) was using his data to test his theories about the nature of different types of group solidarity found in rural traditional areas and urban industrial areas.

CHAPTER 3

Explaining Youthful Crime in Immigrant Communities
How to Do It? How Much Is There?

*A*re the available data adequate for the development of an efficient explanation of how youthful crime emerges in immigrant communities? The conclusion reached in Chapter 2 is that past studies have been inadequate to this task because no explanations have emerged from the cross-sectional study of individual ethnic groups. How then to tackle the question?

I have described the ideal in Chapter 2: Statistics collected across two generations for five or six immigrant groups would permit comparisons using quantitative techniques. Such data, unfortunately, are not available. Despite the markedly different theoretical conclusions of other authors, however, the similarities in their empirical observations remain. That is, a high incidence of youthful crime does occur in strikingly different immigrant groups. As demonstrated by the juxtaposed statements of American social scientists, a Jewish Palestinian youth, and a Mien elder in Chapter 1, despite wide separations in time, space, and settings, the situations of immigrant groups are remarkably similar. Immigration is a process, but how to describe it effectively?

COMPARATIVE HISTORICAL SOCIOLOGY:
DESCRIBING A ROBUST PROCESS

Although the data available from different groups are not, in the strictest sense, comparable, data have been gathered from various immigrant groups. The question is how to put together different types of studies conducted at different times and places in order to make general conclusions. This suggests the use of comparative sociological techniques that rely on the data available. In this process, possible explanations can be eliminated or confirmed (see Goldstone, 1991; Inciardi, Block, & Hallowell, 1977; McGrath, 1984, pp. 247-260; Ragin, 1987).

The advantage of using such techniques is that when we look at data from groups that migrated under different cultural, socioeconomic, historical, and demographic circumstances, we can control logically for potential confounding factors. By doing this, we can isolate the effects of a common factor—in this case, migration. For example, if migrant groups as different as Molokan Russians in early-20th-century Los Angeles, Jews in British Palestine, and Laotians in late-20th-century Sacramento have similar clusters of conditions leading up to high rates of youthful crime, then there is a good chance that the differences among the groups (e.g., religion, historical period, the nature of host society, law enforcement) have been accounted for. Likewise, if we can then apply the model developed for such unusual groups to immigrant groups that have not had high rates of youthful crime, such as Mexican immigrants in 1930s Los Angeles or Koreans in late-20th-century California, and we discover that for these reasons these immigrant groups did not have the same interactions, then we have found further confirmation of the proposed theory.

VALIDITY: ELIMINATING OR CONFIRMING
DIFFERENT HYPOTHESES

Jan Vansina (1991), a scholar of African history, describes how the validity of such comparative methods is evaluated to describe unobservable events. He notes that such an approach achieves a high order of logical validity because it provides explanations for a large number of interconnected elements. The point of such an approach is to find as examples the most unusual cases possible and then identify the underlying processes common to all (p. 250). The emphasis on explaining the "outliers" is of course important, because if this can be done the chances for the model's being applicable to other, more normal, cases that are not part of the sample also improve. In this way, the tests for validity are different from those that would apply if statistical methods relying on the properties of the central limit theorem were being used. For example, in this case, the validity of the hypothesis proposed increases as a larger number of commonalities in the overall explanation (e.g., among education, demographics, and youthful crime) are accounted for. The more this interconnection is accounted for, the more unlikely alternative hypotheses become.

Applying this principal to the issue discussed here, I am making the following claims:

1. There is a process of migration that has an internal logic of its own.

2. This process involves the becoming and disbecoming of group identity as mediated by intergenerational dynamics.

3. This process occurs in the context of unusual structural conditions that are also migration induced.

4. Deviant youthful subcultures are an observable product of this process.

Thus, if the observable (i.e., youth crime) can be explained logically using these assumptions, there is a good chance that the unobservable (i.e., becoming and disbecoming) is also true.

Following similar reasoning, Goldstone (1991) points out that the point of such an approach is to identify a process that has unfolded in a similar (but not necessarily identical) fashion in a number of different historical contexts (pp. 57-58). Such a process is not necessarily a "law," but is a causal statement asserting that a particular sequence will emerge because individuals—in this case parents and their children in immigrant communities—respond in similar fashions to similar situations. If the proposed model is a good one, it can be expected that in a wide variety of circumstances, actors will respond similarly, and as a result, likely action can be predicted and/or explained.[1]

THE PROBLEM OF DEFINITION AND MEASUREMENT: YOUTHFUL CRIME, CRIMINALS, AND DELINQUENTS

Related to the question of validity is that of definition. After all, the validity of a conclusion cannot be specified unless there is a consensus about the process observed. Crime, of course, is a subject that has begged a sound definition in virtually every study attempted. Like fine wine, you know it when you see it, but it is difficult to describe. Gottfredson and Hirschi (1990, p. 3) sharpened this point recently; they point out that criminology is one of the few disciplines that does not control its dependent variable—that is, what is defined as crime. This is because the definition of crime is a political act, and definitions vary across time. Most obviously, possession of alcohol was a crime during Prohibition, but not before or after that period; furthermore, possession of various drugs (marijuana, cocaine, and so on) was not against the law until early in the 20th century. What is defined as a crime also depends on whether or not there is a response from law enforcement. Having noted that, Gottfredson and Hirschi go on to use standard measures of crime in developing their general theory of crime. I take the same shortcut here.

With the above limitations in mind, *youthful crime* is defined for our purposes as illegal acts committed by persons under the age of 25—that is, the age category in which studies have shown (a) that criminal activity is most common, and (b) that criminal activity is most likely to be perpetrated by small groups. A variety of indicators will be used as measures. One measure is official arrest and incarceration statistics. These have been the most commonly used measure of "crime" despite the fact that they exclude acts never officially recorded. Because of this bias, such measures are referred to as either *official crime* statistics or, in the case of juveniles, *official delinquency* statistics. Another useful indicator could have been self-report data. Unfortunately, however, the only ethnic minority for which self-report data have been systematically collected is blacks. The data for other minorities, including specific immigrant groups, are particularly spotty.[2]

Qualitative data can also be used. The qualitative data focus not just on crime itself, but on the social structure of the youth gangs or peer groups that are often involved in illegal activity. Due to a continuing academic and popular interest in the "subculture" of such youth gangs, this is the tradition from which much of the literature about youthful crime in immigrant groups has emerged.[3] This is because most youthful crime is committed by small groups of males, whether immigrant or not. I take advantage of the literature developed from this traditional association for this review.

TESTING THE THEORY

One way of testing the argument is to think of it as an equation in which the variation in the dependent variable "youthful crime" is described. In this case, the variable can be assigned an ordinal value—that is, described as "high" "medium," and "low" rates of youthful crime at a particular time. To identify the effects migration itself has on youthful crime, this explanation is sought in terms of the processes of migration. Four of these conditions were specified in Chapter 2, and include the following:

1. Variability of gender and age structure within the immigrant population, particularly with respect to proportions of at-risk youth within a particular population

2. Variation in the type and quality of group solidarity and internally generated social controls

3. The traditional correlates of youthful crime (i.e., poverty, education, and residence in impoverished central cities) that have been correlated with arrest rates and other indicators of youthful crime

4. What is perceived as being law and how the law is enforced (varies across immigrant groups, times, and localities in a patterned fashion)

The equation would read something like this:

$$\text{Youthful Crime} = \text{Demographics} + \text{Social Control} + \text{Social Conditions} + \text{Perceptions}$$

Again, a way of looking at this equation is to think of the dependent variable as having a qualitative value, such as high, medium, or low.

Where on this continuum youthful crime will be is in turn dependent on how the four independent variables "add up."

Speaking in terms of an equation, it is possible that these independent variables will interact with each other, meaning that it is likely that demographics in particular will affect the type of group solidarity that is possible. For example, a peasant/working-class immigrant population that arrives with a gender-balanced population with a median age of 21 will have a high proportion of fertile people marry each other under normative standards brought from the home country. The fertility levels these immigrants bring "from home" are likely to be fully realized despite the different geographic location. These parents in turn will not be able to socialize their children into conventional host-country values, and it might be expected that there will be a "crisis" of some sort emerging some 15-20 years after the peak of immigration. As will be seen below, this potentially describes the case of the Laotian Hmong refugees in California in the 1980s. It also describes the case of the Molokan Russian immigrants from Russian Georgia who settled in Los Angeles in 1904-1907.

Of course, there are other plausible "outcomes" of youthful crime for such populations. Nevertheless, we can see how interactive such demographic issues are with those of social solidarity and life chances by comparing the young peasant/working-class population described above with its polar opposite. Filipinos provide a good example. The largest immigrant group from Asia to the United States since 1965 has been from the Philippines, and it has included a large number of English-speaking female nurses in the 22-29 age cohort. The unbalanced sex ratio of this group and the professional status and preexisting English facility of these immigrants have combined to produce a high rate of intermarriage with whites and other ethnic groups in the United States. One consequence has been that, unlike the Hmong and Molokan Russians, Filipinos have relatively low fertility levels. Also as a consequence, the population is more dispersed, and due to strong family ties via middle-class American husbands, is more likely that offspring will be effectively socialized into conventional U.S. values. It would be expected therefore that rates of youthful crime would be "low" for Filipinos.

Other groups have other possible interaction effects on group solidarity, rooted in the demographics of the particular groups. An immigrant population that is 95% male and aged 23-32 on arrival (e.g.,

19th-century Chinese) will confront different issues in the socialization of youth, or potential for youthful crime, from one that is composed of large numbers of upper-middle-class professionals with a median age of 39 (e.g., Cubans). These groups are of course different again from the Hmong, Molokans, and Filipinos mentioned above.

Although demographics shape how immigrant groups deal with various issues, institutions also play a role. The emphasis on the historical particularity of each migration is still relevant. For example, as will be seen below, the traditional church-based *sobranie* of the Russian Molokan Church in Los Angeles of 1910 is not the same institution as a bureaucratized social service agency like Lao Family, Incorporated, which directed the delivery of government services to California Hmong in the 1980s.

There is one final methodological point I would like to make. It is important to remember that although each independent variable has an effect on youthful crime, the variables are not constructed with respect to crime rates. For example, in the assessment of the types of social control agencies (i.e., "social cohesion") within a community, the strength of each agency is considered as a communitywide phenomenon, and not simply as it relates to police and youth services. Likewise, levels of poverty and education have broad implications throughout a community, only one of which is youthful crime. Again, the construction of these issues as "variables" is done without respect to youthful crime incidence itself, and is not discussed specifically in the chapter where this is developed as an issue. The same principle applies to the chapters dealing with age and gender structure, as well as perceptions of the law. It is important to do this, however, if the independent variables are to be truly "independent."

METHODS: DEVELOPING THE VARIABLE YOUTHFUL CRIME

In order to develop these variables, I chose a nonrandom sample of California immigrant groups. I had three reasons for selecting the groups, two methodological and one practical. First, all the groups were, in effect, outliers on the dependent variable—that is, groups that had high rates of youthful crime at one time or another, and groups

that had especially low rates of youthful crime. Second, I selected the
groups for their usefulness in controlling for a variety of variables that
could potentially confound analysis. Thus I selected Asian and Mexican groups with both high and low rates of youthful crime in order to
control for race (including the Confucian ethic and the theory that
witnessing a brutal war causes youthful crime in immigrant groups).
I selected two groups from the earlier part of the 20th century and
three from the latter part in order to control for time (e.g., the assertion
that the 1980s were different from the 1920s, and therefore the two
should not be compared). And I chose Mexicans and Molokan Russians from the Boyle Heights neighborhood in order to gain an understanding of why different groups of immigrants who were living as
neighbors could have such different results.

The variations in youthful crime rates for these groups become in
effect the dependent variable. The variables that help explain the
variation in the youthful crime rates become the independent variables. These variables emerge out of the theoretical discussion in
Chapter 2 (also see the equation above).

I also selected cases that had both positive and negative results for
youthful crime, in order to avoid the "sampling on the dependent
variable" problem that has characterized studies of gangs within
particular communities. As I have noted in Chapter 2, a chronic
problem of past studies has been that only cases that have problems
are examined, and then inferences are made to groups that do not have
problems. This is clearly inappropriate.

The immigrant groups selected provided contrast across both the
dependent and the four independent variables, across time, and across
ethnicity. Thus other potentially confounding factors were also logically controlled for. For example, geography was controlled for through
the limitation of the analysis to California groups. The complicated
and tragic history of black-white relations in the United States was
controlled for through the limitation of the analysis to white, Hispanic, and Asian groups, even though the postwar migration of African
Americans to California could very well have generated the same
problems of socialization of youth found in the other groups.

I also selected particular groups because of the comparatively high
quality of the data that were available. For example, I selected the
Laotian case because in 1991 I was involved with a research project
funded by the California Policy Seminar titled "Laotians in the Crimi-

nal Justice System." The analysis might just as well have included Vietnamese and Cambodians, both of which have confronted problems similar to those faced by Laotians in the socialization of youth since migration to California.

I chose the Molokan Russians because of the excellent data collected by Pauline Young in 1932. I chose Koreans in large part because they provide a good contrast to the Laotians, and because a number of authors have written extensively about the Korean experience in California. Mexicans are included because over the past 80 years they have been the largest immigrant group to come to California, there have been a wealth of secondary sources published about the Mexican migration, and this group has had strikingly varied rates of youthful crime.

CONSTRUCTING THE DEPENDENT VARIABLE: SERIOUS YOUTHFUL CRIME IN CALIFORNIA IMMIGRANT GROUPS

In 1991, the California Youth Authority began separating for the first time incarceration data for Asian ethnic groups in California, some of which were specifically immigrant groups. In 1990, the U.S. Census Bureau also released population information for a number of Asian immigrant groups that had not previously been available.[4] Combining these data made possible the generation of rates of offense for "serious juvenile crime."[5] This information, for 1991-1996, is presented in Table 3.1.

As this table shows, there are two clusters of ratios in the groups that have migrated since 1965. One group, the Indochinese refugees from Laos, Cambodia, and Vietnam, have similar ratios of commitment, which rose steadily between 1991 and 1993. The three Indochinese groups, although they come from different backgrounds and live in different parts of California, also share some characteristics that could explain this commonality. In particular, all have passed through similar experiences in the international refugee regime. Koreans and the Filipinos, on the other hand, have primarily been "economic immigrants" and have unusually low levels of commitment. Does this explain the discrepancies in these groups?

TABLE 3.1 Ratios of CYA Commitment, Controlling for Age, 1991-1996

	1991	1992	*Rate Per 10,000* 1993	1994	1995	1996	*1995 Total Male Population, 13-19*
Chinese[b]	6	7	8	12	16	18	33,254
Japanese	10	6	7	9	13	12	10,182
Korean[a]	18	20	22	24	38	39	13,234
Cambodian[a]	123	170	185	184	194	176	6,531
Vietnamese[a]	109	137	155	198	204	194	18,892
All Laotian[a]	105	144	187	209	212	182	10,535
Thai[a]	73	119	140	371	636	730[d]	1,807
Filipino[a]	19	16	19	35	19	20	40,317
White	17	16	15	15	15	15	899,113
African American	266	259	256	235	207	207	124,366
Hispanic[b]	59	71	77	79	82	85	484,072
Total	56	64	63	NA	54	56	1,497,470[c]

SOURCES: Population figures are from the 1990 U.S. Census, and include all 13- to 19-year-olds for 1991 data, 12- to 18-year-olds for 1992 data, 11- to 17-year-olds for 1993 data, and so on. CYA data for Asian groups are from population breakdowns run on December 31, 1996; December 31, 1995; May 31, 1994; March 8, 1993; February 29, 1992; and April 9, 1991. These data include wards and parolees as of those particular dates. Data for whites, African Americans, and Hispanics are from 1991 reports and reports dated December 31, 1996; December 31, 1995; June 30, 1993; and December 31, 1992. These data include institutionalized cases received during the calendar year.

NOTE: In this table, the total population of 13- to 19-year-old males—that is, the population at risk for commitment to CYA—is divided by the total number of commitments to CYA. Ratios for Asian groups cannot be compared with the ratios for whites, African Americans, and Hispanics, as these represent all institutionalized groups received during the year. The Asian groups include those institutionalized as of a particular date. NA = not available.

a. This group has had almost all of its foreign immigration since 1965.

b. This group has large numbers of post-1965 immigrants, but also a substantial population that migrated before 1930.

c. Total does not match the sum of the column because some smaller groups are omitted.

d. The rise in rates for the category "Thai" appears to be due to "Lao" youth self-identifying in this category. See Note 7, p. 118.

Laotians, 1975-Present

Laotians began arriving in the United States as refugees in 1975. Before 1975, there was no significant Laotian population in the United States. Laotian refugees come from three more or less exclusive ethnic groups—Hmong, Mien, and ethnic Lao—that have slightly differing histories. These groups have also had slightly different histories in the United States, and by and large, did not live in the same neighborhoods and cities upon first arrival. This is changing in the late 1990s,

TABLE 3.2 Ratios of CYA Commitment for Three Groups of Laotians, August 1991 and May 1997

Ethnic Group	N August 1991	Rate/10,000, 1991 Only	N May 1997	Total 13-19-Year-Old Population, 1991
Laotians total	104	130	105	7,998*
Mien	19	281	7	approximately 675
Ethnic Lao	60	148	64	approximately 4,053
Hmong	25	76	34	3,270*

SOURCES: Total figures for all Laotians and Hmong are from the U.S. Census. The estimate for Mien is based on a ratio of Mien school enrollments to the total Laotian figure from the U.S. Census. NOTE: This table includes cases in CYA custody only. Parolees are excluded.

however, as all three groups concentrate in California's Central Valley. Perhaps one-third of the more than 300,000 refugees coming from Laos settled in the California cities of Fresno, Sacramento, and San Diego, as well as in Orange County. The three groups have also had different rates of serious youthful offender incarceration during their earlier years, although all three groups have been at the high end. Likewise, examination of the probation records at the California Youth Authority for all three groups indicates that gang activity was a primary correlate of arrest in the early 1990s (Waters & Cohen, 1993). This trend has continued as recently as 1997 (see Table 3.2). However, this was most important in the earlier years with the Mien and the Lao. Hmong did not begin to experience higher rates of arrest due to gang activity until the mid-1990s, and even then it never approached the unusually high rates of the Mien or ethnic Lao.

Gang Activity Among Laotian Youth

The activities of youthful gangs of Laotians began to come to the attention of law enforcement in the late 1980s. Law enforcement correlated the phenomenon with a broad number of issues, such as the proximity of the Southeast Asians to African American and Latino/Chicano gangs in inner-city neighborhoods, breakdown in parental control, and opium abuse by elderly Mien. Of particular interest to law enforcement officials has been the issue of culture. They have observed that in the 1990s Laotian gangs began to resemble the structure of black and Hispanic gangs, and developed "age sets" between Central Valley gangs. Law enforcement officials have noted that they have seen portions of the Laotian gangs originally focused on petty theft, pride, and girls develop organizations involved in rock cocaine and methamphetamine distribution. The Hmong gangs organize home invasions, but, according to some law enforcement officers, continue to have lower rates of arrest. In the process, all three ethnic groups have become more violent and have developed a reputation for "copycatting" Hispanic prison gangs such as Nuestra Familia.

Refugees, social workers, and law enforcement officials alike correlate this rise with a lack of understanding of American child-rearing techniques among refugee parents. Often these explanations are framed in terms of how the child protection laws are enforced. Many refugees believe that it is "against the law" to discipline their children with the corporal punishment techniques they are accustomed to using. There is undoubtedly some truth to all of these explanations. However, they are also after-the-fact explanations, usually of use in explaining situations within only one group, in this case Laotians. As a consequence, such explanations are not easily generalizable to other groups.

Analysis of data gathered from the records of the Sacramento County Courthouse reveals more precisely how the high incidence of Laotian youthful crime emerged in the late 1980s. The first major felony arrests of adult Laotians in Sacramento were for opium and for a murder in 1985-1986 (see Table 3.3). Felony arrests tapered off in 1985-1987. The first arrests of juveniles for gang-oriented crimes, such as car burglary, occurred in 1988. These continued through 1989-1990. This in turn led to arrests for more complex crimes, particularly drug dealing, usually involving the ethnic Lao, in the mid-1990s.

An increase in the Laotian population accounts for some of this increase in criminal activity. However, it does not account for either the sudden emergence of car burglary as an adult crime or the quadrupling in the number of arrests between 1988 and 1989-1990, or for the rate of arrests being sustained through 1995. This is because a different pattern of arrests began to emerge with the formation of youth gangs, such as the Sacramento Bad Boys (SBB) in the Oak Park area of Sacramento. Arrests for auto burglary, marijuana, firearms, and other gang-oriented activities by members of such youth gangs began in the early 1990s. By the mid-1990s, SBB had slowed its activities, although not before a younger set, Against the Law (ATL), became involved in drug dealing. This coincided with other gangs' aging by adopting age-graded sets. This happened at the same time parents were complaining to social workers about the breakdown in the control of

TABLE 3.3 Time Series for Adult Laotian Cases Prosecuted in Sacramento County, 1980-1990

Year	Felonies	Hmong (Vang + Xiong)		Lao (X + Ph)		Mien (Sae)	
1980	0	1		0		0	
1981	0	0		0		1	
1982	0	1		5		5	
1983	0	51		12		11	
1984	4	98		21		56	
1985	2	118		38		148	
1986	1	129		52		234	
1987	0	145		55		228	
1988	4	178		65		281	
1989	15	197		74		343	
1990	13	235	*Felonies*	82	*Felonies*	428	*Felonies*
1991	9	238	3	73	0	419	6
1992	26	240	9	68	1	440	16
1993	58	264	11	71	7	426	40
1994	69	275	19	71	8	425	42
1995	60	279	10	59	9	348	41
1996	106	265	27	77	21	188	58

SOURCE: Data collected from the Sacramento County Courthouse.
NOTE: For comparative purposes, Pacific Bell telephone books were sampled for common surnames in each of the three Laotian groups to generate information about the migration into Sacramento of each ethnic group. These data show that the migration into Sacramento stabilized for all three groups around 1990. Felony arrests of adults continued to rise for all three groups, and as of 1996 had not peaked. Because of the sampling technique, comparisons cannot be made between groups, only within groups. Felonies are disaggregated by group only after 1990.

youth. Youth who were not involved in gang activity often attributed these problems to a failure of the older generation to comprehend the problems of living in U.S. society.

In sum, the statistics from Sacramento and the California Youth Authority indicate that for 10 years or so after the first wave of Laotian immigrants came to the United States, youthful crime in this group was rare. Criminal behavior among Laotian youth became important in the late 1980s, and is still important today. A similar pattern seems to have emerged in the Cambodian and Vietnamese communities. In terms of the dependent variable though, the period from 1975 to 1987 can be labeled one of low or negligible crime, whereas the period from 1988 to 1996 can be labeled a period of relatively high youthful crime.

Koreans, 1970-Present

Korean immigrants are included in this analysis because they are
a "negative case." That is, despite the status of Koreans as an immigrant group, there have been few reports of gang activity among
Koreans, or of more than minor incidents of youthful crime. Such negative examples, of course, are hard to measure, because it is the absence
of an expected pattern that is sought (Waters, 1995b, pp. 519-522).

In the case of the Koreans, I conducted a systematic review of the
substantial ethnographic record concerning their communities. I found
only one mention of youthful gang activity (in 1981), although at one
point the Los Angeles police chief claimed that there was a major
Korean "godfather" figure in Los Angeles's Koreatown who employed
"400 thugs." However, as Light and Bonacich (1988) note, in this
instance police made only three arrests, and never identified the
godfather figure (p. 312).

The commitment rate to the California Youth Authority for Koreans
has also been very low; in 1993 it was 21/10,000 for 13- to 19-year-old
males. The proportion rose slightly by 1995-1996 relative to other
ethnic groups, but it is still extremely low compared with the Southeast
Asian groups. This is consistent with Light and Bonacich's (1988)
observation that "no data indicate that criminal victimization rates
increased in areas of Korean residential settlement" (p. 310).

Examination of the files for the 20 cases of Koreans actually in
CYA custody on December 22, 1993, revealed that, unlike the Laotians, the Korean wards were more likely to be committed for single
serious offenses rather than series of minor offenses. Half of the wards
had been committed for homicide or attempted homicide, rape, and
kidnapping. Only 1 had been committed for auto theft, which was one
of the primary commitment offenses for the Laotians. Only 1 of the
18 wards for whom data were available was born in the United States.

Korean contacts with the law have generally involved business
laws of various sorts, as well as Koreans' roles as victims vulnerable
to inner-city crime (see Raspberry, 1993). The few violations prosecuted tend to be related to licensing requirements, violations of
minimum wage laws, record-keeping requirements, and massage par-
lor violations of prostitution laws. Although such violations may be
traced in part to the marginalization of Korean businesses due to this
group's immigrant status, except for the prostitution, none of these

contacts with law enforcement have specifically to do with young people per se. Significantly, among Koreans there has never been the large number of arrests, or persistently visible gang activity, found in the Laotian and Mexican American communities.

Small businesses owned by Koreans are frequently the targets of robbery, as are other businesses found in inner cities, where many Korean entrepreneurs operate. Light and Bonacich (1988) note that such activity is a source of solidarity for Korean business owners in Los Angeles, in that it gives them reason to press for increased protection from the police (pp. 310-311). The role of the Korean shopkeeper as victim was highlighted during the Los Angeles riots of 1992, when many Korean businesses were reported to be the targets of looters (Freed & Jones, 1992).

Mexicans, 1930s and 1940s

The first major wave of Mexican immigration into Los Angeles began about 1918, and peaked during the 1920s. During the Great Depression in the 1930s, large numbers of immigrants were deported back to Mexico under programs initiated primarily by the city of Los Angeles and the state of California. Between 1910 and 1935, however, the Mexicans were a highly visible and controversial minority (Acuña, 1972, pp. 123-152; Gamio, 1931/1969a, 1930/1969b; Romo, 1983, pp. 89-111). Reports focusing on social problems often blamed the presence of Mexican immigrants, in particular their impacts on schools and on the public relief rolls, their involvement in farm labor unrest and unionization, and their use of marijuana (Mexican Fact-Finding Committee, 1930; Morgan, 1990; Wickersham Commission, 1931).

My literature search turned up no indication of youthful crime activity or gang involvement in the Mexican immigrant communities of the 1920s and 1930s, despite the fact that Mexicans were concentrated in the same East Los Angeles neighborhoods as the Molokan Russians. Indeed, in the two key works published by Manuel Gamio in 1930 and 1931, there is no mention of gangs, juvenile delinquency, or youthful crime of any sort, even though many authors have indicated that the Mexican immigrants were often in conflict with the host country, as their repeated criticism of unionization activities demonstrated. Likewise, there were also frequent arrests of adult Mexican

immigrants for the illegal use of alcoholic beverages during Prohibition, as well as marijuana use. Nevertheless, until at least 1935 actual
arrest rates did not significantly exceed those found in the general
population of Los Angeles County (Wickersham Commission, 1931).

Reports of Mexican American youth gangs first become persistent
in the 1940s. Accounts in the Chicano nationalist literature indicate
that the zoot-suited pachucos, whether judged a problem or not, did
not emerge until the 1940s (Acuña, 1972, 1984; Gomez-Quiñones,
1994; Rios-Bustamente & Castillo, 1986). Popular literature dealing
with the zoot suit riots and sociohistorical accounts (Griffiths, 1948;
McWilliams, 1948) all agree that widespread arrests for many reasons
soared as a result, although they do not specify arrest rates.

Why, then, the absence of youthful crime in the Los Angeles
Mexican community in the 1930s, but not the 1940s? Whether
deserved or not, why did the presence of gangs in the Mexican
American community become an issue at that time, and not earlier,
or later? As in the case of the Koreans, there is no easy answer to this
question. Instead, there is yet another negative case for the dependent
variable, a situation that begs comparative analysis.

Mexicans, 1965-Present

Youthful crime in Mexican immigrant communities is difficult to
specify. In large part this is because definition of these communities
has undergone a number of distinct changes since 1965. Analysis is
confounded by two social conditions. First, as a national group,
Mexican immigrants came to the United States primarily in two
separate waves: one early in the 20th century and another later in the
20th century (Acuña, 1984; McWilliams, 1948; Romo, 1983). Separating the individuals who participated in the two waves is difficult,
because latter-day labeling has lumped them together for statistical
purposes. This has occurred in both census records and the records of
police and others. A second problem in analyzing this group is that
the emergence of Chicano/Latino nationalism means that Spanish-
speaking peoples of non-Mexican origin are grouped together. In some
respects, this is good for this study because a wealth of information
has been generated as a result of this social movement. On the other
hand, it makes specification of "youthful crime in an immigrant
community" in anything more than general terms very difficult.

Malcolm Klein (1971) is one of the few researchers who has dealt with the issue of gangs in Los Angeles during the period 1950-1965. He notes that gang activity and youthful crime were at an all-time low during this period. He puzzles over this absence of activity, because, as he notes, within the same community there was a great deal of gang activity both before this period (i.e., 1940-1950) and after it. In his more recent work, Klein (1995) again emphasizes that gang activity is a product of the 1970-1995 period, when reports on gangs expanded very quickly throughout the country. He does not, however, indicate what role, if any, migration may have played.[6]

It is clear that gang activity developed in the late 1960s, although then it was not organized on the large scale that we find in the 1990s. Writers such as Rodriguez (1993) describe youth who are alienated from any society (Chicano or Anglo) who form cliques to defend themselves against the threats of other youthful gangs. Others, including Vigil (1989), Jankowski (1991), Johnson (1997a, 1997b; Johnson & Cardenas, 1997; Johnson & Cole, 1997), and Padilla (1992), have focused on the descriptive ethnography of particular gangs. Brought together, their work is an indication that gang activity was a persistent problem in Mexican American and Latino communities in the 1980s. However, these researchers offer no indication of the relationship of gang formation to immigration. Moore (1991) is more specific in stating that, by and large, gangs are a second-generation phenomenon; as noted in Chapter 2, she asserts that the notion of multigenerational gang membership is a "myth." Dorothy Torres (personal communication, January 1994), who spent many years working with gangs in East Los Angeles, agrees with Moore on this point; she claims that problems emerge when immigrant parents do not recognize what their children are doing. She recalls occasions when she has told immigrant parents that their sons were involved in gangs, and says that the parents who were born in the United States were more likely to be aware of what was going on.

The assumption of all the reports mentioned above is that youthful crime by Latino gangs is high in California's inner cities. This is an impression supported by law enforcement. In sum, it appears that youthful crime is fairly high in California's Mexican immigrant community, particularly in the urban areas of immigrant first settlement. However, despite the wealth of data collected about gang activity, an effective understanding of the role that different structural conditions play on the formation of youthful gangs eludes researchers. In large part this is because, for the purposes of answering this question, most studies have, in effect, "sampled on the dependent variable" by focusing only on youthful gangs and not on the broader sociocultural context. For example, there have been no systematic studies of immigrant Mexican youth who are not gang members. Nevertheless, Mexican immigration can be introduced to the dependent variable as a case of "high" youthful crime in the 1980s.

Molokan Russians, 1904-1950

Pauline Young's (1932) study of Molokan Russians in the Boyle Heights neighborhood of Los Angeles is one of the most systematic juvenile delinquency studies about an immigrant group ever conducted. Using arrest data, Young describes a wave of youthful crime that emerged between 1923 and 1929, approximately 20 years after the first Molokans arrived in Los Angeles from Russian Georgia (this has been described in Figure 2.2, in Chapter 2). What these data indicate is that from 1904 to 1907, there were only low levels of juvenile delinquency, whereas from 1920 to at least 1927, rates were much higher. After about 1940, rates were probably low again. More recent studies of Molokan youth have focused on issues of assimilation rather than juvenile delinquency (Dunn & Dunn, 1978; Hardwick, 1993).

SUMMARY: THE DEPENDENT VARIABLE

The five comparison groups have been assessed for the dependent variable "youthful crime." The results are as follows (see also the summary in Table 3.4):

- *Laotians:* A high rate of youthful crime emerged about 8 years after the largest wave arrived in the United states in 1981. This wave continued to rise at least until 1995. The focus of this group's youthful crime is gang activity. The earlier arrests involved impulsive crimes, but by the mid-1990s, Laotian gangs became involved with drug distribution. This activity was more of a problem among the ethnic Lao and Mien than among the Hmong.

TABLE 3.4 Estimates of Comparative Rates of Youthful Crime in
Six Groups of Immigrants in 5-Year Increments

Immigrant Group	Cohort	Relative Rate of Youthful Crime	Comment
Lao	1975-1988	low	
	1989-1997	high	
Mien	1980-1988	low	
	1989-1997	high	
Hmong	1978-1988	low	
	1989-1991	medium	
	1992-1997	high?	
Mexicans	1960-1965	low	
	1966-1970	medium	emergence of Chicano nationalism
	1971-1975	high	
	1976-1980	high	
	1981-1985	high	War on Drugs
	1986-1990	high	
Koreans	1971-1993	low	
Molokan Russians	1905-1921	low	arrival and pacifism during World War I
	1921-1930	high	
	1931-1934	high?	
	1935-1939	medium?	community disintegration
	1940-1945	low	
Mexicans	1920-1925	low	settlement
	1926-1930	low	labor unrest; arrests for marijuana and alcohol
	1931-1935	low	Great Depression and deportation campaigns; prohibition ends; labor unrest
	1936-1942	low-high	mass deportations from Los Angeles area
	1943-1950	medium?	Sleepy Lagoon incident; zoot suit riots; World War II
	1951-1953	medium?	
	1954-1980	low?	
	1981-present	high	

■ *Koreans:* A major wave of youthful crime has yet to begin among Koreans, despite the fact that large numbers of Korean immigrants have been in the United States since the 1970s. There is no indication that such a wave will begin.

■ *Mexicans—early group:* A large group of Mexican immigrants settled in East Los Angeles between 1918 and 1930. Many lived in the same neighborhoods as the Molokan Russians, but there is no indication that there were any unusual outbreaks of youthful crime among the Mexicans. The earliest reports of youthful gang activity are from 1940-1945, and seem to postdate the peak of Molokan Russian gang activity.

■ *Mexicans—later group:* A large wave of Mexican immigrants arrived in California between 1965 and the present. A wave of gang-oriented youthful crime emerged in the inner cities of California in the 1970s and 1980s. It is not completely clear, however, how closely related this wave is to immigration, given that most statistics are confounded by fairly imprecise classification of the migration event. One thing that is clear is that in the Hispanic population of California as a whole, youthful crime rates for serious offenses have risen substantially since 1985.

■ *Molokan Russians:* A youthful crime wave started among Molokan Russian immigrants about 1923 and ended by 1939. There is no evidence that it persisted into the 1940s. This wave took place between 15 and 35 years after the group settled in East Los Angeles.

CONCLUSION

There has been a great deal of variation in the amount of youthful crime in the five groups surveyed, both within and between the groups. Thus Molokan Russians went from being a "model minority" in the 1910s to having a high rate of youthful crime in the 1920s. This seems to have ended by the time World War II began. This, in turn, occurred at a time when Mexican immigrants living in the same neighborhoods had a very low incidence of youthful crime. On the other hand, the incidence of youthful crime in the Mexican community rose in the late 1930s, before stopping in the mid-1940s.

Likewise, in the late 20th century, a similar though quicker pattern has been observed among Laotians, in particular. Laotians initially had a fairly low incidence of youthful crime, but by the late 1980s it rose. In the case of Laotians, this varied somewhat among the three ethnic groups, though all were affected. Hmong, however, had a lower incidence of youthful crime, whereas the rates for Mien and Lao were higher.

In contrast, Korean immigrants seem never to have had a significant incidence of youthful crime. It is not yet completely clear why this is so, and the literature sheds little light on the issue.

Finally, there are indications that youthful crime rose in some Mexican immigrant communities in the 1980s, after having disappeared in the 1950s and 1960s.

What emerges from the "dependent variable" is a process that in several groups—including the Molokans, Laotians, and Mexicans—has involved rising and falling rates of youthful crime, often at different periods. On the other hand, the Koreans have never had high rates of youthful crime. The question is, Why? Why at some times do immigrant groups have high rates of youthful crime, and at other times low rates? What do the "independent variables" have to say about this?

NOTES

1. Such methodology of course has its skeptics. Historians who focus on the particularity of historical sequences argue that the search for regularities across time and space is epistemologically flawed. Social scientists, particularly sociologists and political scientists, who focus on the statistical generalizations made possible by the central limit theorem criticize such methods because of the small sample sizes inevitably used. They point out, correctly, that absolute predictions cannot be made, or precise causation determined. But just because these characteristics cannot be measured or observed using statistical techniques does not mean that there is no underlying process that can be analyzed and described. As Goldstone (1991) notes, this type of sociology is useful for pointing out "robust processes," and not for establishing causality, correlation, or laws (p. 58).

2. An exception noted by Empey (1982, pp. 115-116) is Voss's 1966 article about a self-report study conducted in Honolulu. This study had a large number of responses from Japanese American youth, but Voss did not indicate whether these youth were first-, second-, third-, or fourth-generation immigrants. Given the history of Japanese immigration into Hawaii and the rest of the United States, it is likely that many were the descendants of 19th-century immigrants.

3. Klein (1971, pp. 11-18) offers a careful discussion of how academic, police, and self-definitions of gang membership can vary. It is apparent from his work that the use of the term *gang* itself can be problematic. Katz (1988) prefers the term *street elites,* noting that the word *gang* itself is a reification by the outside world of academic researchers and law enforcement.

4. Unless otherwise noted, all 1990 U.S. Census data cited in this volume are taken from the U.S. Census of California, Summary Tape File 2, Table PB 5, which I obtained from the California Department of Finance. Data from the 1920 census are from Reel 233 of the U.S. Census for Los Angeles County.

5. See Visher, Lattimore, and Linster (1991) for a discussion of how similarly collected data from the CYA can be interpreted.

6. The number of illegal immigrants in California's prisons received widespread attention as the 1994 gubernatorial election campaign began. Governor Wilson, according to local press, billed the federal government for the costs of incarcerating 23,000 inmates in state prison (Sample, 1994). It is not clear how Wilson arrived at this figure; however, according to a spokesman I contacted in the California Department of Corrections, on January 20, 1994, there were 12,483 Immigration and Naturalization Service "holds" in state prison, and 4,269 potential holds. There were also 5,860 INS holds on parole. These figures total 22,612, which is close to the governor's number. However, not all INS holds are in fact illegal immigrants, given that many legal immigrants (e.g., refugees) are released into the United States on the condition that they "obey all laws" and have immigration holds placed on them when they are arrested. Convictions of legal resident aliens can also result in holds. The total prison population included 119,000 prisoners and 117,000 parolees. However, the classifications are too imprecise to tell what proportions of these are actually "illegal immigrants."

Part II

*A*nswering the

*Q*uestion Why:

Community and Structure

CHAPTER 4

Demographics and the Process of Migration

*C*riminologists have long recognized that criminal activity is concentrated during youth and among males. In other words, criminal activity is strongly dependent on age. Indeed, this has been implied in many criminological studies. Recent demographic studies have also correlated demographics with life chances in various ways. Finally, age is a very significant category within the legal system, specifying as it does the age of majority and, for the purposes described here, the separation of criminal matters into adult and juvenile.

In recent years, some researchers have used these distinctions to make predictions about when crime rates are likely to increase (Cohen & Land, 1987). Typically, they employ a straightforward calculation in which rising crime rates across the whole population are correlated with a rising proportion of young males within the same population. Criminologists note that arrest rates peak between ages 17 and 20, with the exact ages varying a bit from crime to crime. A typical age range for "youthful crime" would be from about 15 to 23, a criminological distinction that spans both sides of the divide between the legal categories of adult and juvenile.

Also of relevance is the attention that demographers have paid to age. Demographers have pointed out that aside from crime rates, the age and gender structure of a population shapes the life chances of the members of that population across the entire life cycle. This approach has had wide application. For example, Easterlin (1980), the best-known proponent of this idea, has correlated "baby booms and busts" with decreased and increased life chances within the U.S. economy. Guttentag and Secord (1983) applied similar principles to sex ratios that they correlated with the social status of women. Goldstone (1991) was able to trace the origin of state breakdown in the early modern world to birth-driven expansions of population that lead to unusually strong demands on state resources in succeeding generations.

Finally, the criminal justice system recognizes implicitly that age matters by maintaining separate institutions for those under 18 years old (juveniles) and those 18 years old and older (adults). This distinction of course emerges from the broader legal philosophy concerning the age of majority as it pertains to rights and responsibilities relative to voting, contracts, and even the military draft. Notably, however, such laws are not the consequence of the systematic observations of criminologists and demographers regarding youthful crime; rather, they represent a social consensus embedded in morals. Nevertheless, this legal categorization is important, and it is the final interaction with the criminological phenomenon that needs to be considered. Although the legal definition does not seem to have any specific effects upon how people between the ages of 16 and 23 behave (for example, as a group, those aged 18 plus 1 day do not offend at a rate greater than those aged 17 plus 364 days), it does mean that there is a different response by the state to the group described here.

THE DEMOGRAPHICS OF IMMIGRANT GROUPS

Underlying the criminological and demographic studies, and also the legal categories, is a basic observation: Demographics structure life options. In the case of immigrants, the age and gender structure of groups is important, because in their home countries there is selection for age and gender among those leaving in the first place. Few, if any, immigrant populations reflect the demographics of their sending societies. For example, most immigrant populations have an unusually large proportion of young adults, although precise age spreads vary from group to group. Immigrant groups also tend not to have large proportions of particular age groups. For a number of reasons, there are typically fewer small children in immigrant streams, and a larger proportion of adults than is found in either the home or the host society (Gordon, 1990).[1]

Just as important, the demographics of immigrant groups are also unlikely to reflect the age and sex structure of the host society. Most obvious, at arrival, immigrant groups tend to have a higher proportion of young adults than the host society. This effect, however, has long-term consequences, because this unusually large group moves through time together, creating "demographic ripples." For example, they have babies together, perhaps creating an hourglass-shaped age structure in which there is both a large proportion of young adults and a large number of children. Such factors help to shape individuals' social psychological expectations concerning their life chances (Guttentag & Secord, 1983, pp. 21-22). In the case of an immigrant group, these expectations are discussed and legitimated through an ongoing "conversation" within the new "ethnic" community. This is done in the context of the "conversation" that is ongoing in the host society. What this discussion is about is dependent on what individuals are doing, which in turn is dependent on where they are in the life cycle. In sum, demographics matter.

For example, an obvious effect of age demographics can be seen in the "marriage market." A population of immigrants that has an unusually large proportion of single males and/or females is likely to have different concerns from one that does not. Similar conclusions can be drawn about other social characteristics that affect social status. Thus a population founded by large numbers of young immigrant peasants (e.g., Mexicans, Laotians, Molokan Russians) is likely to have a higher number of births than one that is composed primarily of middle-aged professionals (e.g., Cubans, Filipinos, and Koreans). And, relevant for the thesis presented here, populations with a high proportion of young males relative to adults are likely to have more difficulties socializing those young males than are those with lower youth-to-adult ratios.[2]

Table 4.1 illustrates how the age and sex structure of a population affects youthful crime. This table shows the percentage of the population of 13- to 19-year-old males in each of 12 categories from the 1990 U.S. Census as well as samples of two groups from the 1920 U.S. Census of East Los Angeles. As a percentage of total population, 13- to 19-year-old males range from 3.3% for the census category "Japanese" to a high of 8.1% for the categories "Laotian" and "Vietnamese." Given this information, it would be expected that even if rates of youthful crime are held constant, they should be 2.45 times higher for Vietnamese than for Japanese. Thus, putting the observations of the criminologists and demographers together, it should be possible to make predictions about future rates of offense by examining the relative proportions of younger age cohorts. Thus Table 4.1 includes the percentages of children 0-5 and 6-11 years old. These groups are important because they permit prediction of how large the at-risk group will be in coming years.[3]

For example, based on the data in Table 4.1, it is expected that, if all other factors are held constant, Lao and Vietnamese would have the highest rates (as measured in offenses per 10,000 people) of youthful crime in the early 1990s, and "Japanese" and "white non-Hispanics" would have the lowest rates of youthful crime. Likewise, based on the 1920 census, the East Los Angeles Russian population would be expected to have a higher rate of youthful crime from 1920 to 1930 than the Mexican immigrant community of the same time. Finally, predictions can be made about the size of at-risk groups into the future. For example, when the 6- to 11-year-old cohort enters the at-risk age group for youthful crime, Hmong arrest rates should exceed all others for at least 15 years (i.e., from about 1995 to 2010). Vietnamese rates, on the other hand, would be expected to drop relative to the other groups, because the proportion of 0- to 5-year-olds in the 1990 population was smaller.[4]

The potential effects of variations in the sex and age distribution on California's immigrant populations are illustrated graphically in the age pyramids in Figures 4.1-4.8. For example, Figure 4.1 is the age pyramid for non-Hispanic whites in the 1990 census for California. This is, in effect, the "control." The sex ratio is fairly even from ages 1 to 16 and over about age 32. Between ages 17 and 31 there is a slight surplus of males. There are also relatively large numbers of children and young adults relative to the number of people over age 45. Figure 4.1 shows that in 1990, the ratio of males to females in the majority white population was relatively large at all ages. There is a bulge representing the "baby boom" cohort between ages 18 and 43. The number of children relative to the size of this cohort is small, however. The older population (e.g., over age 50) is relatively large.

TABLE 4.1 Percentages of Males in Different Age Cohorts in Selected California Ethnic Groups and Summary Statistics: 1990 Census and 1920 Census Sample From East Los Angeles

Ethnic Group	13-19-Year-Old Males	0-5-Year-Old Males	6-11-Year-Old Males	0-14-Year-Old Males
Black	5.5	6.5	5.0	13.0
Lao	8.1	8.6	9.4	22.0
Cambodian	6.7	9.2	10.8	22.5
Vietnamese	8.1	5.6	4.8	14.4
Thai	5.6	4.4	4.0	10.9
Hmong	7.0	13.6	12.3	29.3
Hispanic	6.9	7.7	4.9	15.4
White, non-Hispanic	3.9	3.3	3.6	8.6
Korean	6.0	4.6	4.5	11.2
Filipino	5.3	4.8	4.8	11.9
Japanese	3.3	3.3	2.9	7.5
Chinese	4.6	4.1	4.0	10.2
Mexican	7.0	7.3	6.2	16.2
Total	4.4	4.9	4.5	11.4

Summary Statistics

Mexican ($n = 525$)	5.9	8.8	5.7	16.6
Molokan Russian ($n = 593$)	7.9	11.5	9.6	22.9

Summary Statistics for Data From 1990 Census—Median Ages

	Males	Females
All California	31	31
Korean	30	32
Laotian	17	18
Mexican origin	21	23
Hmong	10	11
White, non-Hispanic	33	35

Summary Statistics for Samples From 1920 Census—Median Ages

	Males	Females	Total Population
Mexican			
median	23.5	18	21
mean	24.3	19.8	22.1
standard deviation	17.1	16.0	16.8
Russian			
median	16	16	16
mean	20.7	20.7	20.7
standard deviation	17.5	17.9	17.7

SOURCES: For data in the top portion of the table, 1990 U.S. Census, Summary Tape File 2, Table PB5; for Mexican and Molokan Russian summary statistics, 1920 U.S. Census, Reel 233, Los Angeles County, California (for the Mexican sample, all families headed by an immigrant on sheets 5-39 were included; for Molokan Russians, all Russia-born who spoke Russian in S. Pecan Street, S. Clarence Street, and S. Gless Street were included).

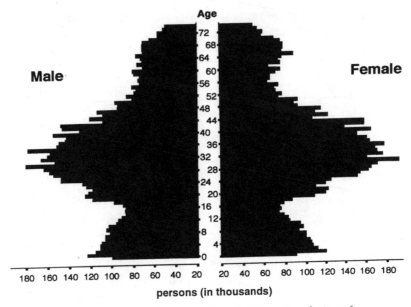

Figure 4.1. Age Pyramid for the Non-Hispanic White Population of California, 1990

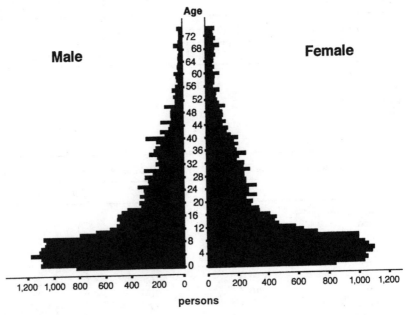

Figure 4.2. Age Pyramid for Persons Self-Identifying as Hmong in California, 1990

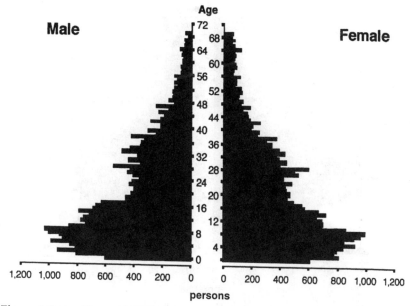

Figure 4.3. Age Pyramid for Persons Self-Identifying as Laotian in California, 1990

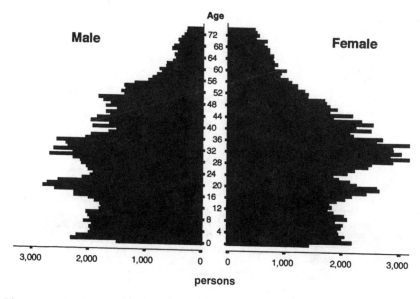

Figure 4.4. Age Pyramid for Persons Self-Identifying as Korean in California, 1990

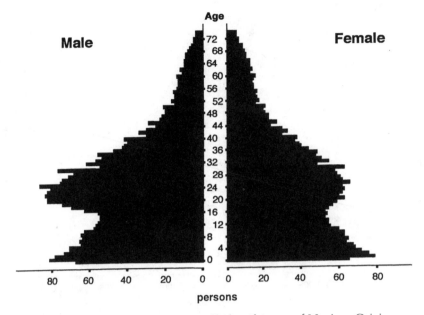

Figure 4.5. Age Pyramid for Persons Self-Identifying as of Mexican Origin
(Whites and Nonwhites) in California, 1990

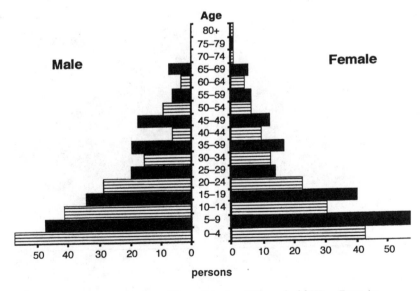

Figure 4.6. Sample of Persons Whose Heads of Household Were Born in
Russia and Spoke Russian, Living in East Los Angeles, 1920 Census

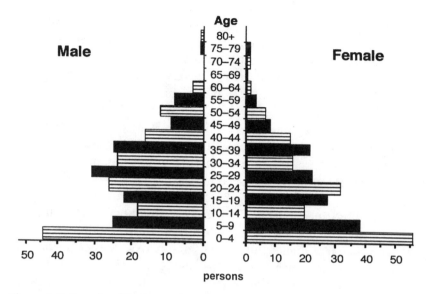

Figure 4.7. Sample of Persons Whose Heads of Household Were Born in Mexico and Spoke Spanish, Living in East Los Angeles, 1920 Census

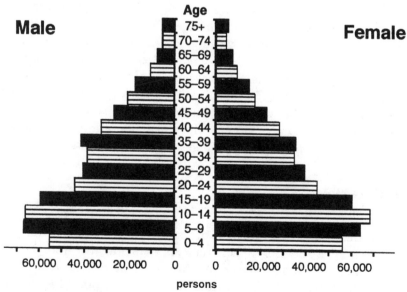

Figure 4.8. Age Pyramid for "Mexican-Origin" Population in the United States, 1940 Census

Are youthful crime rates then simply reflections of population demographics? That is, are youthful crime rates correlated with the proportion of boys at risk for criminal activity in a straightforward, linear fashion? If this were the case, it would be expected that the populations of those committed to the CYA would reflect the proportions of 13-19-year-old males in the general population. In other words, incarceration rates in the CYA should reflect the proportions of Korean, Laotian, and other ethnic groups in the population. This comparison is made in Table 4.2. There is a strong statistical correlation ($r = 0.743$, $R^2 = 0.55$ when $n = 12$ ethnic groups) between the proportion of young males in an immigrant population and the group's incarceration rate in the CYA. But keep in mind that this correlation is about a proportion in the CYA, and not absolute numbers. In other words, the group does not have a higher incarceration rate simply because it has a higher number of boys at risk. Rather, there is an interaction effect, such that groups having more young boys relative to adults have even larger numbers of incarcerations in the CYA than would be expected. But there is no general indication of why having a higher proportion of young boys in a population should cause a higher arrest rate for that same group.

The following examination of each of the groups in the independent variable demography, then, will be aimed at answering one question: How do the different intergenerational dynamics in immigrant groups affect youthful crime rates? A second related question— Why do these youthful crime rates emerge in the way they do?—will be addressed in Chapter 7. There, I will return to the question of demographics and, in the tradition of Easterlin (1979) and Guttentag and Secord (1983), describe why the different types of immigrant demographics result in qualitatively different types of youthful crime waves.

LAOTIANS

More than 215,000 Laotians came to the United States as refugees between 1975 and 1989. These refugees were primarily from 3 of the more than 40 ethnic groups found in Laos: Hmong, ethnic Lao, and Mien. In 1990 in California, roughly 100,000 Laotian immigrants were Hmong, another 100,000 were ethnic Lao, and about 15,000 were Mien.[5] Culturally, these groups are different enough that the

TABLE 4.2 Comparison of "Serious Crime" Rates, as Measured by CYA Incarceration, With Size of 13-19-Year-Old At-Risk Cohort, 1991

| Ethnic Group | 13-19-Year-Olds | | CYA Incarceration Rate, 1991 |
	n	%	
Lao	8.1	1	1/60
Cambodians	6.7	3	1/69
Vietnamese	8.1	1	1/81
Thai	5.6	6	1/111
Hmong	7.0	2	1/130
Korean	6.0	5	1/573
Filipino	5.3	7	1/752
Japanese	1.3	9	1/1425
Chinese	4.6	8	1/1161

1990 census included categories for both Hmong and "Laotian." The Mien, while also culturally distinct, were a smaller group that did not have a separate census category and so presumably were counted in the category "Laotian." On the other hand, other official statistics, such as school enrollment forms and police records, often separated the Mien from the other two groups.

Immigration to the United States from Laos peaked in 1979-1981, when more than 60% of all the refugees who were to come arrived. The most remarkable demographic features of this population have been, first, its subsequent concentration in the Central Valley of California, and second, the extraordinarily high fertility rates found in both the Hmong and Laotian populations. This can be seen in the relatively high proportion of children aged 0-10 as of the 1990 census. In the age pyramids for both groups (Figures 4.2 and 4.3), there are obvious bulges for the population under 10 years old. This is probably because, as Gordon (1990, p. 220) reports, the median age of the immigrants from Laos was very young, ranging from 16 to 19 upon arrival in 1978-1986.[6] Particularly for the Hmong, the young age of this population was a factor that contributed to the large cohort of births in the United States. This circumstance is also in part reflected in Rumbaut and Weeks's (1986) survey, conducted in 1983 in San Diego, California, which found that household size for Lao was 6.7 persons, whereas for Hmong it was 8.2.

This difference is evident from age-specific census statistics for two Laotian census categories, Laotian and Hmong. However, the fertility levels have not been identical in the United States.[7] This is evident from a comparison of Figures 4.2 and 4.3. In both census groups, there is a roughly equal distribution between males and females at all ages. There is also a disproportionately large number of children between the ages of 0 and 17 in both groups. However, the Hmong have slightly more males than females between the ages of 1 and 18. This is particularly striking between the ages of 12 and 18, which would include both immigrant children and a few American-born Hmong.

But the most striking characteristic of the age pyramid for the Hmong is the disproportionately large number of children between the ages of 0 and 12. Indeed, the median age for Hmong males in California is only 10 years, which is substantially lower than that of any of the other groups studied here, reflecting the extraordinary fertility rates of the Hmong in the United States.

The proportion of males 15 and under in the Hmong population was by far the highest of any ethnic group in California. This is also reflected in direct comparisons between the birth cohorts of Hmong and Lao males. Thus, in absolute numbers, Lao are more numerous than Hmong at every age over age 9, whereas Hmong are more numerous at ages younger than 9. In terms of youthful crime, this would mean that if all other things are held constant, the Hmong rate would be expected to be lower than that of the Lao from 1985 to 1995. But, as the large cohort of Hmong youth enters the at-risk age for arrest, if all other effects are held constant, it would be expected that the Hmong rate would rise relative to the Lao.

An advantage of comparing the Hmong and Lao populations is that they are similar on many factors, including time of arrival, experience in Thai refugee camps, family income, and welfare dependency.

KOREANS

Koreans first migrated to the United States in large numbers in the late 1960s, but the largest contingent arrived between 1970 and 1980. The immigration from Korea began in 1966-1968, when professionals and skilled workers were given preferential treatment by the United States in the issuance of immigrant visas. The balance shifted in the 1970s, however, as large numbers began to qualify for admission to the United States as either spouses or siblings of the previous immigrants. Thus migration focused on the newly emergent professional classes of Korea, rather than the working/farming classes found in other migration streams (Hurh & Kim, 1984; Light & Bonacich, 1988, pp. 134-137).

Nevertheless, although the Korean immigrants themselves were, by and large, professionals, they were not always able to reestablish themselves as such in the United States. Instead, many made use of family connections in order to establish capital-intensive small businesses, taking advantage of pooled capital resources and exploiting the labor of skilled, non-English-speaking family members. These practices were facilitated by immigration laws that used family relationships as a criterion for admission (Light & Bonacich, 1988).

The circumstances of their initial migration have resulted in unusual age and gender distributions for Koreans, which can be seen in Figure 4.4. The largest Korean cohort is made up of women aged about 28-38. This population has an unbalanced sex ratio at this age cohort; there are many more women than men. This is consistent with Light and Bonacich's (1988, p. 106) observation that in 1977, there were only 76 male Korean emigrants to the United States for every 100 female emigrants.[8] Unlike the age pyramids for the other ethnic groups, Figure 4.4 shows a substantial "bump" in the distribution of Korean females between ages 25 and 45.

Household size for Koreans is smaller than for the Southeast Asians. Hurh and Kim (1984) conducted a survey in Los Angeles in 1979 and found a mean household size of 3.5 persons, similar to the U.S. average of 3.59 (p. 57).

What these demographics mean in terms of youthful crime is that if all other things are equal there is a higher proportion of Korean adults supervising the socialization processes of the young. As a result, the youthful crime incidence for Koreans relative to groups such as the Lao and Hmong would be expected to be much lower. If all other factors are held constant, it would be expected that the youthful crime rates in the Korean population would be relatively low.

MEXICANS, 1990 CENSUS

Mexican immigration to the United States is a much older phenomenon than that of Laotians or Koreans. There have been two major waves of Mexican immigration in the 20th century, the first in the period between 1918 and 1929, and the second since about 1968.[9] Despite the relatively distant "old" nature of much of the "Mexican-origin" population in the United States, data from the 1990 census indicate unusual characteristics.[10]

Figure 4.5 shows a large number of Mexican males in the 17- to 30-year-old category. This "bump" represents the consequences of recent labor immigration in male-dominated industries, especially farm labor, which attracts "economic migrants." Sex ratios are well balanced in other age groups.

In the Mexican immigrant population there is a substantial proportion of children, reflecting this group's persistently high birthrate (Bean & Swicegood, 1985). Notably, however, the proportion of children relative to the young adult population is not as large as that of the other immigrants from rural areas—Hmong, Lao, Molokan, and, for that matter, Mexicans from the earlier part of the century. The dependent elderly population is relatively small.

Nevertheless, in 1990 there was still a relatively large population at risk in the 17- to 25-year-old category. However, there was also a relatively small number of 15- to 17-year-olds. This is because there was a larger group aged 17-25 who were likely to be immigrants themselves—that is, those who were socialized as children in Mexico and came to the United States as unskilled laborers in service or agriculture.[11] This makes this particular population of Mexicans different from, say, the Laotians or Molokan Russians (see below), for two general reasons: First, the Molokan Russians and Laotians were educated as children in the United States; second, the Mexicans of this age group have gone through a process of self-selection for immigration that the Laotians and Molokan Russians who were born in the United States or migrated as children with their parents have not.

MOLOKAN RUSSIANS, 1920

A sample of the Molokan Russian population in East Los Angeles was taken from the 1920 census tables for the Molokan neighborhood (see Figure 4.6). This sample included all families headed by a Russian-speaking person who was born in Russia. In this way, the smaller but significant populations of Russian-born speakers of Armenian and Yiddish were excluded. According to both Sokolov (1918) and Young

(1932), those Russian-born people who spoke Russian and lived in Boyle Heights in Los Angeles County were by and large Molokan. According to Tripp (1980, p. 76), the population of Molokan Russians was 3,500 in 1912.

In 1920, there was a substantial group of children aged 0-19 in the Molokan population. The older age cohorts were considerably smaller. This population had slightly more males (52.6%) than females (47.4%). The 13- to 19-year-old male population in 1920 (7.9%) was, compared with the modern groups, large. Likewise, there was an extraordinarily large population aged 0-14 (22.9%), about to enter the at-risk ages for youthful crime (see Table 4.1 and Figure 4.6). The median age for males was a young 16.

The large number of children—for the most part born in California— reflects the high fertility of their parents when they arrived in Los Angeles during 1904-1907. In this respect, the pattern seems similar to those of the ethnic Lao and Hmong described above. The census records indicate that all of these children were born to Russian immigrants, and none to California-born Russians. Still, a substantial proportion of the 15- to 19-year-olds were born in Russia, and presumably migrated to the United States as infants or small children.

What this means is that a substantial proportion of the Russian male population was entering the at-risk 15-25 age for criminal activity in 1920-1940. During this period, the adult population supervising these youth would be expected to first decline and then increase as those in the American-born birth cohort themselves became parents.

MEXICANS, 1920 AND 1940 CENSUSES

A sample of the Mexican population of East Los Angeles was taken from the 1920 census. The sample included all Mexican-born heads of households and their families (Figure 4.7). In addition, information was located in U.S. census reports about different populations of Mexicans in the United States.

The majority of the group enumerated in the 1920 census had arrived recently in the United States. Indeed, most of the sample arrived in 1918-1919, although substantial numbers came earlier. This is reflected in the demographics of the East Los Angeles sample group, which had a disproportionately large number in the 20- to 40-year-old

TABLE 4.3 Breakdown in Age Distribution for Los Angeles County's Mexican and Russian Populations, 1940 Census

Age	Foreign-Born				Foreign or Mixed Parentage			
	Mexican		Russian		Mexican		Russian	
	n	%	n	%	n	%	n	%
Under 15					22,660	27	6,700	11
15-24					14,620	17	9,500	15
25-34					6,920	8	8,860	14
Under 35	13,000	15	3,740	6				
35-44	10,160	12	6,320	10	2,960	4	5,080	8
45-54	5,920	7	8,840	14	1,540	2	2,400	4
55-64	3,580	4	6,560	11	660	1	400	1
65-74	1,560	2	2,320	4	380		300	
75+	680	1	720	1	100		20	
Total	34,900	41	28,500	46	49,840	59	33,260	53

Grand totals for the city of Los Angeles

Mexicans 84,740

Russians 61,760

SOURCE: Truesdell (1943, p. 94).
NOTE: Figures are estimates based on 5% samples done by the Census Bureau.

age group (males). The proportion of 6- to 11-year-olds (5.7%) was large, but smaller than that of the neighboring Russians. However, the beginning of a baby boom in this population was apparent in the 0-5-year-old category (8.8%). This group is made up of the American-born offspring of the immigrants. Figure 4.8, which illustrates the age structure of the Mexican-origin population in the 1940 census, indicates that this baby boom probably continued in East Los Angeles.

What this meant in terms of youthful crime was that a "wave" of such crime became possible about 1935, when the first substantial cohort actually entered the at-risk age for youthful crime.

Data from the 1940 census show that the proportion of youth in the Mexican immigrant population continued to rise (see Table 4.3). As a consequence, the median age of the Mexican population in the United States was the lowest (21.2 years) of the 25 immigrant groups reported in the 1940 census. This was true in all categories reported—that is, foreign-born (median for Mexicans = 40.3 years) and native white of foreign or mixed parentage (median for Mexican Americans = 14.2 years). As was the case with the later groups, the Mexican immigrants had a baby boom that resulted in a high proportion of children in the 5- to 20-year-old age group in 1940. As can be seen in Table 4.3, this was true of the Mexican population in Los Angeles County. At the time of the 1940 census, 27% of the "Mexican" population in Los Angeles County was under 15 years old, and 17% was aged 15-24. As Truesdell (1943, p. 5) notes, this was because, of the major sending countries, Mexico was the only one from which migration was not legally restricted between 1882 and 1924.

CONCLUSIONS

What do the demographic data described above tell us about the correlation between size of an at-risk cohort and youthful crime? More specifically, what do they tell us about the two questions posed at the beginning of this chapter? First, how might demographic dynamics affect youthful crime rates? Second, why is the presence of a high proportion of young boys so strongly correlated with outbursts of youthful crime?

Modern Cases (Laotians, Koreans, and Mexicans) and the Question Why

The answer to the "why" question for the immigrant groups surveyed is that the percentages of at-risk youth vary a great deal among groups. There is a strong correlation between rates of serious youthful crime, as measured by the CYA data, and percentage of 13- to 19-year-olds in the population. This correlation is particularly convincing, given the nature of the CYA data; the relationship seems strong. Given the Sacramento County Courthouse data, it seems that this relation-ship spills over into the early adult years in a similarly predictable fashion. Table 4.4 summarizes the variation in the six exemplary groups surveyed. In the case of the four modern groups that have lower CYA commitment ratios, there is a relatively smaller proportion of 13- to 19-year-olds in the Hmong and Korean groups than in the Mexican and Lao groups. Comparison of the actual age pyramids, however, indicates that although the proportions of young males are smaller in the Hmong and Korean groups, there are different future expectations. This in turn is rooted in the social history of each group before its arrival in the United States. A further comparison of the Koreans, Hmong, and Lao (summarized in Table 4.4) provides a plausible example of how this may work.

TABLE 4.4 Summary of Age and Gender Dynamics as an Independent
             Variable

Ethnic Group	Birthrate	Gender Balance	Median Age of Males	Source
Laotian				
Hmong	high	balanced	10	1990 census
Lao	high	balanced	17	1990 census
Mien	high	?	young	
Molokan Russian	high	balanced	16	1920 census
Mexican, 1920	high	male surplus over age 25	21	1920 census
Mexican, 1990	medium	male surplus ages 17-40	21	1990 census
Korean	low	female surplus ages 25-50	30	1990 census

The Koreans came to the United States as professionals, a dispro-
portionate number of whom were female. They also brought with them
attitudes from Korea that included lower fertility rates relative to the
other immigrant groups under discussion. One thing that is likely to
happen in such a population is that there will be more out-group
marriage, with corresponding exposure to nonimmigrant value systems.[12] It is also evident that the adult Korean population will be
monitoring the behavior of fewer children than will, say, the Hmong
population until at least the year 2008, and probably longer.

The Hmong case is different. The Hmong did not have a substantial surplus of either adult males or females. The median age on arrival
was low, and a Third World-style age pyramid emerged as a result of
the group's high fertility rates. In terms of youthful crime, this means
that during the early 1990s the at-risk proportion of the population
for youthful crime remained fairly low. Unlike the Korean population,
this population began to be at risk for high rates of youthful crime in
about 1995, and, if all other things are held constant, it can be expected
that these high rates will continue until at least 2010.

On the other hand, the Hmong have also had the advantage of a
15-year lag between when they migrated to the United States and the
earliest point at which a large portion of the population entered the at-risk
age for crime. This interim period potentially provided the Hmong community an opportunity to establish the social norms needed to deal
with such issues. The experience of the Molokan Russians would seem

to indicate that if all other things hold equal, this lag period may not have the desired effect, and that, in fact, a period of high youthful crime rates will still be the result.

Lao already have the highest age-specific proportion of 13- to 19-year-old males, and the serious youthful crime rate at least for 1991 reflects this (Table 4.1). Relative to the Hmong, a large number of young male Lao were in the immigrant group arriving in the United States. Nevertheless, the Lao population also shows a high fertility rate after arrival. If only the 1990 age pyramid is considered, a high rate of youthful crime would be expected to begin in 1989 and continue until 2010. Thus, although this rate would be expected to be high relative to other groups, relative to the Hmong, all things being equal, it would be expected to be lower, particularly in the early years of the 21st century.

The 1990 Mexican population pyramids are more difficult to interpret than those of the other groups, because of the continued arrival of new immigrants. Nevertheless, the age pyramids do indicate something relative to the process of migration. First, the large numbers of males in their 20s reflect the continuing labor immigration into California during the 1980s. The absence of a similar number of females in this group makes it unlikely that these immigrants will be able to marry Mexican women in the United States. This means that they will return to Mexico, marry non-Mexican women, remain single in the United States, or bring brides to the United States. All these cases mitigate against the emergence of a large pool of males at risk for youthful crime between 1990 and 2000.

However, although the pool of recently arrived Mexican males is unlikely to result in an immediate wave of youthful crime, it is apparent from the age pyramid for 1990 that the fertility rate of the Mexican population is higher than that of the general population (see also Bean & Swicegood, 1985). Nevertheless, fertility is not as high in the Mexican group as among the Southeast Asian groups. As a result, all other things being equal, youthful crime should not be as common in the Mexican population as in other groups.

Early-20th-Century Cases (Mexicans and Molokan Russians) and the Question How

Examination of the demographic data from the 1920 census for the Russian and Mexican populations in East Los Angeles reveals that demographics played a role in how many at-risk males would be present in both populations. For example, on the basis of the 1920 statistics (and 1990s expectations), it is expected that a high rate of youthful crime in the Russian community would have begun in about 1917, as the first large group of young males moved into the at-risk age group. On the basis of the data from the 1920 census, it would be expected that this trend would continue until at least 1940, with a plateau reached about 1927, when the largest group reached age 20. This assumes, of course, that fertility rates in the Molokan population continue to drop, becoming more like that of the host country. There are no empirical data available to indicate that this happened, although demographic theory indicates it should have.

In contrast, the Mexican population of East Los Angeles had different demographics due to a later time of arrival. The cohort of 0-15-year-olds was relatively small in 1920, but there was a large young male population under age 6 in 1920. Assuming that the Mexican immigrant fertility pattern followed that of their Molokan neighbors, the proportion of the at-risk population within the immigrant group would be expected to grow. Nevertheless, without the latter data, it could have been predicted on the basis of the 1920 data that no significant amount of youthful crime would emerge until at least 1932, and assuming that birthrates reached a stable high plateau (as in the case of the Russians, Lao, and Hmong), until about 1940. As demonstrated by the data from the 1940 census, this is probably what happened, despite the confounding effects of later immigration (in the 1920s) and repatriation (in the 1930s).

In sum, it can be concluded that different immigrant groups do have different demographic patterns that affect patterns of youthful crime. This variation occurs across both age groups and gender, and is a likely factor in how group-specific rates vary in youthful crime independent of culture, social integration, poverty, or any other causes typically suggested by criminological theorists. Simply put, the higher the proportion of at-risk youth within a population, the more likely the group is to have higher arrest rates and gang activity. Given the rapidity with which the demographics of immigrant groups change, this means that wide fluctuations in rates of youthful crime can be explained by the relative proportion of youth in populations.

Nonetheless, demographics do not explain all variations in youthful crime. Particularly among the Hmong, Molokan Russians before 1920, and Mexicans before 1938 and after 1943, there were still youthful crime rates lower than what would be expected given the large numbers of young males present. To explore why, the next two chapters examine the effects of social cohesion and socioeconomic conditions.

NOTES

1. See also Waters (1996) for a demographic description of refugees from Rwanda.

2. Populations that have unusually large proportions of young males are expected to have greater rates of criminal activity. This correlation is so strong that Cohen and Land (1987), in particular, have used it to make predictions about homicide and burglary rates. They have predicted that as a small cohort of post-baby-boom births enters the at-risk age for criminal activity, crime rates will drop. Notably, this prediction does not take into account the possibility that the demographic structure of the U.S. population may be influenced by immigrants who could fill the gap left by the "baby busters."

The unique role that demographics has played in the intergenerational dynamics of immigrant communities has been developed by Kim, Hurh, and Kim (1993) in an article that describes the generational differences in the life conditions of Korean immigrants. It was also implicitly recognized in mid-20th-century publications of the U.S. Census Bureau, which enumerate the "foreign-born white stock" and the "white stock of mixed or foreign parentage" as socially significant status groups (see Carpenter, 1927; Truesdell, 1933, 1943).

3. The strength of such variance also varies across time as a group maintains or loses a sense of group identity, for whatever reason. By definition, groups that "assimilate" begin to take on the characteristics of the majority group, and in the process become part of its opportunity structure. Groups that do not assimilate maintain different opportunity structures (Waters, 1995b). This is of course inherent to any concept of the maintenance of group identity and is central to the process of becoming and disbecoming discussed in Chapter 1. For example, in the case of modern middle-class Filipino immigrants who become part of the majority opportunity structure quite quickly for any number of reasons, demographic issues will have different effects from those they have for Hmong from Laos who "assimilate" more slowly and imprecisely, despite the fact that the two groups arrived in the United States at the same time. Likewise, group identity for the category "Japanese" will mean something different from group identity for the category "Cambodian," despite the fact that the two are represented as equivalent discrete variables in the census data. For a detailed discussion of the mechanisms of this, see Waters (1995b).

4. Truesdell (1943, p. 5) published data about the wide variation that he found in the 1940 U.S. Census. His descriptions illustrate well just how much variation there can be in immigrant groups. For example, for all foreign-born in the United States in 1940, the median age was 38.1 years. For the category "foreign-born white," it was 50.9 years, and for "native white of foreign or mixed heritage," the median age was 29.4 years. For the category "total foreign white stock" the median ranged from 21.5 years (Mexico) to 48.2 years (Northern

Ireland). For the category "foreign-born white," the range of medians was 40.3 years (Mexico) to 58.0 years (Sweden). These differences presumably reflect when the larger migrant flows from those countries stopped, rather than the actual structure of the population. Thus the most recent arrivals who were Mexican arrived in 1910-1925, and the Swedes stopped arriving in about 1900, with an average age for "foreign-born" in 1940 being considerable higher.

For the category "native white of foreign or mixed parentage," the range of medians was from 14.2 years (Mexico) to 45.4 years (Germany) These variations reflect the shift in the immigration laws that occurred in 1924. In that year, the immigration of Europeans was, for all intents and purposes, stopped, and only Western Hemisphere immigration (especially Mexican) was continued. Truesdell published data for 25 European and North American countries.

5. The Lao were the majority dominant group in Laos. All people from Laos of whatever ethnic identity are referred to as *Laotians*.

6. See also discussion of fertility rates in Bean and Swicegood (1985, pp. 9-36). These authors discuss how fertility rates in minority groups are likely to adjust over time.

7. Long (1993, pp. 52, 62) has noted that the birthrate in the Hmong refugee camp of Ban Vinai, in Thailand, is about 4.55% per year, and the proportion of the population that is under age 15 is 45%. Evidence from the 1990 U.S. Census indicates that Hmong immigrants have been exceeding even this high rate. In 1990, the proportion of the U.S. Hmong population aged 15 and under was 60%.

8. Notably, however, this is an increase in the ratio reported in the 1970 U.S. Census, when there were 68 per 100 (Hurh & Kim, 1984, p. 55).

9. In between, American labor demands were satisfied with the "temporary" bracero program.

10. As a common category, this means that self-identified Mexicans are likely to include a large number of first- through third-generation immigrants. This is different from, say, the Korean or Vietnamese census categories, which include primarily immigrants and their children. Bean and Swicegood (1985) have also commented about the problems associated with using the changing labels the Census Bureau has associated with the census classification of the "Mexican"-origin population. For example, during different census years, there have been census categories for "Spanish-surnamed," "Mexicans," "Hispanics," and "Latinos." At times, such groups have also been regarded as a separate "race."

11. There is a general consensus that this group was undercounted in the 1990 census.

12. Intermarriage with other ethnic/racial groups also leads to individuals' self-identifying as members of those other groups.

CHAPTER 5

Social Cohesiveness and the Process of Migration

S olutions to the problem of youthful crime have long focused on the amount of control a particular community exercises over its young males. Supervised activities—typically through athletic leagues, boys' clubs, schools, churches, nationalist movements, ethnic revivals, and social welfare agencies—and other forms of local collective life are among the solutions that have been suggested often, with some success. That such programs can contribute to controlling youthful crime is not really doubted.[1] However, it is also recognized that in a broad sense, organizations that are able to provide such control are often specific to the ethnic groups concerned, and are outgrowths of local collective life. These are very different from agencies funded from the outside, which, as Shaw and McKay (1942, pp. 184-186) pointed out long ago, are found in areas of both high and low delinquency.[2]

The advantages of such "homegrown" organizations is that often their explicit purpose is to develop biographical links for members among their experiences before, during, and after migration. These links are often expressed in a manner that emphasizes a unity with the home country. Thus Mexican immigrants describe their migration as a "return to Aztlan," Hmong refugees emphasize their role in what has come to be called America's "secret war" in Laos, and Chinese reburial societies repatriate the remains of deceased Chinese to their natal villages. None of these efforts is aimed specifically at delinquency, but it is plausible that such agencies temper the inevitable disruptions that occur across immigrant generations.

But the effectiveness of such agencies of social cohesion probably varies through time, as both demographics and social welfare conditions change. As noted previously, this variation has an internal logic related to the same intergenerational processes of becoming and disbecoming out of which youthful crime also emerges.

To develop "social cohesion" as an independent variable, it is necessary again to step back from the issue of youthful crime per se and consider the types of institutions that could exert the social controls that may limit youthful crime. Effective institutions necessarily create conditions through which norms are transmitted across generations. Indicators of how effective they are can be found in issues apart from youthful crime, such as control of exogamy, recruitment of new leadership, and the relative health of community-based institutions.

The story of the Molokan Church in Los Angeles is a good example of how the strength of an immigrant institution can vary across time. Both Sokolov (1918) and Young (1932) have marveled over the amount of control this church exercised over different parts of the community. Indeed, Young devotes many pages to ethnographic descriptions of "tradition" and church rituals that were strong at the time she studied, in the late 1920s (pp. 30-97).[3] As a focus for social cohesion, the strength of the religious community, or *sobranie*, cannot be doubted: The communitywide resistance of Molokan Russians to the World War I draft is perhaps the best example of this. The *sobranie* was powerful enough to make an effective case for the exemption of every single Molokan male from the military draft. This meant that in 1918, the group continued to hold powerful sway even over an emerging cohort of males reared in the United States. And yet, by 1930, a burst of youthful crime emerged out of a crisis between parents and youth. And by the time the United States entered World War II, Molokan males reared under the auspices of the church *sobranie* were going to war; indeed, Molokans in San Francisco even erected a plaque honoring the 100 Molokans who fought in World War II (Tripp, 1980, p. 160).

Each immigrant group is presented with similar group- and period-specific challenges—and opportunities—for maintaining group solidarity. And yet, in a country with the powerful assimilative forces of the United States, most also eventually fail to maintain traditional norms and institutions. Indicators of this failure include youthful crime and gang activity among boys and out-marriage among young women. However, how and why such failure occurs is still highly group specific; as a result, it can be considered a variable of the process of migration in and of itself. This is because social movements as singular as the Molokans, and as militant as the Chicano nationalist movement, do have effects on how well the broader community transmits the cultural values of the past and manipulates the cultural values of the present. Below, I describe how such institutions have worked for each exemplary group.

MOLOKAN RUSSIANS

The *sobranie* of the Molokan Church was central to the Molokan way of life. As in the case of most traditional institutions, its focus was on the elders, who had been trained in sacred religious doctrine and ritual. This authority was maintained through ritual requirements for dress and diet. Ostracism, or shunning, was used to enforce the sanctity of the codes.

The focus on "tradition" gave the community a strong source of shared goals and, despite the upheavals caused by persecution in Russian Georgia and resettlement in the United States, provided a consistent moral pillar against which social action could be judged. The *sobranie* was the strong reference point during World War I, when solidarity was maintained through resistance to the military draft. This resistance included the imprisonment of several young men and repeated petitions to the federal government for exemptions.[4] In many ways, this is an impressive testament to the moral standard the Molokan elders maintained despite the difficulties caused by migration from a peasant society in Russia to urban Los Angeles.

Ironically, the influence of the elders, although strengthened by persecution in Russia, migration, resettlement, and World War I draft resistance, deteriorated not during the difficult times immediately after arrival in the United States, or for that matter under the pressures exerted by the demands of the World War I draft, but later, in the 1920s.[5] This time was marked by the rebellion of youth who were receiving more benefits from their new society than had the previous generation (Young, 1932, pp. 160-216). In the case of the boys, Young writes that the symptom was juvenile delinquency, whereas with the girls it was marriage with non-Molokan boys. This was accompanied by the deterioration of skills necessary to maintain the ritual integrity of the *sobranie,* including fluency in the Russian language, familiarity with church rituals, and obedience to the dietary and dress codes of the elders. Notably, these issues continue to be the focus of the "New" Molokan Church of Woodburn, Oregon, which is today the remnant of Molokan presence in North America (Hardwick, 1993).

Young (1932) attributes the breakdown of the Molokan *sobranie* in the 1920s to the young people's extended periods of education in American schools. From this idea, she develops a Molokan-specific model of culture change in which schooling itself is the causal variable leading to a breakdown in the control of the *sobranie* over the youth. As Young points out, this change inevitably led to separation from the intense involvement needed to sustain religious continuity. As an issue, this came up frequently among the women Young interviewed in the late 1920s. For these women, the power of the *sobranie,* and its use of ostracism, was most likely to be felt when they were dating or contemplating marriage to non-Molokans. This thought extended across Molokan society. Young (1932) quotes Anna Pavlova, a 26-year-old Molokan who arrived in the United States as an infant. The interview took place about 1930:

> There was a Russian fellow who wanted to marry me. He was about eight or ten years older. . . . My father told me that his parents were coming over one evening to make the marriage proposal for their son. I told my father I could not be bothered, that I had a "date" and must keep it. My father figured that the fellow was too old for me and told these people that these days the girls choose for themselves. . . . I continued to go out with the American fellow. My parents became more and more anxious about my future. I wanted to marry him. My father would shake his head and look at me very sad. . . .
>
> There was a time in Russian-Town when every American fellow who had a Russian girl would get beaten up. . . . You

see our men believe that they are boss, but in the American home the woman is looked up to, and naturally our girls want to get as much recognition as is due them, and prefer the American men. . . .

. . . Well, I myself have counted up twenty-seven Russian girls who married Americans, or Italians, or Mexicans, who are very unhappy. Most of these girls live with their husbands for six months or so and then they come home. They are looked down on and nobody wants them. Only three Russian fellows have married out. (pp. 172-173)

The language that Anna Pavlova uses shows the deterioration of the moral cohesion that had held youth and their parents together. It is of course also what would be expected given the process of becoming and disbecoming that takes place during migration. There is the inevitable uncertainty as to where loyalty and solidarity lie; her mixed attitudes toward marriages to "American fellows" in large part reflect this. Anna Pavlova seems uncertain whether it is a good thing because "our girls want to get as much recognition as is due them," despite her claim in the next paragraph that "most of these girls live with their husbands for six months or so and then come home." Young calls such attitudes a "cultural hybrid" and notes that they inevitably sap the traditional sources of group solidarity, in this case the church *sobranie*. An odd bit of rebellion that Anna Pavlova relates illustrates this well:

Something happened at my wedding which I will never forget. During the confession the elder asked if I have ever drank, smoked, danced, or played cards. I sure did feel funny, as I was guilty of all four things he asked. He looked so steadily into my face, and I looked back at him; I don't know what struck me, for I said quite positively, "No, I never have." He sure did look queer at me. . . .

I hardly ever go to church now. . . . I don't like to go to sobranie because some women look down on me. They say I am too Americanized. . . .

It sure is strange. I don't like to live like my mother does, but I can't live like the Americans. Sometimes I think I am "advanced," as my parents say; but sometimes I just don't fit in anywhere. (quoted in Young, 1932, p. 174)

At least one other factor may be relevant to the maintenance of solidarity: the capacity of a community to reproduce the leadership. The elders who had established the Los Angeles Molokan Church in the early 1900s, during the migration itself, were dying by the late 1930s. During the elders' long "reign," younger leaders were unable to command the respect of the community or to develop the ritual knowledge that the founders demanded. Even if they had been so inclined, they could not spend the time needed to acquire the religious knowledge necessary for the perpetuation of the rituals because of the time demands of their work schedules in the urban industrial economy of Los Angeles.

As a result, emigration of Molokan Russians out of East Los Angeles and into the suburbs of Los Angeles accelerated as the elders died. According to Moore (1991), the exodus was complete by the mid-1940s. Bill Waroff (personal communication, November 1993, February 1994), a member of the Molokan Russian community who was a boy when his family moved out of Boyle Heights, has related an example of how this occurred. He recalls the death of his elderly grandfather and grandmother as being the immediate cause of the family's move to the suburbs. Both grandparents had been pillars within the church, able to demand the participation of their children and grandchildren. After their deaths in the late 1930s, however, the family's involvement with the church declined. A strong indicator of the significance of this change is found in the high armed forces enlistment rates of Waroff's Molokan Russian cousins during World War II. This is in marked contrast to the response of the Molokan Church during World War I, when communitywide resistance to the draft represented high social costs for all concerned. When I asked Waroff about World War II, he told me that a number of his cousins had served; he had not even been aware that the draft had been an issue during World War I.

Hardwick (1993, pp. 174-179) provides a longer-term view in her biographical study of Molokans. She emphasizes that today, Molokan identity is based primarily in religion rather than in ethnicity, particularly in urban areas. According to Hardwick, the Molokan communities with the strongest religious identity are maintained in the rural areas of Kerman, California, and Woodburn, Oregon. The colony that began in Los Angeles has virtually disappeared into the suburbs and these rural settlements.

MEXICANS IN THE EARLY 20TH CENTURY

Mexicans migrated into California during the 1920s, but they did not have an institution analogous to the *sobranie*. The Catholic Church, although important to the immigrants, did not demand obedience in all facets of life as the *sobranie* did. Likewise, as Romo (1983, pp. 142-148) points out, in comparison with the church involvement of other Catholic immigrant groups, such as the Polish and the Irish, the Mexican churches in Los Angeles were well attended but poorly subscribed to by the immigrant parishioners. Romo attributes this, first, to the continuing attitude of "sojourning," that is, a belief by immigrants that they would return to their home country; and second, to a lingering anticlericalism among the immigrants that originated in the days before and after the Mexican Revolution, when the church played an active role in Mexican politics.

Nevertheless, as one person I interviewed, Vince Macias (personal communication, January 1994), made clear, the church in the 1940's was a sanctuary respected by both youth and police. He described the church as a place police would not enter, making it something of a safe haven for youth. His description puts the parish priest at the center of the moral order within the community. He noted that the priest was respected by the police and by the youth, as well as by their parents:

> The church was regarded by all as a safe place. We would run into the church, and the police would stop at the door. But then we would have to deal with the father. Everyone respected him, and even feared him. It was safe, since the police wouldn't rough us up, but the fear of what the priest thought was almost as bad.

Macias went on to point out that this made the church an especially important institution in the early 1940s, when gang-type confrontations among Mexican American youth, sailors, and the police were common: "It wasn't like today, though. The church was still respected even by those of us who did not attend mass."

Youthful escapades aside, World War II arrived for the large cohort of Mexican American youth coming of age in East Los Angeles and elsewhere. The youth in East Los Angeles were quickly taken into the military. The large proportion of veterans among Mexican Americans after World War II meant that veterans' associations became an important focus of group solidarity (Griffiths, 1948; McWilliams, 1948).

SOCIAL SOLIDARITY AND GANG ACTIVITY
IN EAST LOS ANGELES, 1940-1950

Modern accounts of Mexican American gang activity often trace its origins to the boy gangs of the early 1940s and the "zoot suit wars" of June 1943. The latter were confrontations between Mexican American youth living in East Los Angeles and U.S. sailors who were shipping out of the Los Angeles port to fight in the Pacific. Vince Macias remembers the period preceding the zoot suit wars as being one during which rival gangs of soldiers and Mexican American youth would fight using chains and clubs. The fighting quickly became polarized around race. *Time* magazine (1943) noted that police were often involved after the fact, when they arrived to "arrest the victims," who were typically the Mexican American youth ("Zoot Suit War," 1943). According to Macias, the confrontations lasted for about a year, before the number of Mexican Americans in the military increased so much that sailors' forays into the Maravilla neighborhood of East Los Angeles ceased because of "an unwillingness for our own kind to fight our own kin." *Time,* using the traditional emphasis on immigration status to explain the situation, noted a

> basic American problem: the second generation. Their fathers and mothers were still Mexicans at heart. They themselves were Americans—resented and looked down on by other Americans. Jobless, misunderstood in their own home and unwelcome outside them, they had fallen into the companion- ship of misery. ("Zoot Suit War," 1943, p. 18)

Such descriptions are, of course, typical of the explanations given by the contemporaries of Shaw and McKay. Suggested solutions focused on the establishment of boys' clubs and the initiation of other settlement- type activities that emphasized integrating youth into the larger society (see Sherman, 1943). This, it might be added, was also accomplished by the enlistment of Mexican Americans during World War II.

A number of institutions aside from the church and gangs appeared in the Mexican American communities of Los Angeles during the 1930s and 1940s. Among the earliest of these were the labor unions, which recruited immigrants during the 1920s and were particularly active in protecting employment rights during the Great Depression (Acuña, 1972, pp. 153-176; Gomez-Quiñones, 1994, pp. 381-385). The labor unions often had the effect of radicalizing the Mexican American population relative to the Anglo center. The Mexican Consulate, on the other hand, played an ambiguous role. Focusing at times on the right of Mexican workers to form unions and at others on assisting in the repatriation of workers who were unable to find employment in the United States, it provided a more conservative focus for solidarity (Balderrama, 1982).

As an immigrant group, Mexicans often stand apart as an exception in discussions of assimilation, especially when assimilation is judged according to conventional measures such as naturalization and exogamy. Naturalization rates for Mexicans and Canadians have, historically, been the lowest in the United States, perhaps owing to the presence of easily crossed land borders (see Portes & Rumbaut, 1990, p. 120; Taylor, 1931). Exogamy has also often been lower among Mexicans than in other immigrant groups, possibly because of the high concentration of Mexican immigrants within specific geographic areas. However, judging from Panunzio's (1942, pp. 692-693) estimates that out-marriages between Mexicans and Mexican Americans and others between 1924 and 1933 in Los Angeles County constituted about 17% of all marriages, it can be assumed that the Mexican immigrant community was not a cultural island. Despite the immigrants' segregation into ethnic enclaves, exogamy was common within 20 years of the main migration from Mexico.

Mexican Americans from East Los Angeles also had unusually high rates of enlistment in the U.S. armed forces during World War II. Military service, along with a high casualty rate, meant that the attentions of the large cohort of young Mexican American males were directed overseas. After the war, this high rate of military service also affected the types of voluntary organizations that emerged in Mexican American communities. Among these were the American G.I. Forum, which became active in the protection of Mexican American veterans' civil rights, and G.I. benefits. The League of United Latin American Citizens (LULAC) was important in the protection of middle-class Mexican American interests from about 1946 to the mid-1960s. Both groups focused their efforts on the elimination of discrimination while advocating integration of Mexican Americans into the larger American society (Allsup, 1982; Marquez, 1993).

MEXICANS, 1960-PRESENT

The next major wave of permanent Mexican migration into the United States began in the late 1960s. The presence of a substantial Mexican American community in East Los Angeles and other southwestern cities meant that the new immigrants had established communities as destinations (Bean & Tienda, 1987; Horowitz, 1983; Massey, Alarcon, Durand, & Gonzales, 1985). Thus, although many Mexican Americans moved out of places like East Los Angeles after World War II, these areas remained substantial ethnic enclaves. The experience of modern Mexican immigrants, then, has been different from the experiences of other modern immigrants (e.g., Laotians, Vietnamese, Cubans, and, in some places, the Chinese), who did not have a persistent preexisting social identity shaping their options.

This circumstance, in combination with perhaps a more pernicious discrimination than encountered by other groups, meant that institutions developed in urban areas such as East Los Angeles based on a nationalistic Mexican American ethnic identity (Williams, 1964). Again, unlike the ethnic identities of other groups, this identity is distinct to the United States, and is not necessarily the consequence of a migration-induced shift in cultural values.

In the 1960s, this identity became labeled as *Chicano*. This was a consequence of both the urban-based Chicano movement and the farm labor movement (Romo, 1983, pp. 163-171), both of which developed in the United States and both of which had more to do with a stable U.S.-based identity than with institutions imported from Mexico. The presence of both social movements and the emphasis on "La Raza" have led to a persistent social identity with which new Mexican immigrants must deal. Thus, although few Mexican immigrants may actually identify with the term *Chicano* (Keefe & Padilla,

1987, p. 38), the presence of such a social movement provides a cohesive alternative to the middle-/working-class culture that was the sole option of past white immigrants to California, such as the Molokans. In turn, this has resulted in a more developed ethnically based political movement than, say, the Laotians, Molokan Russians, or, for that matter, earlier arriving Mexican immigrants were able to generate. The gains of the Chicano social movement(s) with respect to bilingual education programs, affirmative action programs, and so on have, from the perspective of the immigrant child, present a "third option" to the culture of the parents and the culture of the host country. How does this affect youthful crime and the intergenerational transmission of norms? I address this issue at the conclusion of this chapter, where I draw comparisons of the Mexican immigrants to groups that do not have such an option, and finally in Chapter 8, where I assess the presence of this third option against the dependent variable itself.

LAOTIANS

As noted in Chapter 2, the three Laotian groups include the ethnic Lao, Hmong, and Mien. These groups have maintained relatively separate communities in the United States, and have different forms of group solidarity. Researchers in the United States have taken advantage of this fact in assessing how the formation of social solidarity can vary from group to group.

The Hmong brought strong leadership with them from Laos that has been able to reestablish itself in the United States; this leadership continues to maintain its influence through various social service agencies. Lao Family, Incorporated, a social work agency funded through a combination of federal grants and paid memberships solicited from within the Hmong community, is the most important of these. In response to concerns of the Hmong community about crime and other social issues, Lao Family "persuaded" groups of Hmong to take up residence in rural areas of California's Central Valley.

As a source of social cohesion within the Hmong community, Lao Family has been important, especially during the 1980s. Founded by the charismatic Hmong leader Vang Pao in 1978, Lao Family is typically described by members of the Hmong community as their "government." Its strong role in dispute resolution as well as in mediation among the Hmong, social service agencies, interpreters, schools, and law enforcement has mitigated many of the kinds of resettlement problems faced by other Laotian groups. One consequence seems to be that, despite socioeconomic conditions similar to those of the other Laotian groups, and higher birthrates, Hmong college attendance rates have been higher (Waters & Cohen, 1993).

The effectiveness of the Hmong leadership was first evident in the late 1980s, in the movement of large numbers of Hmong into small Central Valley towns. As a consequence of the direction of the Hmong leaders, small towns like Linda, Willows, and Oroville have substantial Hmong populations. The organization of the Hmong community is best illustrated by an example: In 1989, an apartment complex owner in Willows, a town of about 6,000, arranged for the Hmong leadership to take a helicopter tour of the complex; this resulted in the arrival of about 600 Hmong (Helzer, 1993). The movement of large numbers of Hmong from inner cities to such small towns was an explicit response of the Hmong leadership to inner-city crime and the many temptations that gangs were offering Hmong youth. Notably, neither the Mien nor the Lao were able to coordinate similar moves.

The once omnipotent presence of Lao Family in the Hmong community began to deteriorate in the late 1980s, as a result of pressure from the federal government for the agency to serve non-Hmong as well. This in turn exacerbated internal tensions in the Hmong community. These tensions, however, have been capitalized on by a new generation of Hmong leaders, who by 1996 were organizing demonstrations in response to provisions of the 1996 welfare reform bill that would deny federal SSI benefits to noncitizens. Among these leaders were college-educated Hmong who were savvy in the production of media events. Neither the ethnic Lao nor the Mien, who were also affected by such provisions, mobilized similarly high-profile opposition.

The case of the ethnic Lao provides a marked contrast to that of the Hmong. Despite the fact that ethnic Lao are the dominant group in the hierarchy in Laos, they have a much lower profile in the United States. Despite relatively high social status brought from Laos, they have been unable to reestablish any overall leadership in the United States. This includes an apparent breakdown in the Buddhist faith as an organizing institution of Lao society: Christian denominations have had success in seeking converts in the ethnic Lao community.[6]

Even "Lao" as a separate ethnic identity has become questionable. Many young "Lao" instead present themselves as "Thai," an identity option available to them in the United States due to similarities in the two cultures.[7] The presence of members of the Lao royal family in the Central Valley has not proven adequate to establish a source of leadership.

Mien are known for being the most fragmented of the Laotian groups, and are now split into a number of factions. About half have converted to various Christian denominations, whereas the rest remain focused on traditional forms of worship, which have undergone a revival (Habarad, 1987; Waters & Cohen, 1993). Some 10 years after most migrated to the United States, however, divisions between elders and the young have, if anything, widened, as the cohort of American-educated young people drifts away from traditional religious practices which depend on prolonged apprenticeships. In 1993 it was widely acknowledged among members of the Mien community that the skills and memories, both oral and written, that have been at the core of the traditional Mien ritual life are inaccessible to the young people because of the emphasis they must place on economic activities (T. Waters, 1990).

Young Mien have persistently sought to reorient Sacramento's Mien community in order to deal with the persistent social problems confronted by that community. One example of this attempt was the Young Adult Mien Association, which was founded by young men who had jobs within the social work bureaucracy and who wanted a base from which to make requests for grant money. The leader of the organization described the cleavage within the Mien community to a writer for the *Sacramento Bee*: "The older generation has almost no power in terms of working and controlling. . . . Communication is the most difficult part of their lives. But the young kids can learn and adapt to American culture" (quoted in Magagnini, 1994b, p. A1). This agency is one of several that have been started by factions within the community. Despite the acknowledgment of the cleavage described above, it has been able to attract the attention of American press and government in ways that traditional Mien leaders have not (see Magagnini, 1994b).

As a potential source of social cohesion, it is difficult to imagine how the Young Adult Mien Association could bridge the intergenerational gap and reconnect the young people to their elders, who would normally be the instruments of social control. More than anything, the prominence of the association's effort is evidence of the vacuum in traditional sources of social solidarity. Notably, other organizations established by ambitious young people are also described in Whyte's (1943, 1993) book about an Italian immigrant neighborhood in Boston, as well as in Young's (1932) ethnography of Molokan Russians. In both cases, the agencies also proved ineffective at realizing their long-term goals of providing a new spirit for community identity.

During the early 1990s, substantial numbers of Mien began to drift into family-focused strawberry-growing enterprises. The more successful farms involve the intensive cultivation of 2-5 acres of land using family labor. Marketing is through both bulk sales and roadside stands, which take advantage of young English-speaking family members. Whether these enterprises will form a basis for future Mien social solidarity remains to be seen.

The conditions described above—that is, strong social cohesion in the Hmong community and social fragmentation in the Mien and Lao communities—may be explicable in the context of the different age structures of the groups (see Chapter 4). I address how these interactions may work in Chapter 8.

KOREANS

The Korean American community is well-known for a sense of social cohesion apparent in the strength of both its churches and its business associations. Light and Bonacich (1988) discuss this phenomenon most articulately in their chapter titled "Reaction and Solidarity" (pp. 300-328). And although Korean business associations, child labor, *kye* savings associations, and the like are often "self-exploitative," they present opportunities for the monitoring of youth. Such opportunities were not taken by the ethnic Lao or Mien immigrants during their first 5-10 years in the United States. On the other hand, there is no single dominant institution in the Korean immigrant community such as the Lao Family for the Hmong or the *sobranie* for the Molokans.

An unbalanced sex ratio has led to a great deal of exogamy in the Korean community, which has made the persistence of Korean social institutions potentially more difficult. Anecdotes will serve to show the response of some Koreans to this situation—a modern-day version of what Molokan Russian boys did to American boys who dated Russian girls (Young, 1932). A former roommate of mine who eventually married a Korean woman recalls being warned by the woman's brother not to call his sister again. Modern telephonic relationships being what they are, however, the brother was never able to carry out any threat. A former Korean female student of mine described how a similar confrontation occurred in her family: "My sister told my dad that [I] would probably not marry a Korean. She told me that he didn't like that, but he hasn't talked to me about it."

Like Mexican immigrants, but unlike the other groups under discussion, Koreans also have a consul general who maintains a strong interest in the affairs of the Korean community. Also like Mexican immigrants, Koreans have an "easy exit" option for children who are unable to cope with the exigencies of American life, in the form of a quick return to Korea. This has the effect that the Korean population, much more so than the other Indochinese refugee groups, is self-selected for "good behavior" even as the younger people get older.

SUMMARY

Each of the surveyed groups has attempted to maintain a collective identity in the United States. Typically, these attempts have taken the form of the establishment of voluntary associations designed to maintain biographical links to the groups' shared social experiences before, during, and after the migration event. These have focused primarily on such areas as language, marriage, and religion. However, there has been variation both among groups and across significant time differences in how effective such agencies have been in asserting moral authority over prospective members. The following list summarizes how this happened are for all of the exemplary groups (see also Table 5.1).

■ *Laotians:* The primary focus of group solidarity for Hmong has been Lao Family, Incorporated. However, this agency was not able to extend its loyalty beyond its Hmong base. Within the substantial Hmong community, however, it has been able to maintain cohesiveness through the use of both traditional Hmong sanctions and manipulation of access to American social institutions. The authority of this agency has faded, but other analogous

TABLE 5.1 Summary of Social Cohesion as an Independent Variable

Ethnic Group	Formal Institution	Persistence Across Generations	Relative Strength	External Events	Institutional Persistence
Laotian					
Hmong	Lao Family	?	strong	—	1978-1989?
Lao	Lao Family	none	weak	—	1978-
Mien	various	none	weak	—	
Molokan	*sobranie*	variable	strong	World War I draft	1905-41?
Korean	churches	strong	medium	—	1970s
Mexican	labor unions	strong	medium	UFW	1930s, 1960-1970s
	Catholic	strong	medium	Mexican politics	1920s-
	Chicano movement	variable	medium	Vietnam War	1960s-
	veterans' organizations	none	medium	World War II	1946-1960s

ethnic-based organizations are emerging to take its place. Neither the Lao nor the Mien have had a comparable institution. Perhaps as a consequence, religious conversion (typically to Christianity) and other "symptoms" of rapid social change have been more common in these communities than among the Hmong. Agencies designed to maintain ethnic identity have typically failed. One symptom of this is the apparently large number of ethnic Lao youth presenting themselves as "Thai" to the broader social world. Exogamy has yet to emerge as an issue in any of the Laotian communities, because so far there has been no substantial cohort of American-raised females who are of marriageable age. The exogamy that I am aware of has, by and large, been between Southeast Asian groups, and not with white Americans.

■ *Koreans:* Solidarity within the Korean community is generally regarded as high, despite the dispersed character of the community. Business associations, chambers of commerce, Korean consulates, Korean churches, and *kye* associations are among the bases for social solidarity and continuing reproduction of institutions brought from Korea. On the other hand, an unbalanced sex ratio has led to a great deal of exogamy, which has made the persistence of Korean social institutions questionable in the long run.

■ *Mexicans, 1920-1950:* Solidarity within the Mexican community of 1930s Los Angeles was focused on the Catholic Church and/or labor unions. High rates of military service in World War II refocused some of this solidarity onto veterans' organizations and LULAC after the war. Such agencies typically emphasized assimilation as a social goal.

■ *Mexicans, 1960-present:* Mexican Americans have established a strong separate identity in California. Much of this has been focused by the Chicano nationalist movement that emerged in the 1960s and has tried to establish Chicanos as a group with interests different from those of the "Anglo" majority. This is a potent force that has refocused the efforts of organized labor, the Catholic Church, the education establishment, and neighborhood organizing in California's Mexican immigrant communities. The large size of the potential constituency means that it could become one of the most powerful electoral blocs in the state organized along ethnic lines. But the same assimilation processes that have affected other immigrant groups in the United States have blunted the hopes of the more extreme nationalists. Studies show that exogamy rates are relatively high, particularly in the third generation (Keefe & Padilla, 1987). Likewise, across generations there is a pronounced deterioration of Spanish-language skills.

■ *Molokan Russians:* Until the 1930s, the focus of solidarity within the Molokan Russian community was the *sobranie*. After that time, there was a rapid deterioration of group identity as many individuals moved to the suburbs. The church was reconstituted later, but not as the all-encompassing focus of community solidarity it had been between 1905 and 1930. Often this reconstitution was found to be most effective in rural areas.

CONCLUSIONS

Issues of social cohesion do not exist in a vacuum. They are interrelated with issues of demographics, residence, the broader social community, and poverty. Nevertheless, as an issue in and of itself, social cohesion can stand as a variable. Some communities have strong

social institutions and others do not. Groups that have such institutions should be able to control youthful crime rates better than those
that do not. Or, put in specific terms, if all other things are held equal,
an immigrant group that is able to maintain a *sobranie* or a social
service agency such as Lao Family should have lower rates of youthful
crime than groups that do not. As Shaw and McKay (1942) point out,
this is because such social institutions affect how well communities
can transmit social values between generations, and this ability is a
critical element in explaining why youthful crime emerges more
forcefully in some communities than others.

Likewise, the effects on group solidarity of outside events are
important. Two examples are the challenges that the pacifist Molokans
made to the military draft during World War I and the role that military
service in World War II played in creating a postwar focus of identity
for the Mexican American community in agencies such as the American G.I. Forum and LULAC.

The question, however, is: How well do such agencies work? Are
their effects trivial or significant? Further questions include the following: Particularly in the context of the strong predictive value of age
structure in determining the incidence of youthful crime, is social
cohesion affected by an increase in the proportion of children in a
population? How does the erosion of group boundaries across time
(i.e., assimilation) affect group identity and cohesiveness?

I attempt to answer these questions in Chapter 8, when I make
comparisons among all of the immigrant groups analyzed. At this
point, however, it is important to note the obvious conclusions that
can be drawn from the material presented in this chapter:

■ Community agencies can be important mediators of intergenerational relationships. However, this is not always the case, and
there are often problems with the emergence of leadership cliques
that represent only one extreme of the age continuum—that is,
either the elders or the youth. Further, Shaw and McKay (1942)
draw a distinction between agencies that are generated from
within the immigrant community and those from without; it is
not clear how the roles of these two kinds of agencies may differ.

■ The role of a community-based agency can change over time.
Shortly after an immigrant group's arrival, a group-based social
service agency may be a unifying force, facilitating the estab-

lishment of biographical continuity within the community; later, the agency may serve as a conservative force, attempting to perpetuate the authority of the "graybeards." Still later, the agency may take on the role of interest group advocate, expressing the integrative ambitions of potential leaders. In interpreting social solidarity as a variable, it is important to recognize the varying roles of community agencies.

NOTES

1. Malcolm Klein (1995) has recently made an articulate argument that some types of gang intervention can facilitate increased gang activity. Gottfredson and Hirschi's (1990) theory of social control can also be interpreted in a fashion that sheds doubt on whether programs focused on 13- to 25-year-old youth will be as effective as those focused on younger children.

2. See also Whyte (1943, 1993) for a description of voluntary associations in an Italian American neighborhood of Boston. The relationship between issues of social control and crime is also addressed directly by Gottfredson and Hirschi's (1990; Hirschi & Gottfredson, 1994) theory of social control.

3. Moore (1991) claims that the Molokan community disappeared from Boyle Heights by the late 1940s due to migration to the suburbs. Hardwick (1993) indicates that the Molokan community was active in Los Angeles, although there were also a few persistent communities in rural areas of California's Central Valley and San Francisco. An index search of the *Los Angeles Times* turned up references to Molokan cemeteries in Los Angeles and Molokan identity in Baja California, but no references to any type of church activity in the greater Los Angeles area between 1990 and 1997. Hardwick (1993) documents the activity of the Molokan Church in the 1990s. The newsletters to which she subscribes indicate that the "New" Molokan Church in rural Oregon is still active (S. W. Hardwick, personal communication, February 1996).

4. The case of six young men imprisoned for failure to register for the World War I draft was the focus of this solidarity (see Dunn, 1976, pp. 103-105; Young, 1932, pp. 131-136). As a consequence, the War Department granted an unusual group exemption to the Molokans, and no Molokans served in World War I.

5. For a theoretical discussion of this issue, see Waters (1995b).

6. In 1991, I witnessed a court case in which a Lao Buddhist monk found it necessary to seek social security payments on the grounds that he could no longer practice his "profession" due to an inability to sit in the lotus position for long periods of time. Had traditional forms of social solidarity been working, this would not have been an issue, and the local community would have provided for the monk whether he was able to sit in the lotus position or not.

7. This phenomenon was pointed out to me by Robert Vryheid, an anthropologist who has worked in Thailand, Cambodia, and San Diego for many years. The young Lao he met in San Diego, he noted, introduced themselves to him as "Thai," an identity that in the United States is apparently more prestigious than "Lao." Kathy Negri of the California Youth Authority told me that she believes this phenomenon is occurring based on what she has seen of probation records. For a discussion of situations in which white Americans choose their ethnic identities in similar ways, see Mary Waters's book *Ethnic Options* (1990).

CHAPTER 6

Status Adjustment, Socioeconomic Mobility, and the Process of Migration

*T*his process of migration typically includes an attempt to climb a socioeconomic ladder. At the same time, declines in social class or status are also commonly associated with migration, particularly during the period immediately following the migration event. As I have noted in Chapters 1 and 2, these changes can result in profound status shifts within the family, as children move into positions of authority. In some cases, they also result in shifts in status between men and women.

Shifts in social status involve more than just changes in relations within the family. They also involve changes in how immigrant adults are viewed by peers, both inside and outside the immigrant community. For example, the male head of an immigrant peasant family typically loses status in the urban United States, where his skills and knowledge become obsolete. On the other hand, the authority of a traditional priest may rise as his or her community experiences improved economic circumstances brought about by the availability of jobs or welfare benefits. Both of these situations have occurred in the Mien and Molokan communities of California.

The ability to maintain or to acquire socioeconomic status is often associated with youthful crime. An example is the Vietnamese, who are often divided into two groups: the "first wave" of 1975 refugees, who are said to have low rates of youthful crime due to their high socioeconomic status in Vietnam; and the later group of "boat people," who are often said to have higher rates of crime owing to their lower socioeconomic status in Vietnam (Caplan, Whitmore, & Choy, 1989; Smith & Tarallo, 1993). Undoubtedly, there is some truth to this theorized association. Prior economic status and skills brought from the home country undoubtedly have effects on youthful crime rates. But such characteristics also have effects on birthrates and on a group's ability to maintain cohesiveness, which are the variables described above. To tease this factor out, it is necessary to see whether socio-economic status does in fact correlate with youthful crime rates and how it interacts with other factors. In other words, assuming that the popular model described above for Vietnamese is accurate, it can be assumed that the groups analyzed here will have similar patterns; that is, those coming from peasant backgrounds will have high rates of youthful crime, and those coming from "middle-class" backgrounds will have low rates. This is in effect a "falsifiable" hypothesis that can be checked against the groups in this study. In this way a third independent variable can be developed. Like the preceding discussions of demographics and social solidarity, the description developed below is independent of the discussion of crime.

As is the case with other characteristics, a loss or change in social status is time dependent. At the extremes, the immigration experi-ences of medical doctors from the Korean elite are different from those of Hmong hill tribespeople from Laos. However, individuals in both groups probably experience loss of social status. For example, the Korean doctor with one or two children becomes an entrepreneur, or maybe a medical technician, but probably still lives in a suburban home. The Hmong farmer/soldier who has six children, on the other hand, is more likely to live in an inner-city apartment and collect Aid to Families with Dependent Children (AFDC). Both have experienced major shifts in social status, but the results vary. In turn, such changes affect other factors relating to the process of migration, such as fertility, residential mobility, and views of the law. Nevertheless, status changes are likely to occur in a patterned fashion. Youth living in the upper-middle-class suburbs will probably not acquire the habits of inner-city gang members, whereas immigrant youth whose families settle in inner-city areas very well may.

As a variable, however, the issue of status is different from other issues discussed previously. Most important, within immigrant communities, prestige is related to qualities brought from the home country. Social cohesion, in contrast, although it may be rooted in meanings brought from the home country, is dependent on structures that are developed in the new country. The discussion below addresses the processes of status change and socioeconomic mobility for each of the six groups under study.

LAOTIANS

Most Laotians in the United States were associated with the military in Laos, although small numbers were also involved in the civil service. For the most part, adult Laotian immigrants were not well educated and did not speak English well when they came. Their military activity included service in both the government army and the semi-independent Hmong units. The Laotians benefited from U.S. federal refugee funds at the time of resettlement after 1975. Later, large numbers of the former soldiers qualified for federal SSI benefits; a problem arose when these benefits were withdrawn as a consequence of the 1996 welfare reform bill in 1997, as it became questionable whether they would continue to qualify.

SSI benefits, in combination with their large families, tended to keep them out of the workforce, given that AFDC payments to large Laotian families often exceeded entry-level wages. The development of ethnic enclaves in urban areas means that the bulk of the Laotians are concentrated in the inner cities of Sacramento, Fresno, Oakland, and San Diego. The exception to this rule is the large number of Hmong who have been able to reestablish themselves in the apartment complexes of small Central Valley towns between Visalia and Redding. In some of these towns, the Hmong, who typically occupy one of the few apartment complexes in a rural town, may represent up to 10% of the population and, because of their high birthrates, one-third of the school-age population (as they do in Willows, California).

Between 1978 and 1995, there was nevertheless a steady move off of welfare by Laotians, and toward paid labor. The first to make the move were the young men (and occasionally women) who served as interpreters for various social welfare agencies or as bilingual teacher's aides. Since then, there has been a steady movement of young adults into more traditional working-class occupations, including factory work, automobile repair, strawberry farming, military service, clerical work, and jobs at specialty stores, fast-food restaurants, and convenience stores. By the mid-1990s, Hmong in particular were attending California universities, and small numbers had entered law enforcement, become teachers, or entered other white-collar occupations. Particularly in the case of small business, this was within the context of the larger Southeast Asian community, in which Vietnamese businesses are often dominant.

A result of this mobility pattern is that, unlike their parents, many young immigrants have received some high school education and/or technical training in the United States. As a result, the upward status mobility of Laotians in the context of the United States has often been accomplished by the younger people in the family. Older people, including the elders who traditionally hold high status, tend to be excluded from this rise. An exception is found in the Hmong community, where some high-status elders are able to maintain status through leadership positions within Hmong-controlled social service agencies. These agencies typically focus on liaison activities between the refugee community and the American social service sector.

In sum, Laotians who moved to the United States started as dependents of the social welfare system. Small numbers of young adults began to move into social welfare occupations as translators during the first years. This movement represented more the need for language skills on the part of social welfare agencies than the need for status reproduction within the Laotian communities. The result was a fast rise in social status of skilled young people relative to their elders. Later, as a cohort of Laotians with some American education matured, a variety of working-class service occupations became available to younger people. Particularly among the Mien and Lao, the young people made these gains while living in the inner cities of California.

This opened a variety of urban occupations for the youth to move into. However, it also exposed them to the pressures of living in the inner city, including gang activity. Hmong, to a certain extent, compensated for this by moving to rural communities where such pressures—and opportunities—were not as great.

Thus what would be expected if socioeconomic status were a contributing factor for youthful crime in Laotian communities is a fairly high level of such crime in the years after arrival, with a decline in later years as refugee families moved into the workforce and out of their neighborhoods of first settlement. In particular, it would be expected that those living in urban areas would have higher rates of involvement with gangs, whereas those who resettled in rural areas would not.

KOREANS

Koreans are well-known for owning small inner-city shops and running them by using family labor—a process that Light and Bonacich (1988) call "self-exploitation." The 1980 U.S. Census reported that 13.5% of employed Koreans in the United States were self-employed or nonpaid workers in a family business. This rate was higher than for all other ethnic groups, and the proportions were even higher in cities that had Korean population concentrations, such as Los Angeles (Light & Bonacich, 1988, pp. 6-8). Nevertheless, the proportion was not so high that such activities dominated the economic focus of the community. After all, 86.5% of the employed Korean population was working in other sectors.[1] Koreans' success in their entrepreneurial activities was ironically highlighted by the experience of Korean shop owners in Los Angeles during the 1992 riots, when their shops were often the targets of looters.

Nevertheless, as Hurh and Kim (1990, p. 31) note, this success in entrepreneurial activity was the result of downward mobility; many Korean immigrants had higher status in their home country. Korean immigrants to the United States have come disproportionately from the middle and professional classes in Korea, but they have typically not been able to reestablish themselves as such in the United States. Nevertheless, their higher status has meant that they have not been exposed to inner-city neighborhoods in the same way Laotians have.

Nevertheless, as has been the case among Laotians, the route out of the ethnic community for Koreans has often been through children socialized by American high schools and universities.[2] Members of the second generation appear to be trying to reestablish the middle-class professional roles that their parents left behind in coming to the United States. A particularly articulate student of mine described her own memories of this status loss in the following fashion in August 1994:

> My parents were professionals in Korea. My father worked for a newspaper which his family owned and had even published some novels. My mother was a doctor. I remembered when we first came to Ohio [when I was 6 years old], my father had promised us a better life. But all there was was a small apartment. . . . Even at that young age I knew that something strange was going on.

In the 15 years since they arrived in the United States, this family has been able to reestablish itself financially and send a daughter to the University of California. However, the status changes that the family has experienced have been substantial. The novelist-doctor couple are now the proprietors of two convenience stores in Southern California.

As writers who have described the Korean experience emphasize, Koreans who have succeeded as the "petite bourgeoisie" of the inner city have in large part been immigrants who are, by both American and Korean standards, well educated, and who have enjoyed some social status in Korea. Both Hurh and Kim (1984) and Light and Bonacich (1988) imply that such ethnicity is persistent, or more "adhesive," than that found in other immigrant groups. This argument is based primarily on the observation that it is easier to reproduce transplanted relationships in businesses emphasizing family connections than in a community that has an economic base in industrial employment. There may be something to this argument, at least for the 13.5% of the Korean immigrant population working in such occupations. However, it remains to be seen whether the Korean children now entering American universities will be able to maintain, or will be interested in maintaining, such ties into the next generation.

Although many Korean businesses are located in inner cities, the successful owners of these businesses often live in the suburbs (Hurh & Kim, 1984, pp. 62-72; Light & Bonacich, 1988, p. 225). In large part, the success of Koreans as a group is probably due to the large proportion of economically active adults in the Korean population.

In terms of social mobility, older Korean immigrants probably have more downward or sideways mobility in the long run than other groups. This is because they started out at a higher status level, having brought substantial skills from a well-educated society. However, in terms of a hypothesis about the nature of youthful crime, this does not necessarily say much. Rates of such crime would be expected to be low among Koreans due to the high social status brought from the home country, although the rates might be expected to rise slightly as the immigrants become aware of the status loss that is often associated with immigration.

MEXICANS, 1920-1950

Mexican immigrants into Los Angeles in the 1920s found employment in the railway yards or as itinerant farm laborers. Their income levels were consistently lower than those of the surrounding communities (Griffiths, 1948; Mexican Fact-Finding Committee, 1930; Wickersham Commission, 1931), and their occupational status was firmly blue-collar. Farm labor also played an important role in the Mexican immigrant community; however, at no time was even a majority of the immigrant workforce employed as farmworkers. Indeed, typically two-thirds of California's Mexican population is found in urban areas, both in the present and in the past.

During the Depression, there were law enforcement crackdowns on Mexicans resident in the United States. This, in addition to the regular movement back to home villages in Mexico, led to both a decline in the population of Mexican-born living in Los Angeles and a slowdown in the growth rate of the Mexican population. Although there is little statistical evidence to back up any claims about who stayed and who did not, it is apparent that having American-born children provided an incentive for immigrants to remain. Large families, coupled with continued residence in working-class East Los Angeles, pushed Mexican Americans toward an economic experience similar to that of other immigrant groups up until the 1940s. However, as the large cohort of young males came of age, World War II arrived.

Enlistment of American-born children of Mexican immigrants in the
U.S. military was unusually high during World War II and provided a
social discontinuity that opened routes out of the Los Angeles barrio
for many (Griffiths, 1948; McWilliams, 1948). Returning soldiers had
fundamentally different outlooks on life, and they used the G.I. Bill
and other military benefits to leave East Los Angeles for the suburbs
during the 1940s and 1950s (see Allsup, 1982; Marquez, 1993).

Permanent immigration from Mexico into the United States virtually
ceased from 1930 to 1965. During this time there was apparently an
accelerated movement of permanent residents out of East Los Angeles
and into the middle-class suburbs. However, perceptions of this move
vary. Millions of temporary immigrants arriving in the United States
under the bracero program (1942-1965) helped to maintain preexisting
social networks into Mexico, in addition to developing a perception
that there was a constant resupply of Mexican immigrants between
1920 and the present.

It is not clear what this circular migration means in terms of
youthful crime, but it is assumed that some upward social mobility
from what has been found in Mexico is a consequence. Nevertheless,
relative to the broader American population, socioeconomic status
continued to be low among Mexican immigrants, and for this reason
it would be expected that relatively high levels of youthful crime should
be persistent across time if poverty itself generates youthful crime.
The exception might be the postwar period, when a great number
of Mexican Americans moved out of the barrios and most of the
Mexicans who participated in the bracero program returned to Mexico at the end of the harvest season.

MEXICANS, 1960-PRESENT

The Mexican immigrant population in California is younger and less
educated than the native California population. These immigrants
tend to be paid less than natives, and are more likely to be found in
blue-collar professions. Farm labor continues to be dominated by
Mexican immigrants. However, as in the past, at least two-thirds of
the Mexican immigrant population is employed outside the agricultural sector. Employment levels tend to be comparable to those of the

native-born. The Mexican-born labor force in California is large, and has, at least until recently, continued to expand. In 1991, it was estimated that one of every four new entrants into the California workforce was Mexican-born (Vernez, 1993, p. 147). This connection between Mexico and the United States has become so important in recent years that it has begun to reshape California' culture, particularly in the southern counties.

Owing to the size of the Mexican immigrant population and the proximity of the Mexican border, California's immigrants from Mexico have assumed a unique role in the social status structure of the state. The large size of the population movement means that Spanish language skills are reproduced to a far greater extent than are the language skills of any other immigrant group. The structures necessary for the reproduction of Mexican culture are present in California, in contrast to the situations of more dispersed groups.

Because of the sustained movement of Mexican immigrants into California, as well as the size of the immigration, it is more difficult to make generalizations about this group than about other groups. However, it seems that the social status of Mexican Americans as a separate status group has led to their having opportunity structures separate from those of the larger Anglo culture. Notably, this is not the case for other groups, such as Laotians and Molokans. In terms of socioeconomic status, large numbers of Mexican immigrants have moved from rural Mexico to a modern urban environment. This involves, by some measures, a distinct improvement in socioeconomic status, even though it also implies exposure to urban poverty.

MOLOKAN RUSSIANS

Molokan Russians brought few skills from Russia that they could use in urban Los Angeles. Peasant farmers in Russia, they soon became disoriented by the urban life of Los Angeles. On an economic level, the men were soon employed in the Boyle Heights lumberyards, and the women mostly remained at home. With the passage of time, younger men were also able to seek more stable employment; by the 1920s, they too were working in lumberyards, or as mechanics. Women also occasionally found work as retail clerks (Young, 1932). Young (1932) also notes that the status of the Molokan women increased in the United States relative to their situation in Russia. This applied to relations within the family as well as their position in the larger world. This was an uneven process, as is illustrated by the Hardwick's history of Tanya Desatoff, a woman born in Russian Georgia in 1894; Desatoff was married in Los Angeles in 1909, had 12 children, traveled widely, lived 40 years in East Los Angeles, and died in 1984 (Hardwick, 1993, pp. 174-179).

Movement out of the suburbs was coincident with class mobility as well as exogamous marriage (Dunn, 1976; Sutherland & Cressey, 1974; W. Waroff, personal communication, November 1993, February 1994). Thus coincident with changes in youthful crime rates came changes in class and a breakdown of what was left of group solidarity.

In terms of youthful crime, what would be expected for this group are fairly high rates of youthful crime in the period just after immigration, before men were able to get jobs in the lumberyards. This would be expected to decrease as the men moved into permanent jobs and families were able to buy their own homes in the 1920s.

SUMMARY

Immigrants to California have had a variety of experiences with respect to socioeconomic status changes after their arrival. A summary of these changes for each of the six analyzed groups is offered below (see also Table 6.1).

- *Molokan Russians:* Molokan Russians were peasant farmers in Russia, but in California they became urban laborers, and generally engaged in various types of unskilled labor while living in East Los Angeles. After an initial period of disorientation in 1905-1920, economic conditions began to improve as families were able to establish a working-class niche in Los Angeles or move to rural areas. The status of women, in particular, improved in the United States.

- *Mexicans, 1920-1950:* Like their neighbors in East Los Angeles, most Mexican immigrants became blue-collar wage laborers, many (but not most) of whom were in seasonal agriculture. The

TABLE 6.1 Summary of Socioeconomic Status as an Independent Variable

Ethnic Group	Previous Occupations	Education Level	U.S. Residence	U.S. Economic Activity
Laotian				
Hmong	soldier/farmer	negligible	rural/urban	welfare; blue-collar work
Lao	soldier/farmer/ bureaucrat	literate	urban	welfare; blue-collar work
Mien	soldier/farmer	negligible	urban	welfare; blue-collar work
Molokan	peasant	negligible	urban	laborers
Korean	professional	12+ years	suburban	small business proprietors
Mexican, 1920-1950	farmer	negligible	urban	urban labor; farm labor
Mexican, 1960-present	farmer	approximately 8 years	urban/rural	blue-collar work; farm labor

enlistment of large numbers of young men in the armed forces during World War II provided a way out of East Los Angeles for many.

■ *Mexicans, 1960-present:* Mexican immigrants to California in the late 20th century have been employed in the blue-collar sector and have often been able to take advantage of social networks within the Mexican immigrant community. The overall education level of immigrants from Mexico has been comparatively low. However, the extraordinary diversity within this large group makes generalization difficult.

■ *Laotians:* Many Laotians in the early 1980s lived on refugee benefits and various federal and state social welfare programs. Since the late 1980s, however, increasing numbers of Laotians have begun to move into blue-collar jobs. Large number of youth, particularly Hmong, also have begun attending California's colleges and universities. This is potentially a route into the middle class.

■ *Koreans:* Koreans suffered a loss of status upon arrival in the United States. This is particularly true for professionals from Korea who have been unable to practice their professions due to language difficulties and licensing requirements. As a result, a disproportionately large number of Koreans have established themselves in large cities as shop owners and entrepreneurs. In this fashion, they have been able to generate family incomes while effectively utilizing the human resources available within the immigrant community and the social networks unique to Korean communities in California and elsewhere. Large numbers of Korean youth are making their way into California's universities. It is not known whether this will be the path for the Koreans into a more settled middle-class existence.

CONCLUSION

A complicated picture emerges from the comparisons drawn in this chapter, but a few generalizations can be made. First, it is not inevitable that poor peasant groups that cross broad cultural distances will experience outbursts of youthful crime. The Hmong, Mexicans, and Molokans had cohorts of young boys present in their communities early after their immigration who did not necessarily initiate waves of youthful crime. This is a characteristic they share with their higher-status Korean counterparts.

Likewise, an argument of relative deprivation is difficult to sustain. Judging from the literature, Koreans have suffered more downward mobility than have peasants immigrants from various places. This, too, does not correlate well with outbreaks of youthful crime.

Although the above does not directly refute what Smith and Tarallo (1993) have written about the difference in youthful crime between first-wave Vietnamese immigrants and boat people, it does raise questions about whether theirs is an adequate explanation. Certainly, there is no indication of a simple cause-and-effect relationship between rising socioeconomic status and falling rates of youthful crime. Discussion of the Vietnamese, however, is beyond the purpose of this chapter. Indeed, it is doubtful whether any data are available that separate first-wave Vietnamese from boat people for either demographic indicators or indicators of criminal activity. However, what the data do point to, if issues of socioeconomic status are to be considered, is the need to consider age distribution in the population as well. By themselves, socioeconomic status correlates do not cause outbursts of youthful crime. Rather, they are common correlates with some factors that do in fact lead to youthful crime. What could these be? What is the relationship between poverty and these seemingly nebulous "other factors"? I address these questions in Chapter 8.

NOTES

1. The census category is of course imprecise. Presumably, a number of Koreans working for other Koreans are paid to work in the family business, and therefore are not in the category.

2. In a 1991 survey of entering freshmen at the University of California, Davis, Koreans and Filipinos are the discrete immigrant groups for which data are available (Low, 1992). Of the entering freshman class, 46 students, or 2%, self-reported as Korean. The Korean students reported a median family income of $45,000 per year, which is significantly higher than that reported by Southeast Asian students ($15,500), but a bit lower than the universitywide median of $56,750. They also reported in unusually high numbers that both of their parents attended college (78.8%). Interestingly, the Korean students reported a relatively low "level of comfort" when interacting with members of other racial or ethnic groups.

Part III

Answering the Question How

CHAPTER 7

Legal Pluralism and the Understanding of Youthful Crime

> Hence it is inherent in the nature óf legal systems that they can never become fully coherent, consistent wholes which success-fully regulate all of social life. One formal, logical manifestation of this [is] that legal rule-systems include general principles of applications and interpretation which can themselves be inter-preted in a variety of ways. Such rule-systems invariably include ambiguities, inconsistencies, gaps, conflicts and the like.
>
> *Sally Falk Moore, Law as Process, 1978*

WHY LEGAL PLURALISM?

Up to now, I have been examining the possible preconditions for youthful crime in immigrant groups—that is, under what conditions do these groups experience outbursts of youthful crime? This is in keeping with sociological traditions that emphasize social structural conditions. Sociologists ask: Under what conditions are there likely to be high rates of crime (or poverty, or family formation, or discrimina-tion, or welfare dependency)? Some conclusions have of course emerged from this discussion. For example, it is clear that in many groups, the existence of a fairly large cohort of at-risk males is probably the major prerequisite. It is also apparent that preexisting cultural factors ("a culture of crime") are probably not causal for outbursts of youthful crime. Likewise, the socioeconomic expectations of an immigrant group are important only in the context of a large cohort of at-risk

135

males. In this respect, the focus of this discussion of youthful crime has shifted away from the particular correlates associated with specific groups, as discussed in Chapter 2. Still, there is no real understanding of what happens once these structural conditions are met.

An answer to this question might be provided by the "legal pluralists," social scientists who study situations in which two or more legal systems coexist (Arthurs, 1985; Falk Moore, 1978; Geertz, 1983; Griffiths, 1986; Merry, 1988; Mertz, 1994). Legal pluralists start with the observation that "every functioning sub-group in a society has its own legal system which is necessarily different in some respects from those of other subgroups" (Pospisil, 1971, p. 107). Or, in other words, for a group to be a group, its members must share a consensus about what is the normative order.

Legal pluralists note that in the normal course of events, individuals move among different rule systems as they move among the groups to which they owe allegiance. For example, in my own daily life, I move from the normative order in my house in the morning (where my wife has normative expectations about what role I play in the morning) to my car, which I drive on a highway where there is a normative expectation that if I do not exceed the speed limit by more than 10 miles per hour I will not get a ticket. I then go to the Sociology Department at my university, where the department secretary enforces norms and rules about photocopying, scheduling, add-drop cards, petty cash vouchers, and myriad other procedures needed to keep the department functioning. Perhaps in the evening I might go to a meeting at my child's school, where there is yet another set of expectations for how I will behave and the role it is legitimate for me to play. Overarching all of these interactions are the "juristic," or hegemonic, written laws of the state of California and of the United States. As someone born and socialized in the United States, I have an intuitive understanding of when and how these laws should be permitted to be used to order normative understandings. Indeed, I am usually able to shift among all the different situations in my day with subconscious ease.

Legal pluralists investigate what happens when two systems of law are operating simultaneously. Often in this work, they have looked at colonial situations in which European law was imposed on preexisting legal structures that may or may not have been written. What they have found are patterns of how imposed state law begins to enter preexisting normative orders. In this process, the imposed law at times becomes the tool of the colonized. For example, demands by Africans for independence from European powers in Africa have typically been framed in appeals to Western law, rather than to the coexisting law of the indigenous social order.

Further development of the legal pluralist position has come from studies of Western societies, where it is clear that interpretations of the law and legal system vary among subcultures (Arthurs, 1985; Merry, 1986). Merry's (1986) study of working-class attitudes toward the legal system illustrates well the difficulty of understanding the ideals of written state laws in the context of the limitations of the available legal system (i.e., police and courts). The litigants she studied "emerged from their encounters with the law with a more complex understanding, having experienced the dual legal ideologies embedded within the American lower courts. One of these ideologies expresses the dominant American vision of justice provided by the rule of law, the other a situationally based, lenient, and personalistic vision of justice produced within the local settings" (p. 253). To put it in terms legal pluralists would use, these litigants went into the system with one understanding of what the literal written law is and came out with another understanding of what the justice system can actually deliver (see Appendix A for a cross-cultural example). As Merry goes on to point out, "winners" in formal legal situations are often those most able to move back and forth skillfully between the two alternative systems of norms, something that lawyers and other court officers are trained to master.

If it is difficult for working-class Americans to understand the workings of the American legal system, imagine what it is like for the immigrant parent who must interpret the inherently dual nature of American legal ideology. Imagine further that this parent must see the system through the eyes of his or her children, who serve as interpreters and intermediaries. The result is likely to be multiple layers of misunderstanding, as alternative normative systems are used to legitimate successive decisions. It is of course easy to see that the result will be confusion. It is not uncommon for this confusion to be interpreted as insularity on the part of the immigrant or racism on the part of the police and courts. Such generalizations may be true in some cases. However, they miss the complexity in which the alternative normative systems of police and immigrant are reproduced through the compromises necessary to order social action coherently. After all, despite the confusion, the legal system continues to be reproduced (see

Hammond, 1991). But how to describe this process? Benda-Beckmann (1988, pp. 897-898) says that a description should start with the presumption that there is more than one normative legal order in any society. This, he writes, is the departure point for any type of empirical research, and this is what Merry did when she studied middle-class litigants. The danger, Benda-Beckmann continues, is that a "multiplicity" of "intertwined" strands exist, and the result is that we come full circle to another muddle. In other words, jumping to the conclusion that things are "multiple" and "intertwined" is as imprecise as concluding that immigrants are inherently insular or the police are inevitably racist. Griffiths (1986) describes this complexity: "Legal reality is an unsystematic collage of inconsistent and overlapping parts, lending itself to no easy legal interpretation, morally and aesthetically offensive to the eye of the liberal idealist, and almost incomprehensible in its complexity to the would-be empirical student" (p. 4).

The process through which youthful crime emerges in an immigrant community, however, provides a good illustration of the principles of legal pluralism, because the relevant actors occupy comparatively well-defined social fields. In the immigrant community, there is clearly a normative system brought from the home country. In opposition, there are positive written laws and strong normatively grounded views on the part of the police about the nature of the immigrant community and the origins of any new problems. In describing the fact of this opposition in this chapter, I will realize two objectives. First, I will clarify the problem of how youthful crime is consistently amplified in immigrant communities having large numbers of young males. Second, I will describe the principles of legal pluralism inherent to immigrant situations.

In order to examine how youthful crime emerges in immigrant communities, I will start with a theoretical discussion in which I will evaluate how the data needed for this analysis can be approached. This is followed by a presentation of the data, and the chapter ends with a summary and conclusions.

THEORETICAL APPROACH: DESCRIBING YOUTHFUL CRIME AND LEGAL PLURALISM

The preceding three chapters have been concerned with the prerequisites of the high incidence of youthful crime in immigrant communities—

the "why" of the explanatory equation about youthful crime in immigrant communities. As tools for understanding why youthful crime emerges at particular times, such variables are critical. However, age structure, group solidarity, poverty, and social status, although they may correlate with rates of youthful crime, do not themselves describe how relationships develop among immigrant parents, their children, and law enforcement. And this "how" should be at the heart of any description. After all, if you ask a youth, parent, or police officer involved in an outburst of gang activity why one group has high rates of youthful crime and another does not, no one will comment on the demographics, social cohesion, or social status of the groups. Instead, they will focus on how well different parts of the community understand the meaning and nature of law.

To answer this question, it is necessary to investigate what Luhmann (1985) describes as the structure of the legitimacy of law. More specifically, it is necessary to investigate how "cognitive normative expectations" brought from one country affect how another set of cognitive normative explanations found in the new country are utilized. In the case of immigrants, it is of course inevitable that there will be "ambiguities, inconsistencies, gaps, conflicts and the like" (Falk Moore, 1978, p. 3). These inconsistencies are not random, particularly when they are shaped by a patterned social process such as migration.

Legitimation of Law in Immigrant Society: Cognitive Acquisition and Contingent Rules

Luhmann (1985, pp. 199-200) calls law a process of decision making that is dependent on a preexisting expectation that a certain act will elicit a particular response. In traditional societies such as the Hmong and Molokan, the structures of expectations are grounded in natural law—that is, are believed to be God-given and immutable gifts of the Holy Spirit (Molokans) or of one's ancestors (Hmong). For such groups, this means that the roles of both parents and children are rooted in tradition, and therefore incontestable. Disruption of this system by appeal to another normative system, even the modern state, inevitably causes confusion and disorientation. As a consequence, the "ambiguities, inconsistencies, gaps, conflicts and the like" (Falk Moore, 1978, p. 3) inevitably multiply, causing disruption of both the home and the host systems. In cases where there are large numbers of young boys, the result is a rise in the incidence of youthful crime.

Despite the ambiguities, however, legal expectations are evaluated by the "normal person" as part of the consistent and coherent whole having a logic specific to the social group. In other words, there are shared expectations that if individual X commits a particular act, the state will respond in fashion Y. What is more, individual Z will perceive the state's responses as being morally proper.

In order for laws to be effective, it is necessary that all concerned share the same "contingency" rules for social action, so that every actor can predict (more or less) how others will respond in specific situations. This means that to manipulate a system of criminal law effectively, one must have a command of the normative expectations of the citizen, the police, the courts, and others involved. To be equal participants, all individuals involved in a particular case must be able to understand the viewpoints of all other participants. For the law to be an effective arbiter of social interaction, the defendant must be able to look at the case from the perspective of the police, and vice versa. Likewise, defendant, witnesses, attorneys, and judge must all make normative assessments for action based on how they believe the others will respond. For example, the judge presumes that the defendant does not want to go to jail and that all witnesses will be bound by the symbolism of an oath. The defendant in turn needs to assume that the judge will enforce the positive written law, that the defense attorney will observe the norms of confidentiality, and that the district attorney and police will observe the rules of evidence. Lawyers, police officers, and others who are part of the proceedings will likewise make similar assumptions about the roles of others. This is a fairly straightforward process in a society where potential defendants, lawyers, and police officers have all been socialized into the same role expectations (see Appendix A).[1]

In the case of the immigrant, however, the decision-making process is plural, and includes two separate systems of legal contingencies that may be only tangentially related.[2] The difficulties inherent to such a dissonant situation follow from differences not only in what is defined by positive law as "criminal," but in the responses to criminal behavior. For example, most societies define the use of someone else's automobile without the owner's permission as morally reprehensible and contrary to any positive law. Indeed, this is something that Hmong "traditional" law and American law share. Nevertheless, the rules for how such a situation is dealt with, and the roles that particular social actors take in that situation, vary from society to society, in particular with regard to how the inevitable discrepancies between law and the application of law are resolved (or ignored). For example, when the car is recovered and the thief caught, what is the legitimate way for the car's owner to seek compensation? How can he or she seek retribution? When is it proper to utilize extralegal solutions? Can the positive written law be overlooked if the thief simply returns the car? How is closure reached? Only when such issues are satisfactorily resolved, or at least ignored in a legitimated fashion, is the legal system effective.

The discussion below addresses how the acquisition of legal norms has taken place in the Mexican, Laotian, Korean, and Molokan Russian immigrant populations. As will become apparent, this process occurs in a patterned fashion even among groups as different as the Hmong, Mexicans, Koreans, and Molokan Russians; that is, there is a pattern to how immigrants handle contacts with the law during the process of becoming and disbecoming.

Just how important a jurisprudential sense is in the context of migration becomes evident when the inherent relationships among norms, the law, and the state are added to the equation. A legal system does not exist in a vacuum, although to the immigrant it may seem to. For the ideal-typical immigrant, the legal system of the host country is not a unified whole grounded in historically specific norms and events, as it is for the native (Falk Moore, 1978; Fitzpatrick, 1992). This is because the ideal-typical native has been socialized into the expectations of a particular jurisprudential system, whereas the immigrant has not. The gradual, time-dependent acquisition of these norms is part of the process of immigrant becoming.

In order to show how this complicated process takes place, I present below an analysis of some ethnographic material. This discussion will demonstrate that even when culture is controlled for, there is a patterned process in which the contingency rules for legal behavior are legitimated (see also Appendix B).

Methods

Controlling for Culture/Immigrant Group

To determine how immigration in and of itself may affect the acquisition of legal norms, it is necessary to control for ethnic group/culture. Integration of a group into a new society is a dynamic process, negotiated between the host-country norms and those that are remembered by the immigrants themselves. In order to show how this process varies, I examine below the relationships between the exemplary groups and the American legal system through accounts offered by the different groups across time. The "variable," in other words, is the story of how a relationship develops through time between the immigrant group and the legal system. The accounts come from groups at varying places in the migration process, including those who migrated as adults, those who migrated as older children, and those who migrated as young children or were born in the United States. Despite the fact that each example is culturally specific, these stories reveal common patterns in how immigrants view their relationship to the law during the process of migration. This procedure effectively controls for the confounding variable "culture."

Controlling for Variations in the Law Enforcement Community

An immigrant group's situation also influences the attitudes of host-country law enforcement personnel and how they define their own relationship to the immigrant group. This happens as law enforcement officers necessarily develop specific attributive accounts to explain the behavior of unfamiliar groups. Such accounts are local products of the interaction between the immigrant group and the law enforcement personnel in the locality where an immigrant enclave forms. Often first encounters are important, because they initiate the "historical memories" within the subcultures of law enforcement and the immigrant community. Future reference is always made to such understandings. This process is particularly important as police officers and social workers begin to acquire specific information about a particular immigrant group, by first categorizing and then attributing certain behaviors to groups of people. This categorization is typically done using assumptions specific to the subculture of law enforcement. This can result in particularly empathetic officers who serve as intermediaries between law enforcement and the immigrant community, but it can also result in uncomfortable situations, particularly when individuals a step or two away from the new communities try to fit accounts of illegal activity grounded in an immigrant subculture into the preexisting bureaucratized categories. Notably, use of such labels can result in new social categories that have far-reaching consequences.

How otherwise arbitrary labels can affect youthful crime was clearly demonstrated in December 1993 and January 1994 by television and newspaper accounts of home invasion robberies in the Sacramento community (see Magagnini, 1994a, 1994b, 1994c). Although virtually all accounts of the robberies indicated that only Laotians were the victims as well as the perpetrators, the preexisting category available to police officers and press was "Asian American." As a consequence, prevention and protection efforts focused on the category "Asian American." The result was that most of the press attention, as well as police programs, took place in the context of Vietnamese restaurants and involved Chinese American spokespersons.

This example illustrates how powerful categorization can be with respect to ethnic labels such as *Southeast Asian* and *Hispanic*. These two labels in particular are both products of the U.S. bureaucratic system, and as ethnic categories do not have social significance anywhere other than in the United States—there is no *Hispanic* in Mexico or *Southeast Asian* in Thailand. These terms simply do not specify significant social categories in the home countries of those so labeled. Consider, however, the significance of such ethnic labels. The result of the bureaucratic label *Hispanic* is that, for the first time, the behavior of a third-generation Chicano is relevant to a Cuban immigrant, because in the United States they are both placed in this category. Or a Vietnamese refugee's behavior reflects on the reputation of a Filipino immigrant, as both are labeled *Asian*. At the extreme, such labeling can be used as an excuse for arrest sprees. In a more common and general way, it results in the imprecise categorization of specific behaviors based on observations of individuals who, from an ethnographic perspective, may be only peripherally connected. Nevertheless, how individuals are perceived, no matter how ethnographically imprecise, affects how culture will be generated for succeeding generations. Through such a mechanism, the explanation eventually becomes part of the fixed ethnographic record, at least when the anthropologist shows up to write it down.[3]

A second example of how subculturally specific beliefs can shape police views is the commonly expressed view in law enforcement that Vietnamese (and often by extension all Southeast Asian and/or Asian immigrants) do not trust the American police because bribery is so common in Vietnam (or Southeast Asia, or Asia in general).[4] This belief seems to have its origins in either the Vietnam War or the early days of the refugee exodus from Vietnam, when the Vietnamese "other" first became defined by American norms. Whether or not this was ever "true" in a positivistic sense is immaterial. What is relevant is that this belief has shaped the interactions of police and immigrant Asian communities as they have integrated during the process of migration.[5]

The point is that any new legal interaction between immigrants and authorities is a potential source of mutual misinterpretation, as both groups assign labels and categorize behavior based on preconceived notions. Given the culturally/morally grounded expectations inherent to the law, it is not surprising that both groups do so in imprecise fashion. But out of the imprecise structured reordering of legal contingencies, the relationships between immigrant groups and law enforcement are socially reconstructed.

Conclusions: Criminal Law as a Dynamic Variable

In an ideal-typical situation, the normative bases for the laws, the society, and law enforcement all form a logical and balanced triad (see Figure 7.1); the law is consistently legitimated through, to borrow Luhmann's (1985) phraseology, a "mixture of cognitive/normative expectation of normative expectation of cognitive expectation of normative expectation" (p. 204) that is shared by the public, consistent with social structures, and shared by law enforcement. These shared expectations include not only the written positive law, but also the legal norms on which the legal pluralists focus. Figure 7.1 represents the ideal-typical situation, in which two separate systems are legitimated independent of each other. Among the issues implied are the unwritten norm-based assumptions about when it is moral to use the law and when it is not. Unlike most ideal-typical constructions, however, this is not only a social science tool. Such a balance is also implicit to the "legitimating myth" that underpins the positive law in State A.

Such a balance is also found in Society B, which also has a law and state that are legitimated by the normative structure of the society. Now, what happens when a group of people from Country B migrate to Country A? The physical change in location means that they become subject to the laws of Country A. However, the individuals who make up this group were socialized in Society B, and will continue to legitimate their own social actions according to the norms of Society B.

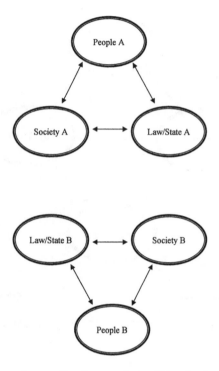

Figure 7.1. Relations Among the Expectations of People, the Laws, and Society: The Ideal-Typical Situation

This is not, however, what social network analysts call a "stable triad." That is, there will be a tendency for the immigrant group to try to eliminate the implied "dissonance" (see Figure 7.2). This has typically meant that as children are socialized by the institutions of Society A, a stabilizing leg is established between Society A and the immigrant group A/B. The eventual result is that the flow of normative institutions from Society B to the immigrant group disappears. This is the ideal-typical pattern for a country like the United States, and in particular explains fairly well the assimilation of Europe's 19th- and early-20th-century immigrants into U.S. society. This is presumably what has happened to "assimilated" groups such as the Molokan Russians. It is also what has happened to ethnic minorities that have acquired separate indigenous identities different from those of their home countries. A good example of this is the "Chicano" identity, a U.S.-based social category that sustains itself independent of its origins in Mexican migration to the United States.

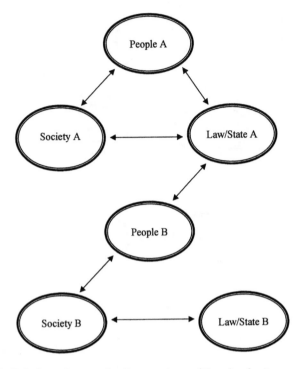

Figure 7.2. Relations Among the Expectations of People, the Laws, and Society: An Unstable Triad

However, there is also a second logical pattern: State B can "reclaim" its immigrants by having the power of the state follow them to their new country. This is what happens during the expansion of countries into neighboring areas where immigrant groups have established a separate presence. Examples of this type of dissonance include present-day Hong Kong, where Chinese "society" rejoined the Chinese "state/law" in 1998. Colonial situations in which state and law were European but the society continued to be local have also proved to be unstable. This is one of the reasons that European nations abandoned their African colonies after a comparatively short period (60-80 years) of occupation.

But how does this work in practice among immigrant groups? Earlier in this chapter, I quoted Luhmann's (1985) convoluted description of the contingent decision making necessary for legal action: a "mixture of cognitive/normative expectation of normative expectation of cognitive expectation of normative expectation" (p. 204). In the context of the above discussion, how could it be expected that immigrant groups—with their inherently attenuated socialization into American legal norms, unusual demographics, and fragmented social structure—would be able to legitimate and perpetuate normative structures? How do norms for legal action influence what individuals do within the immigrant group, as well as how their behaviors are understood by law enforcement and the broader social community? In the following section, I present examples related to all of these issues.

CASE STUDIES: CHANGING LEGAL EPISTEMOLOGIES

Presented below are case study examples that illustrate immigrant community views of older persons, middle-aged persons socialized in both the immigrant and the host societies, and young persons socialized primarily in the United States. These come from a variety of published sources as well as from my own interviews and observations. Also included are examples from the popular media of how the law enforcement "subculture" views immigrant groups and of some typical views of the general public regarding immigrants. The examples are developed most fully for the Laotian and Molokan cases, but there is also some material dealing with Mexican cases, and I present a very brief discussion of Korean perceptions of legal issues.

What all these examples show is a pattern found in the process of migration, in which positive law is used and misused or understood and misunderstood by different groups at different social locations. Although each account is culturally embedded, all immigrant youth— be they from the Mien, Mexican, or Molokan community—have views reflecting socialization in American public schools. Likewise, the approaches of the police, social workers, and other law enforcement authorities are patterned by similar laws and norms. The result is that the authorities deal similarly with all arrested immigrant youth, with language difficulties, and so on, whether they are dealing with Mien youth, Mexican youth, or Molokan youth. Immigrant elders and parents, although shaped less by direct contact with the broader society, also respond in a patterned fashion to those (i.e., youth) who are shaped by that society.

Laotians

Laotians brought to the United States from Laos and from Thai refugee camps have very specific norms for dealing with the misbehavior of youth. The ethnographic record indicates that among the most common and effective methods is ostracism from the social group (Tapp, 1988). The "traditional" ideal for Laotian Hmong may be described in the following manner:

> Actual punishment of the criminal did not fall to the court, but fell to the lineage of the criminal. In such societies, it is the lineages which must pay the fine, and it is the lineage which in turn must police itself. This policing was done by first, the loss of face within the lineage, and in an extreme, several Hmong explained, a habitual offender would be made to "disappear" by his own lineage, i.e. ostracized or perhaps killed in the forest. The disappearance of this person was then recounted to children in the form of a moral tale designed to both teach ethical behavior and insure social order. It needs to be emphasized, though, that unlike the ideals of the American system, social order was not developed through "correction" or "punishment" of an individual, but through the need of a group of people (i.e. the clan or lineage) to protect its name throughout the highland villages. (Waters & Cohen, 1993, pp. 16-17)

In other words, there is a "civil" focus of the law in which compensation and self-regulation are emphasized rather than punishment or rehabilitation by the modern state. Most important, punishment is the prerogative of the offender's own clan, and not of the state. Such social control can, of course, be highly effective in many circumstances. However, it does not have any standing legally or normatively in the United States, and as a result does not articulate well with what American social control agents expect to hear.[6] Nevertheless, accounts for misbehavior offered to U.S. authorities by Laotians focus on the usurpation of parental authority by American laws regulating the treatment of children in general and corporal punishment in particular. Such attributions can be contextualized in both American and Laotian social systems in a legitimated fashion, whereas statements about ostracism cannot.[7] The opinion of a Mien elder is representative of how the traditional Mien community responded to the upsurge in youthful gang activity in 1991-1993:

The young ones won't pay attention to our traditional councils anymore, because the government doesn't permit them to have any authority over their own. We can't enforce our will. In Laos, they would have had to listen to their elders, or they would have been severely beaten. Here the government won't let us enforce our decisions, though. So the kids run wild. They are good students in elementary school and junior high school, and even do better than the American kids. But then in high school everything goes wrong, and suddenly the American kids are doing better than ours. Please explain to the government that if we were permitted to handle our own problems, everything would be much better, and our young people would be good citizens and students. (quoted in Waters & Cohen, 1993, pp. 55-56)[8]

This Mien elder provided a specific attributive account in the context of the continuing misbehavior of his nephews, who had been arrested numerous times.[9] It is embedded in a system very much like that described above in the quote from Waters and Cohen. Policing, in the elder's view, is the responsibility of the offender's clan, not of the state. Significantly, this view is embedded in assumptions about what the relation of the government should be to a semi-independent political body. This is the situation that was found in Laos under the idealized conditions described above.[10] In this respect, the view is a mix of accounts adjusted to meet the expectations of American values dealing with compulsory education and the law, but still embedded in subconscious assumptions about social relations (i.e., the role of elders and government) brought from Laos.

A Hmong social worker, about 30 years old at the time of the interview, provides, in 1991, a more nuanced view of how the two systems could effectively interact. Keep in mind that, unlike the case of the Mien, the Hmong were, in 1991, relatively well organized, primarily through the agency Lao Family, Incorporated (described in Chapter 5). One consequence was that the Hmong evolved effective strategies, legitimated within their own community, for describing how the American legal system could be made to work in the situations in which the Hmong found themselves.

We don't teach about [American-style] remorse, because "sorry" is not enough. I remember that in [the American] high school I had trouble with a white kid who messed with me.

The teacher came and made him tell me that he was sorry. But that was nothing. What is "sorry"? Only words. The Hmong seek compensation for an offense. Without compensation the situation is not righted, and words are not compensation. . . .

So I asked the teacher if I could attack him [my tormenter] and then simply say that I was sorry. [After all, this is what the other student had in effect done to me.] But I was told no. How can you win in a situation like that? Just saying "sorry" means nothing in our [Hmong] society. (quoted in Waters & Cohen, 1993, pp. 63-64)

Here, the informant, who is something of a modern Tocqueville in his approach to American culture, is poking fun at the difference between American assumptions of remorse and Hmong conceptions of proper civil compensation. He reframes the question in terms of compensation for a wrong, which is what the Hmong legal system, as well as many others, assumes is the purpose of law. He says that in the Hmong legal epistemology, there would be a need to exact monetary compensation from the offender or his family in order to assure that the act would not be repeated. Saying "sorry" is worthwhile only in the symbolism "mythology" of American social interaction. The teacher, who was embedded in American legal assumptions, probably did not understand the informant's joke.[11] What this Hmong informant does, in effect, is make fun of what Fitzpatrick (1992) calls the "myth" necessary for the rationalization of American positive law.

On a different issue, the same informant went on to describe how stepping outside of the American mythology can be used to manipulate American police practices. My notes on his comments are as follows:

My informant complained about slow response times by the police, and had a story about the problem to illustrate the point. He claimed that the police response time improves only if a woman is reporting or some serious crime is occurring. "To get the police to come, you call and tell them that you are beating your wife. Or, better yet, you say that a burglar is making trouble. If you call and just say that a prowler is hanging around, you can call two, three times. Every 10 minutes or so. What works, though, is if you call the fire department and report a fire. They come much faster, and in the process, scare away the prowler. This is good, but then the firemen complain because you have made a false report. How do you win in a situation like this?

Again, these remarks show insight into the underlying "mythology" of American police response that is unlikely to be found among individuals embedded in American legal culture. Unlike in his first story, however, in this one the informant is poking fun at the pluralistic nature of American law. Like the story about remorse, it is "cute" and reveals an unusually keen awareness of American legal epistemology.[12] Potentially more problematic, however, is the informant's view of how control of juvenile delinquency can work within the Hmong community:

> Young people are warned [by the Hmong elders] once when they mess up. If they mess up again, then no one will come to assist them or bail them out when they get in trouble with the police. . . . In the case of auto theft by a youngster, I may even report my own nephew to the police. It is my responsibility and, no, my brother will not resent this. I am doing my duty by reporting to the police, particularly if the nephew has already been warned [by the elders] about a previous offense. (quoted in Waters & Cohen, 1993, pp. 63-64).

Such a view may be problematic because it assumes that the category "elders" will be perpetuated as a means of Hmong social control into the future, even though the routines of life through which Hmong society is being reproduced in California are focused on a modern industrial life in which elders will ultimately have little status. The threat is that, as happened with the Molokans, the new lifeways will exclude the elders over a period of time.

The underlying problem in what the Hmong informant describes is that, although his humor indicates keen insight, a parallel understanding of Hmong and American jurisprudential epistemologies is difficult, if not impossible, to maintain. Such a system would assume a steady supply of young "de Tocquevilles" like this informant embedded in two cultures and who, as a consequence, could observe the irony in situation after situation even after Hmong society has been completely reproduced in the United States. The following example illustrates why the continued production of so many Hmong de Tocquevilles is problematic at best.

A 24-year-old Hmong teacher's aide in one of Sacramento's schools offered a view of how traditional councils work. This woman had come to the United States in 1978 at the age of 9, and was speaking to a reporter (McGrath, 1993). She had probably lived from 1975 to 1978 in Thai refugee camps, and likely was born in one of the many Hmong military/refugee encampments in Laos in 1969. According to the article, she has three children, a fact that presumably legitimates her status as a woman within traditional Hmong society, although in American society (i.e., that of the reporter) it is her status as a teacher's aide that is important and the reason her opinion was solicited in the first place. Indeed, as a woman living under traditional conditions, her views about gangs and the problems of raising youth would probably not be solicited by Hmong elders. Her views are important in the context of an American newspaper, in which they were reported.

> In Laos our people would go to the mountains and cut trees or plant fields, but here they have laws regulating everything, and if you don't speak English, it's hard to understand. . . . I know what [my people] are feeling. I try to make them comfortable. (quoted in McGrath, 1993, p. A2)

Her assertion that there are laws in the United States, but in Laos life was uncomplicated because all they did was "cut trees or plant fields" is, according to any positivistic ethnographic record (as well as common sense), inaccurate. There are complex laws and norms in Laos, as there are in any society. The question, however, is, When a Hmong woman offers such a view in the first place, and it is privileged by an American newspaper reporter, what does this do for the reproduction of Hmong culture in the United States?

When migration is assumed to be a process, a plausible answer suggests itself. Ethnographic naïveté about one's own family is understandable in the context of the "unbecoming" that is occurring in the Hmong community. By comparing the views of the Hmong social worker and the Hmong teacher's aide, we can see how this process is "making" sense to Hmong in a fashion that is slow and halting. The next step is to ask what this means for the maintenance of the "mythical" nature of the law, as well as the continuing reproduction of both American and immigrant society.

Fitzpatrick (1992, pp. 72-76) points out that the mythical nature of modern law is embedded in the assumption that "the other" has no law. He notes that in order for there to be modern law, it must be contrasted with a "savage state." He quotes from the description of the land of the savage Cyclops in *The Odyssey* to illustrate: "Ulysses and his company . . . 'came to the land of the Cyclops race, arrogant lawless beings who leave their livelihood to the deathless gods . . . have no assemblies to debate in, they have no ancestral ordinances. . . . and the head of each family heeds no other, but makes his own ordinances for wife and children' " (p. 72).

In a halting fashion, the teacher's aide quoted here seems to have reached a similar conclusion that the "other" she is describing—that is, ancestral Laos—had no law. This conclusion is based more on her own socialization in refugee camps and the United States than on any ethnographic fact. On the other hand, if one thinks through the process of migration, it is not surprising that people of this woman's experience and generation have reached such conclusions. The law she knows comes from the United States, and she has evaluated it using the contingency rules she has been socialized into in this country. As a consequence, she does not interpret the practices of her elders as a parallel alternative law (as the Hmong social worker does), but as the misunderstandings of an out-of-touch older generation who need to be made to "feel comfortable." At a certain point, the "other" became defined to her as an absence of relevant norms, rather than as an independent set of norms, as it was for the Hmong "de Tocqueville" quoted above. Not coincidentally, it also probably matches the reporter's need to write the story in a "we-they" form that his readers expect. If Fitzpatrick is right about the mythical nature of law, this would seem to be a necessary precondition for integration of the teacher's aide's generation into the American system of legal norms.

Finally, compare the three examples provided above: the Mien elder, the Hmong social worker, and the Hmong teacher's aide. Only the social worker expresses a thorough understanding of both cultures and how they can be integrated. The other two lack knowledge, either about the American system or about the Laotian system. The Mien elder's views of child abuse laws are inaccurate, and the Hmong teacher's aide's understanding of traditional systems of social control are imprecise.

However, although such problems may be inherent to the process of migration, they also occur in a context where, myth or not, the legal system must change and respond. The influence of the U.S. legal system is of course necessarily hegemonic relative to that of the imported Lao system. The necessarily dominant all-pervasiveness of the American system limits how such mutual perceptions can develop.

Let's look at this relationship. The imprecision is there because the Laotian system can maneuver only within the context of the socially legitimated legal tools provided by the American system.[13] However, the opposite is also true: The American system, hegemonic or not, can operate effectively only in the context of the Laotian system, weak and withering though it may be. The limitations. are illustrated by the following description of a murder investigation which was related to me by a police officer. The officer had a keen sense of the ironies involved in conducting an investigation in which very different concepts of criminal responsibility existed. The murder resulted from a fight between gang members over the favors of a young Mien girl. In our interactive discussion about the incident, the police officer's comments reflected a number of different issues. The ironies presented by the competing epistemologies of "guilt," however, are especially important to consider here. A synopsis of our conversation follows (adapted from Waters & Cohen, 1993, pp. 57-58):

> The girl had been the girlfriend of a Mien gang leader who had been arrested and sent to juvenile hall for a period. When he returned to his gang, he found out that his girlfriend had been "partying" with another member of the gang. Words were exchanged between the two competitors, with the result that there was an alignment of gang members loyal to the returned leader and of members who sided with the girl's new friend. The uncle of the challenger also appeared during the argument (bear in mind that the relationship of uncle is an important one in Mien and Hmong societies).
>
> At this point, the leader left the scene. Sometime thereafter, there was a melee in which the uncle of the challenger was attacked. In the attack, the uncle received a knife wound to the leg; a large artery was severed, and the uncle bled to death.
>
> This attack was apparently witnessed by a number of people in the area. During the investigation, all witnesses indicated that the responsible party was the gang leader, a person who, because of his record, was well-known to the

police. However, the police could not arrest the leader because he did not participate in the beating or hold the knife that caused the fatal wound; for that matter, he was not even physically present during the attack.

There were, however, witnesses willing to say that the gang leader was the responsible party. They reasoned that, had the leader not started the argument that led to the uncle's death, there would never have been an attack and the uncle would be alive. In other words, by Mien reckoning, the actual participants, including the person who held the knife, were victims of the circumstances created by the gang leader. In addition, the witnesses reasoned that if only the knife wielder was arrested, then the threat of further assaults would remain, because the leader would be free. As the leader, he would take revenge on those who reported his followers. On the other hand, if the leader was arrested, the actual knife wielder, who was a follower, would not necessarily take revenge, so further threats to the community would be removed and the peace of the community would be protected.

In many respects, this type of reasoning has a certain appeal. Certainly it makes some sense even to Americans grounded in individualistic rather than corporate-type concepts of criminal responsibility. However, such reasoning does not have any basis in California law, which assumes that the persons who participated in the beating and the individual who held the knife all had free will and were not victims of circumstances initiated by the gang leader.

A consequence of these differing concepts of responsibility and social action is a persistent mistrust on the part of immigrant groups concerning what the police can do to protect public safety.

The problems noted by the police officer in this case are those of a keen and thoughtful observer. However, as he admitted, an effective and trusting relationship between law enforcement and the immigrant community cannot come out of such differing views of criminal responsibility (see also Appendixes B and C), even when all involved have the best intentions. Indeed, when I interviewed a deputy from the Sacramento Sheriff's Office in 1997, he indicated that this case (along with others) continues to be a factor in the intensified mistrust of law enforcement within the Mien community. There has been no "closure" in this situation, and mistrust had grown.

Thus, just as the views of the Hmong social worker and teacher's aide reflect evolving interpretations, how agencies of social control form such views also influences how these relationships develop. Particularly among individuals who are several steps removed from those directly involved, the insight that emerges out of practical experience decreases, with the result that officials draw more and more on their own experiences with nonimmigrants to define new and novel situations presented by immigrant groups.

Formation of Views on Laotians by Law Enforcement

Agencies of social control necessarily form their own explanations for behavior out of preexisting, culturally embedded discourses. For example, in the 1980s and 1990s, discourses about gender and cultural relativism were common in the United States. A common way of framing the Hmong experience in the United States has been to say that Hmong refugees are "time travelers" of some sort, because they have in effect moved from the 16th to the 20th century. Sherman (1985; cited in Moore-Howard, 1987) has described it in this fashion:

> The Hmong made one airplane flight from the sixteenth century to the twentieth century. Within the space of seventy-two hours these mountain people were taken from bamboo-thatched huts in refugee camps . . . and put into two- and three-bedroom apartments in Philadelphia, Minneapolis or other American cities.

Moore-Howard (1987) elaborates by noting that this means that "a proud group of people from the hills of Laos were faced with learning skills and making decisions four centuries apart in time." This metaphor of the Hmong as time travelers provides a convenient, and probably effective, way for Americans to grasp the changes the Hmong have faced in the United States. It is of course ethnographically inaccurate (the Hmong in the 1960s were very capable of waging 20th-century warfare), but such views shape how the competing sets of contingency rules are perceived.

Such assumptions are often reflected in courtroom discourse designed for American juries. The result is that courtroom battles often focus on "cultural defenses," with greater attention paid to the American legal requirements involved than to the formal ethnographic record. Two exemplary cases are described below: an opium case in Sacramento and a rape case brought against a Hmong defendant in Minneapolis. These two cases have little in common, other than the manner in which the role that the current American discourse about gender and cultural relativism (i.e., multiculturalism) was used to attempt to legitimate, albeit unsuccessfully, the case for the defense. Defense attorneys in both cases framed their arguments in gender-based terms that have a great deal of legitimation in the American society from which the attorneys and jurors were selected.

The Opium Case

In 1990-1991, U.S. Customs agents made a series of arrests for opium trafficking. In these cases, the defendants typically received opium shipments at a variety of post office boxes rented in post offices throughout Northern California (see Waters & Cohen, 1993, p. 33). Because the cases involved customs violations, they were tried in federal court.

The case described below followed another federal case in which an acquittal was obtained after a "cultural" defense was made following the expert testimony of an anthropologist witness from the Center for South and Southeast Asian Studies at the University of California, Berkeley. Such testimony was disallowed by the judge in the case of *USA v. Liw Kuan Saechao* (file 2:CR87-292, June 26-29, 1991), described below. Nevertheless, the defense based its case on a number of points about "culture" and "gender" that emerged out of this defense. The following account is from a *Sacramento Bee* article published after the jury had found the defendant guilty:

A Mien tribeswoman stood before a federal judge Monday and pleaded tearfully for mercy from a legal system clearly at odds with the cultural practices she was taught in the remote hills of Laos.

Liw Kuan Saechao, a 39-year-old North Highlands woman, was sentenced to 41 months in prison. . . .

> Saechao's attorney, . . . Suzanne A. Luban, argued during
> the trial that her client was merely obeying the request of one
> of her elders when she drove to the Elverta post office in
> January and picked up a package containing the opium.
>
> Mien tribal customs call for younger people to be subser-
> vient to their elders, particularly younger women, according
> to Luban. . . . [Judge] Garcia seemed convinced on this point
> saying, "It appears that this defendant was importing the
> opium at the request of the elder." (Bernstein, 1991, p. B1)

Suzanne Luban told me after this trial that Saechao had refused a
plea bargain that would have resulted in a prison term of $6\frac{1}{2}$ months in
what Luban felt was a difficult case to take to trial. In order to illustrate
the point about obedience that she had made during the trial, Luban
pointed out that Saechao refused to accept the plea bargain only after
consulting with her male relatives, particularly her uncle, who felt,
owing to the Mien understanding of the concept of "agency"—that is,
that Saechao was only the "courier" in this case—that she was not
punishable.[14] In court, Luban tried to validate this point by claiming
that the Polk Street Apartments, around which the defendant's social
life revolved, were more like "a Mien village" than an American apartment complex. She went on to explain that the post office boxes that
the defendant had rented as opium drops were the "same idea for Mien
as hamburgers are for troops in Saudi Arabia." In other words, she tried
to frame a potentially criminal situation in terms recognizable in the
broader discourse about the nature of culture in which the jurors had
presumably engaged. In order to accentuate the strangeness of the case
and strengthen her "cultural" defense, on the final day of her testimony
the defendant wore traditional Mien clothing.

The Rape Case

Minneapolis, Minnesota, has the oldest Hmong community in the
United States, and as a consequence has a relatively large number of well
educated and sophisticated Hmong social workers. Many of these social
workers are in a particularly powerful position, between recently
arrived refugees and the American social service agencies that administer
contracts to provide social welfare services. In 1991, a well-educated,
high-status Hmong who was a job counselor used his position to

convince newly arrived Hmong women to go to hotel rooms for "job counseling," and he then had sexual intercourse with them. The defendant of course argued that the sexual acts were consensual, and the victims argued that the sex was coerced. This resulted in particularly unusual defenses focusing on how "Hmong culture" views rape.[15] The arguments attracted the attention of a writer for the *Twin Cities Reader*, which published a sympathetic description of the defense:

> From a traditional Hmong perspective, a married woman's consent in sex is immaterial because she is the property of her husband and has no independent right to consent. Traditional Hmong, therefore, perceive the primary victims of the [alleged] acts—whether they be rape or consensual sex—to be the cuckolded husbands.
>
> Some culturally assimilated Hmong, including a number of leading Hmong feminists, likewise believe the trials were about adultery, not rape. They are appalled by the guilty verdicts, which they attribute either to the court's cultural ignorance or to a racist impulse to repress any Asian man who dares to succeed in this country. They question whether the scanty evidence presented in the cases would have ever convicted a white man. (Hammond, 1991)

The generalizations made in this article illustrate well how difficult it is to mix the "mythology" of law from two cultures. Nevertheless, the defense attorney tried to do so by drawing on the broader discussion of multiculturalism and gender. In this way, she was even able to make plausible a claim that the primary victim in a rape is a man who was not even present. The power of an argument rooted in such terms is illustrated by the fact that the story was presented by a lawyer, a person attuned to jury sensibilities, and published in a popular journal like the *Twin Cities Reader*. The story reduces the complicated Hmong marriage traditions that the ethnographic record describes as the consequence of negotiations between clans (see Tapp, 1988, pp. 88-91) to "a woman's consent in sex is immaterial because she is the property of her husband." Not only that, the lawyer, newspaper reporter, and a few Hmong women find it strategic to label such a position as "feminist" in an attempt to legitimate the argument. The use of such a distinctly American (as opposed to Hmong) category as "feminist" is similar to describing the views of the "assimilated," despite the fact that the issue being described is unfamiliar in both Hmong and American culture. Certainly it is highly doubtful that an American feminist would have advanced such an argument about marriage and rape.

What the Opium and Rape Cases Have in Common

In both of these cases, unusual situations were forced into categories that were already available to the attorneys and for which they hoped there would be some sympathy from the jurors. In both cases, the defense attorneys forced the issues into a broader discussion of cultural relativism ("It's in their culture, so it must be okay—free will and rape are different in their culture") and gender (the woman was powerless; she did not have free will). However, in doing so, they had to adjust the way Mien and Hmong cultures are being reproduced to the types of accounts demanded by the American legal system. At the same time, however, they adjusted, legitimated, and reproduced preexisting American cultural norms about the other—those that have to do with cultural relativism and gender.[16]

Laotians, Youthful Crime, Police, and the Social Category "Gang"

Police officers who focus on youthful crime are interested in putting the crimes they observe into preexisting legal categories shaped by their own subculture, which, although based in the law, also has strong unwritten norms. As in popular discourse, these subcultural norms affect how they will approach their jobs, which in turn influences how the immigrants will respond. Just as the cases discussed above were shaped by popular discourse, the subculture of law enforcement fits new youthful crime in immigrant communities into familiar discourses—discourses about gangs and gang activity.

In the late 1980s, such discussion of "gangs" was important, because youthful crime was framed in this way in the popular media, law enforcement, and the law itself. Common usage of the term *gang* usually fell somewhere between the legal definition, which called a gang any group of three or more people who come together to commit illegal acts, and more social science-oriented definitions, which focused on "opportunistic groupings." Two examples from the Laotian experience follow, the first from a column written by a *Sacramento Bee* columnist and the second from police testimony, which is reproduced from a court record. In both examples, police officers attempt to explain youthful gang activity in Laotian communities using preexisting categories. A reporter for the *Sacramento Bee* wrote:

> Severe alienation drives Hmong youngsters to seek acceptance elsewhere—such as street gangs. "There is definitely an element that is assimilating a part of the culture we'd rather they didn't," says Sgt. Ralph Coyle of the Sacramento Police Department's Gang Unit. "Asian gangs have adopted many of the characteristics of the more established street gangs—the turf, the weapons, the violence." (McGrath, 1993, p. A2)

Police officers typically developed their typologies for what was expected—and probable—for Hmong youthful crime based on the social categories already available to them. In this case, the focus resulted in two ethnographic distortions: "street gangs" and "Asian." For the police, such categorization evokes a series of normative expectations for identifying possible actions and reactions. In this example, these expectations resulted in a search for "turf, weapons, and violence," expectations that in part are based in the previous experience of police with Hispanic gangs (turf) and Vietnamese gangs (weapons and violence), respectively. The argument is in effect a functional one, where categories are observed and a familiar consequence/cause, in this case "assimilating a part of the culture," is assumed. As is typical with functional arguments, other categories that might have been "assimilated" are ignored. For example, even considering the narrow categories of "gang" and "assimilation," other things not included might have been crack cocaine (a drug associated with black gangs), heroin (a drug associated with Hispanic gangs), methamphetamine (a drug associated with whites), car theft (a Mien gang habit), and burglary (a white nongang crime). In other words, although there may be some cross-cultural learning going on, the grouping is described as such primarily because "gang" is the preexisting category available to the officer. In such a context, what is noteworthy about the above account is not what it tells us about gangs per se, but what it says about how police officers frame issues raised by new immigrant groups.

A similar example comes from records of the Sacramento County Municipal Court:

> "Going to play." Police claim that in SEA gang culture, this means stealing. "Jay-Jay" stopped at Sacramento High School on the morning of the incident to invite Sin Hin to go "play." This resulted in an armed robbery and the arrest of three Mien youth on a theft and weapons charge. Police testify that these boys are members of the "Sacramento Bad Boys" gang. The police say that the identifier for this gang is only tattoos; i.e. that they are not territorial like other gangs. Nevertheless, they may be acquiring the other characteristics of gang activity, including territory, and special language. (trial transcript, Sacramento Superior Court, July 25, 1990; case of Senom Saelee, file 98067)

For a time in 1989-1992, the Sacramento Bad Boys (SBB) were a major source of mayhem (car theft, firearms, petty theft, assault) in Sacramento's Oak Park area, particularly among the Mien community. As a "gang," however, the SBB were a social category only for themselves and the police. Mien in the community had never heard of the group's name in 1992, although they were well aware of the crimes committed by the boys. As the notes above illustrate, however, the assumption on the part of police led to another set of expectations—that is, that the group was "moving toward" the preexisting category "gang" in a way that would resolve the dissonance between the established definition of law enforcement and what was observed by police officers.

In contrast, Mien contemporaries of the Sacramento Bad Boys perceived the same individuals differently. Mien who were more distant from the authorities—but tied closely to the gang members through kinship relations—had never heard the name Sacramento Bad Boys and knew only in a general way that their cousins had formed a gang of sorts. More typically, they considered the cousins a group of kids who hung out together and were in trouble a lot, whereas they thought of "gangs," if the word made their vocabulary, as the Crips and Bloods of popular culture.[17] The 20-year-old cousins who lived across the street from the SBB leader dubbed by police "Sacramento's number one Mien criminal" had a harsh view of his activities, but they had never heard the name Sacramento Bad Boys. They attributed the depredations of their cousin to a combination of split personality and all-consuming desire to acquire money, rather than membership in the SBB. Indeed, the only people who were aware of the name Sacramento Bad Boys within the Mien community seemed to be Mien interpreters associated with the police, and presumably the gang members themselves, who had SBB tattoos. "Assimilation" of such activities was never mentioned by any young Mien informants not associated with the police, despite the assessment of all concerned that the same individuals were bad people who committed major crimes. The differences between Mien and police perceptions lay in how the issues were framed and explained.

Another Sacramento Mien gang in 1991 was the Polk Street Boys, or PSB. Elders who lived in a building sprayed with PSB graffiti were unaware that there was a "gang" of that name when questioned about it directly. This means that the large letters spray-painted on their building were socially unimportant to them and, as a result, cognitively invisible. They were, of course, aware of the numerous ganglike crimes that the Polk Street Boys had committed, and of the individuals involved (see Appendixes C and D). Paradoxically, however, they had not connected the crimes to the graffiti on the apartment walls or to other indicators that are "obvious" in the broader culture. In other words, within the Mien culture of the adults interviewed, graffiti were not a means of communication as they were within the youth culture.

In this formulation, the point is not that either side was right or wrong in terms of positivistic social science, but that acts that all agreed were legally criminal were explained in different fashions. However, this happened in a patterned fashion: Persons in positions of authority hastened to force their understanding of deviance into the preexisting categories found in the American judicial system, whereas individuals in the immigrant community pushed toward an understanding of the phenomenon in terms rooted in the preexisting legal categories they had brought with them from Laos. This situation is not very different from a defense attorney's using the category "Hmong feminist" in arguing before an American jury that a rape charge should be viewed as an issue of adultery.

The Gang and the "Mythology" of Law in Laotian Immigrant Communities

Does this mean that gangs and youthful crime would be absent from immigrant communities if there were no "myth" of the "gang" within American law enforcement culture? The answer of course is no—or, rather, sort of. The concept of the "gang" is a legitimating explanation. That is, it is a way of framing a number of discrete events—auto burglaries, fighting, and weapons use, and the like—committed by small groups of youths. In other words, there would still be car burglaries even if the police called these groups something else. Organizing the concept into a discrete category such as "gang," however, has significant consequences for how both the police subculture and the subculture of the immigrant community address the issues concerned. The irony is that in the process of learning to manipulate such categories effectively, the very source of the generational conflict from which it emerges is likely to disappear.[18]

Molokan Russians

According to Young (1932), the interpersonal relationships between the Molokan Russian immigrants and the broader social world "rarely permitted an intimate or complete view of each others' lives" (p. 128). Certainly the examples described above for Laotians illustrate such circumstances well. Misconceptions also occurred across the generations with reference to parenting, often with effects analogous to those found in present-day Laotian communities. One of Young's interviews with the parents of a rebellious youth is reminiscent of what the Mien elder quoted above described as happening in the Laotian community. In both cases, the focus is on what is perceived as meddling by a larger welfare bureaucracy attempting to control child abuse:

> Our children get the notion that they are overworked, that large families are a detriment, that our homes are crowded, that they are entitled to live and act like city folks. . . .
> We try to make them see our way; we plead with them; and if that fails, what can we do? Children need discipline. God chastises those whom he loves. Beating should be our last resort. At first there was no complaint, but soon these kids were told by our neighbors, welfare workers, and teachers, that this was a free country and a father couldn't beat his children. I'll never forget when a father was taken over to the police station for strapping his boy. The whole Colony was on its feet in no time. One of our brothers arrested! Ivan Ivanovitch, a kind-

hearted man, arrested—for beating his youngster into obedience! Ivanovitch has not beaten another one of his little bums
as hard. He is afraid of them now, and they know it. They hold
the upper hand over him. "I'll give you a thrashing." "I'll have
you arrested," settles it all. (quoted in Young, 1932, p. 138)

On the basis of this observation, Young herself ironically concludes
that "the Molokans have little conception of a system of discipline
independent of family authority. When they were unable to exercise their
authority, they became confused, uncertain, inconsistent. They felt that,
in spite of the increased care and prolonged attention given to the child,
he was not theirs in the same sense that he was before" (p. 138). This
conclusion is ironic because, of course, in the Molokan situation Young
herself describes, the *sobranie* certainly had a "system of discipline
independent of family authority." Again, the problem was that this
sobranie "system" did not fit within preexisting bureaucratic categories
of the modern state, and therefore did not even exist, even to an observer
as thoughtful as Young. At least as significant, it also became effectively
invisible to the immigrants themselves, who, in searching for the
functional equivalent of a social worker from a bureaucracy, found
nothing that was obvious. Therefore they concluded that the occasional
violent act that the parent administered was the source of control, and
not the wider social context generated by the *sobranie*.

As in the account by the Mien elder, the interpretation of child-
protection laws by the Molokans was imprecise. It was not so much a
question of what the law was empirically, but how the law, its agents,
and its tools were interpreted. In 1920s California, the statutory law
was different from the law today. Nevertheless, the Molokan elders
made the same misinterpretations as many immigrants today, arising
out of the us/them divide of the immigrant situation. This divide in
turn became institutionalized within the immigrant community, in
the form of social norms shaping social action. These norms in turn
become legitimated in the form of oral stories or "myths" told and
retold in the community—and occasionally by social science researchers. An example is this story, related to Young by an American
teacher more than 20 years after the actual event:

The young [Molokan] children were eager for outdoor play. We
would not keep them away from the playground equipment,

but the girls were not dressed properly to use it. They came in long, wide dresses and underskirts, no bloomers underneath. Many panties were given to the school, and we made a great fuss over them, admiring the lace edging and the whiteness of the material, until the children were anxious to put them on. They liked them, but we anticipated a disturbance among the older brothers and sisters. We called them in and admiringly showed them how cute the little ones looked. A burst of laughter met us: "Girls wear pants here?" and we insisted that they were not pants but panties—nice fine panties. "And do teachers wear panties? You wear panties?" If worst came to worst, I was prepared to show them what I wore. After that the situation was settled. "In America girls and women wear pants, too." The mothers took notice and copied the pattern. That was the end of that difficulty. (quoted in Young, 1932, p. 151)

In this case, the consequences are fairly trivial, hardly the stuff from which out-of-control crime waves emerge. Indeed, it is not even necessary that these events actually ever happened as related. What is significant is that it is out of the telling and retelling of such stories that the two normative orders come to accommodate each other. It is out of the telling and retelling of such "mythical" stories that the normative expectations of the immigrants and the host country slowly begin to adapt to each other (see Luhmann, 1985, p. 204).

In the case of the Molokans, the stories describing social roles necessarily occurred in the context of generational change. As with the Laotians, this took on different forms, depending on the generations of the individuals involved. The following example, which is from Young's book, deals with young people who have been socialized into both the American and the Russian societies and show a sophisticated understanding of each. In this respect, these individuals are not very different from the cocky Hmong "de Tocqueville" described above:

"Don't give anyone a chance to say that a Russian is no good, that he has no honor, and can't behave like a good citizen." This appeal to the young by the young has brought astonishing results. Individual probation officers report a decrease in delinquency among Molokan youth from 20 to 50 percent during 1931. . . .

"... We understand each other, and there is enough talent in our group to do everything covered that we can do everything by ourselves. ... We have lots to learn but have discovered that we can do a great deal ourselves," they remark.

It is too early to foresee the consequences of their activities, but it is already evident that new spirit animates Molokan youth—a spirit developed within, and expressed through, their own rank and file. At times there is even evidence of a true cultural revival which seems destined to sweep the ranks of the youth, but again new defections occur with such rapidity that it is increasingly apparent that in the end sectarianism is not wholly able to resist the insidious penetrating corrosiveness of urban life. (Young, 1932, p. 271)

When Young was writing, in 1931, it was not completely clear what this new "spirit of biculturalism" could offer. The Molokan youth believed that somehow the two were not inconsistent; that the routines of a peasant sectarian life were not inconsistent with those of urban industrial Los Angeles. As Young notes, such bicultural institutions undoubtedly can have some effect on youthful crime. However, it was not so much the revival of Molokanism that would determine what would happen to the Molokan community, but the "defections" that were occurring in the form of out-migration and out-marriage.

In large part, I suspect, this happened because the skills necessary for maintaining and reproducing both sets of normative structures are rare, and are limited primarily to the better educated and more sophisticated. The following account illustrates well how difficult it is to move between the legal systems of two societies; Young describes the speaker as a 38-year-old woman who has been deserted by her husband:

I swear out warrant [for my husband's arrest]. Whole month go by. I go to prosecutor's office and they say: "We don't know where [your husband is]. We can't arrest him if we can't find him. You give us address and we will put him in jail." I wrote to his parents a nice letter and promised to send money to their son, and they give me address. I give it to prosecutor, who says: "We must wait three months, and if he don't send money we arrest him." Haven't I waited more than three months? They say: "That's law." Law—yes—but give me money to live on while law waits three months. I go to other charity place. My husband at last arrested and put on rock pile, and he pay me $45 first month.

His parents were screaming mad and blame me for jailing their son, a Molokan. I tell them I was forced to file a complaint on him. Nobody wants to look at me. They all refuse to talk to me. No husband, no parents, no friends, and no money. (quoted in Young, 1932, p. 225).

By going to the authorities and attempting to balance the competing sets of norms between her two societies, this woman was ostracized from both. This is reflected in her inability to reconcile the conflicting legal norms in which she, as a Molokan immigrant, finds herself. Young's own description of this incident reflects the complexities inherent to maintaining and reproducing parallel legal systems:

> The woman lost caste in the [Molokan] brotherhood because she let herself be persuaded to take legal action against her husband, without giving him an opportunity to be "saved" by the *sobranie*. Few workers, indeed, realize that Molokans do not identify courts, police systems, and "man-made laws" with communal social order. These stand for a power which is incomprehensible because outside the experience of the spiritual brotherhood. Molokan peasant sectarians are accustomed to think of laws only as divinely revealed—immutable and unchangeable. . . . Furthermore, Molokans appealing to social agencies lose caste in their own group. The Molokan brotherhood is embittered against members with whom outside agencies alone must deal. (p. 225)

The assumption of "immutability and unchangeability" is a reference to the contingent nature of modern law, in which everything is negotiable, as opposed to the immutable God-given law the woman was socialized into in Russia and searched for in the United States. How could the Molokan woman, as an immigrant, switch from one immutable system to another? How is it possible to be a "we" and be able to shift between both sets of law? How does a Molokan switch from the immutable authority of the *sobranie* to the authority of the bureaucratic legal system? Law enforcement, on the other hand, is more aware of the dual nature of plural law, although it must also continue to legitimate a preestablished set of plural legal norms. And whereas law enforcement personnel can enforce laws while still being aware of their mutable nature, there is no way for an "us" to maintain two independent sets of norms simultaneously.

Imprecision by Law Enforcement: Youthful Crime and the Police

In 1910, a juvenile court judge called the Molokan elders together to explain why civil marriage is important in American society. Arranged marriages and the Molokan custom of "giving away" their children in marriage had raised questions about the "selling of girls." This resulted from a misinterpretation of Molokan customs and the demands of the day for legitimacy in childbirth. In any event, Judge Taft must have handled the situation well, because civil licenses became legitimated and after that date were sought for Molokan marriages (Young, 1932, p. 145). This story began to be told and retold as a means of legitimating Molokan identity in Los Angeles. Also common, however, were overgeneralizations about the nature of how Molokan society worked, written by social workers:

> The whole idea of Molokan authority is wrong. The elders dominate the lives of the younger group until they have not a soul they call their own. Some of the young fellows are efficient, straight thinkers, but they are set aside by the gray-beards. . . . And the elders are not as wise as the community believes them to be. A clever American real estate man can sell any idea to these simple-minded peasants. They are catching on now and can't be fooled easily, but many families have suffered because of inefficient leadership in the Colony. . . .
>
> Their leaders intimidate them and exploit the loyalty of the group, and they endeavor to deep them from assimilating our American efforts. They condemn those who appear advanced and progressive. (Young, 1932, p. 136)

To the modern "multicultural" ear, these views sound harsh. However, they are not all that different, except in tone, from those of the Hmong teacher's aide quoted above, who implied that there are no laws in Laos. In each of the accounts, the assumption is that what is from the past is archaic, and the desirable future is one of assimilation into the more sophisticated American society. Inherent to this opinion is the idea that moral questions about the nature of good and bad are somehow more complex in the United States than in Laos or Russian Georgia. This is an important part of the American legal mythology, where assimilation continues to be an important cultural touchstone.[19]

American Law Enforcement Looks at the Molokan Community

Less charitable views were found among persons who were a step or two away from direct involvement with the Molokans. The categories available to them were more general than those available to persons who had more intimate contact with this unusual group. One consequence was the development of an "Americanization" movement in the 1910s and 1920s. Americanization programs started with the fixed social category "American" and assumed that the "other"—that is, immigrants—were moving toward assimilation into that category.[20] Such a generalization of categories, of course, meets the bureaucratic needs of the state. A cynical Americanization teacher framed the nature of the movement relative to the Molokans:

> We conceive the Americanization problem of the Molokans on the wrong basis. We either stuff them with patriotism or we go to the opposite extreme and attempt to arouse them to the beauties of Russian literature, music, and art. The teacher is seldom sufficiently versed in Russian culture even to discuss it intelligently. She may have picked up a few ideas by a second-hand process, but she really doesn't understand the deeper implications nor the spirit of the Russian nation. And besides, the Molokans are not Russians culturally. Aside from their racial origins and the language, they have little in common with other Russians. . . . We assume that the young people have a burning desire to know something of Russian history. They seem to be much more eager to know the latest American inventions, fashions, inventions, manners, American heroes and writers. One of the most intelligent Russian girls scorns Gorki. She hungers for Shakespeare, Vachel Lindsay,

American art, American museums. . . . The method of instruction of the adult illiterate has not changed in proportion
to the many advances of instruction of children, and the
classes are not conducted by specialists in Americanization.

Most [Americanization] teachers know little about Molokan
culture, and what they do know about it does not appeal to
them as worth fostering and promoting. They laugh up their
sleeves about the "Jumpers." (quoted in Young, 1932, p. 154)

Like the more recent use of the broad category "Asian Americans"
to describe the perpetrators and victims of home invasions robberies,
the use of the general category "Russian" had important consequences
for how the Molokans were perceived. Again, this is an example of how
categories are created in the host country to accommodate the relations
understood to be possible within the bureaucratic system. In this case,
the social category "Molokan" was meaningless to the bureaucratic
system—to put it in modern terms, there was no category "Molokan"
on census forms, just as today there is no category "Mien." As a
consequence, the schools latched onto the closest plausible category,
Russian, which includes the literature of Gorki, but not Shakespeare. As
a phenomenon, this is structurally similar to having a Vietnamese
spokesperson talk about home invasions within the Mien community,
or to using the category "gang" to talk about all youthful crime.

Mexicans, 1920-1950

Mexicans have had a long history in California. Despite the
relatively small proportion of Mexicans resident in California from
about 1860 to 1910, being Mexican in California has always implied
a distinct social status. This probably has its roots in California's
origins as a Mexican frontier colony captured by Anglo-American
adventurers during the Mexican American War of 1846-1848 (Gomez-
Quiñones, 1994; Rios-Bustamente & Castillo, 1986). As a consequence, Mexican immigrants in the 20th century have never had the
"blank slate" that other immigrant groups, such as the Molokan
Russians and Laotians, have had. In the 20th century, there has always
been a local romanticizable past for Mexicans, which could of course
be used as an internal source of group identity—indeed, the Chicano
movement is based in this. But such a past can also be used by

out-groups to stigmatize and exclude. In terms of youthful crime, this has meant that renegade "banditos" have occupied a special place in the relationship between Mexican immigrants and the larger culture.[21] Griffiths (1948) offers this description:

> In police and sheriffs' stations throughout the state today, picture displays show Mexican "criminals" and "bandits" of the early [19th century] days of California, and there are show-cases with guns and other souvenirs that were used in the fights. Occasionally, too, you see a black-framed picture of a police officer killed by a Mexican in line of duty. Such facts and folklore become a real part of the rookie officer's indoctri-nation. Policemen and sheriff's deputies add stories of their personal experiences with "those sneaky greasers—who knife you as soon as look at you." False arrests, unjustifiable beatings, and sometimes the tragic deaths of Mexican youths at the hands of officers who shoot first and think later are the natural conse-quences of the usual prejudice intensified by such training.
>
> Prejudice is returned by prejudice, and the Mexicans do not like the police any better than the police like them. There are many corridos telling of mistreatment of Mexicans in California by deputy sheriffs and the police. Other stories are handed down from generation to generation. Old Mexicans will tell you of the intimidations and years of "pushing around" they have taken from local police. Small children tell countless embroidered stories of police injustice that have become neighborhood folklore. The stories of the teen-age boys and girls who are the frequent victims of this injustice carry the familiar ring of persecution. (pp. 201-202).

As this passage illustrates, unlike the Molokans or Laotians, Mexi-can immigrants arriving in the 20th century have always had a distinct social status, even though in absolute numbers their 19th-century predecessors in California included very few people living in what were then sparsely populated backwaters. This preexisting social status meant that new immigrants dealt with entrenched stereotypes that shaped both their opportunities and their relations with law enforcement.

Perhaps as a consequence, community views about the law and law enforcement among Mexican immigrants tend to be much more negative than in either the Molokan or Laotian examples, even in the late 1930s and 1940s, when the issue of youthful crime in Mexican immigrant communities first emerged in Los Angeles. Thus, whereas there was shame associated with arrest, there also was a shared mutual antipathy between the Mexican community and law enforcement, whether the focus was on youthful crime or crime of an "adult" nature, such as the marijuana arrests of the 1930s (Morgan, 1990). Resolving this antipathy was at the root of a *Los Angeles Times* editorial that focused on the "zoot suit riots" of 1942-1943—the fights that took place between sailors passing through Los Angeles on their way to World War II's Pacific theater and Mexican American youth then living in East Los Angeles. The editorial's slant is implicit in its description:

> The . . . [issue] pressing then, not only is to get to the bottom of the social causes which result in zoot suit gangsterism but also during that process to discourage as far as possible the loud and unthinking charges that the fault lies exclusively in racial prejudice, police brutality, or Fascist tendencies of the constituted authorities. There can no more be justification for these unsupported assertions than there could be for a defense of unlimited mob violence. It would be as unfortunate, on the one hand to advocate cleaning up of the situation by military action alone as it would be to say that sailors and soldiers at the outset did not have the right to defend themselves from zoot suit attacks. ("Time for Sanity," 1943, p. 1. Copyright, 1943, Los Angeles Times. Reprinted by permission.)

This version of events is of course one-sided, and does not reflect the subtlety of the conflict, but it reveals the context in which youthful crime in East Los Angeles developed in the 1940s. One consequence was a distrust of law enforcement on the part of Mexican immigrant parents, who, under "normal circumstances," might have been blaming their sons' "gangsterism" on lax enforcement of the laws on the part of the police and usurpation of parental authority, as have Laotian and Molokan parents. The situation also resulted in the management of the problem in a fashion that showed a higher awareness of legal ethics and norms. A very different description of the same series of incidents appeared in the New York-based *Time* magazine:

For two nights the mobs of soldiers and sailors had found poor hunting. In long caravans of cabs and private cars they had toured the Mexican sections, armed with sticks and weighted ropes, crashing into movie houses, looking for zoot-suited pachucos, the little Mexican-American youths. But they had found only a few dozen, and not all of them even wore zoot suits. They had broken the jaw of a 12 year old boy. Said the boy, in the hospital: "so our guys wear tight bottoms on their pants and those bums wear wide bottoms. Who the hell they fighting, Japs or us?" ("Zoot Suit War," 1943)

Parents and youth alike may have had similar views of the police and "zoot suiters," but that did not mean that they necessarily shared interpretations of social action. The community may very well have had a large number of youth suffering from the "second-generation problem." However, part of this second generation was able to respond with the savvy of the 12-year-old with a broken jaw who offered an early-day sound bite to *Time* magazine from his hospital bed: "Who the hell they fighting, Japs or us?" [22] Two men whom I interviewed about their boyhoods in East Los Angeles, Vince Macias and Joe Astin, agreed that their parents "did not know what was going on." Nevertheless, neither recalled in their community the cooperation between parents and police that Molokan and Laotian parents sometimes searched for; nor, for that matter, was I able to find any mention of such cooperation in descriptive accounts.

If anything, the two descriptions above from mass-circulation periodicals of the time reveal the breadth of misunderstanding that the zoot suit riots led to. One result was a particularly high level of political awareness among Mexican American activists about how to deal with the police. This included author/journalist Carey McWilliams's using public sentiment concerning the wrongs suffered by Mexican Americans to organize the community in the 1940s and 1950s.[23] Sociologist Joan Moore (1991) comments:

Police prejudice and brutality were related issues helping politicize East Los Angeles. For decades, both city police and county sheriff's officials delivered racist "explanations" to account for Mexican-American youth problems—always accompanied by a storm of protest from the community. For decades, organized labor—Mexican-American locals, in particular—

joined with Mexican-American civic organizations and the Community Service Organization (CSO) in protests against police brutality. Between 1948 and 1954, the CSO conducted thirty-five investigations into police brutality against Mexican Americans. (p. 17)

As a consequence of these circumstances, the legitimation—and trust—process needed for normal policing activity became harder to establish in the Mexican immigrant community, further complicating the misunderstandings implicit to the immigrant situation. The experience of the early Mexican immigrants was thus different from that of either the Laotians or the Molokans. Also contributing to this difference was the segregation of the Mexican community, continued migration from Mexico into the East Los Angeles neighborhoods of first settlement, and the geographic proximity of the border.

Mexicans After World War II

Little was written about the East Los Angeles Mexican community between the time McWilliams (1948) and Griffiths (1948) wrote and the emergence of an extensive literature that came out of the 1960s Chicano nationalism movement. Moore (1990, p. 17) has noted that the "moral panic" initiated by the zoot suit riots lasted until the early 1950s, but there are few descriptions of youthful crime among Mexican immigrants between about 1950 and 1980. This is, in part, because there seems to have been a shift in how the Mexican immigrant community identified itself and its role relative to the broader American community. Both McWilliams and Griffiths were still focusing on the assimilation ideal popular in the 1940s, and early influential Mexican American organizations such as LULAC and the American G.I. Forum, mentioned previously, also had this emphasis on assimilation. On the other hand, more recent literature describes a process in which a new social identity was emerging, some of which came out of the "romanticizable past" that the zoot suit riots provided.

Joan Moore (1990) provides perhaps the best example of this newer genre, focusing as she does on two gangs that evolved in East Los Angeles between about 1935 and 1990. Moore notes that World War II in particular caused a great discontinuity in the gangs, because the military pulled large numbers of the older boys out of the neighborhood who might otherwise have been gang organizers. She asserts that the persistence of the gangs has been a result of both the problems of integrating immigrant youth into the system and continuing migration from Mexico: "This meant that the legitimate institutions remained comparatively marginal and the alternative structures—the gang—could become institutionalized" (p. 6).

Koreans

The Korean immigrant community has generated little youthful crime; indeed, when involved in such crime at all, Koreans are most often the victims. As proprietors of convenience stores in urban neighborhoods, Korean shopkeepers are often the victims of armed robbers. Confrontations between African Americans and Koreans, in particular, have highlighted how Koreans view the criminal justice system (Freed & Jones, 1992; Lee & McMillan, 1992; Raspberry, 1993). Most of these confrontations have been the result of shopkeepers' protecting their stores against people they perceive as robbers or shoplifters. The Latasha Harlins case in Los Angeles, in which a Korean shop owner shot and killed a 15-year-old African American girl whom she thought was shoplifting, is a well-known illustration of this conflict. The shooting resulted in a manslaughter conviction on the grounds that the shopkeeper believed that the Harlins had a weapon. The judge in the case handed down a suspended sentence, saying that the "cross-cultural circumstances," and not intent on the part of the victim, were the cause of the shooting. This result was widely applauded in the Korean community and widely condemned in the African American community.

Misinterpretation of American laws occurs commonly within the Korean community, particularly with reference to the rotating credit associations, or *kye*, commonly used as a banking alternative. Light and Bonacich (1988, p. 257) describe the widespread rumors that emerged out of arrests for fraud in the conduct of *kye*. Many in the community came to believe that *kye* itself is illegal, although it is not, and this impression was in turn amplified by a story in the *Korea Times*, which reported that "kye itself is illegal according to American banking law." As Light and Bonacich note, this was an error; it is only *kye* fraud—that is, the deceptive operation of a *kye* pool—that is illegal.

The Korean example is interesting here not for its lack of accounts about youthful crime—that would be expected from any community with such a low proportion of young males. Rather, the Korean case is interesting because, despite the differences between the experiences of Koreans and those of other immigrant groups, it reveals similarly imprecise assessments of the U.S. legal culture.

SUMMARY AND CONCLUSIONS

The "How" of Youthful Crime in Immigrant Populations

This chapter has shown that in the groups described at length above, relations developed with the law enforcement community in similar ways. This process occurred in matters of both youthful crime and other normative issues. The important point is that the dialogue between normative systems occurred across generations during the process of becoming and disbecoming. Likewise, this was a complex dialogue, occurring both as formal law is written and as it is enforced. In the migration process, this dialogue is often mediated by young people who are attempting to straddle both systems. These young people often have some success; on the other hand, given the lack of continuous socialization into both systems, it is difficult to believe that the understandings, or "mythology," of the old system will be reproduced and legitimated in the new society.

The commonalities among the groups may be summarized as follows:

- There were mutual misinterpretations of the legal contingencies used by both law enforcement and the immigrants. Both law enforcement and the immigrant community made inaccurate "ethnographic" attributions to explain the behavior of the other. This at times resulted in stereotyping. Such behavior, although perhaps undesirable, is also very normal when an immigrant group enters a new society. This is patterned by the preexisting subcultural assumptions of each group. In the case of law enforcement, this pattern is caused by subcultural norms, as influenced by the wider political community. In the case of the immigrant group, it is the result of home-country values, or at least what become idealized/romanticized as such.

- Particularly on the part of people socialized outside the United States, there was a search for explanation in remembered/ romanticized examples of normative behavior. Often this took the form of a specious correlation—for example, assuming that a specific form of social control, such as extreme corporal punishment, is the practice out of which social control emerged, rather than broader normative understandings.

- Youth socialized in the United States often judged their parents' reactions based on American standards. The inexplicability of parental actions in American terms sometimes resulted in the assumption that life in the romanticizable past was "normless," or without the rule of rational law. In the cases discussed here, this new identity included both mainstream *American* and the U.S.-generated *Chicano*.

- The conflicts resulted in a legal pluralism that could, for a period, lead to a liminal state in which no system was dominant within the immigrant community. Out of this liminal state, waves of youthful crime emerged.

Acquisition of Legal Norms: Three Patterns

Three different patterns of relations between the legal system and the immigrant group emerge from the examples cited above, two of which involve parent-child relations. Thus, although all groups utilized normative standards brought from their home countries, there were variations in how this process worked itself out.

The first pattern is found among the Laotian groups and the Molokan Russians. This might be termed a second-generation model, because the immigrants themselves, as well as observers, claimed that the problems were rooted in the strain between youth socialized in the United States and their parents, who attempted to assert control using techniques and assumptions brought from the home country. These groups assumed that the police and parents would be allies, but only if the two could reach a more effective understanding.

The second pattern is seen with the Mexican immigrant group and is characterized by the emergence of a persistent identity as an ethnic minority. Here, the same patterns of youthful crime emerged. However, because of the presence of a preexisting identity and shared social knowledge, normative calculations were more precise. As a consequence, although there has been the same migration-induced conflict between parents and youth, there has not been the assumption that the problem lies in a lack of understanding on the part of police and parents. Rather, persistent discrimination and marginalization are blamed, with the consequence that youthful gangs take on an institutionalized identity, albeit one not approved by parents or law enforcement.

Finally, the Korean example indicates that normative misjudgments about the legal system are inherent to migration situations, and are not only a product of parent-child relations.

The Second-Generation Problem and "Assimilation": Molokans and Laotians

Similar methods for responding to the host-country legal system emerged in the Molokan and Laotian immigrant groups, despite their very different origins. In all groups surveyed (Molokan, Hmong, Mien), there were initial attempts by parents to assert the old forms of social control, often with a degree of success. The Molokans and Hmong come quickly to mind as being the most successful in doing this. In both cases, imported institutions embedded in traditional respect for high-status elders preserved some form of social consensus. Among the Molokans, this consensus persisted until after the draft resistance movement of World War I. In the case of the Hmong, it is not yet clear how long it will persist.

In the Molokan community, the control of the elders was reduced by the inevitable aging of the elders at the same time that the children were being socialized into new social identities in public schools, typically at the expense of imported ideals. Clearly, one symptom of this was the emergence of a wave of youthful crime in 1920-1935 as the elders confronted youth who had been rapidly socialized into American society. Something similar seems to be happening among the Mien today. It remains to be seen whether what is emerging in the Hmong community now will turn out to be analogous, although it is clear that there is that potential.

The Mien and Lao never developed institutional touchstones as strong as those of the Molokans and Hmong. This seems to have set off a pattern of youthful crime in their communities at an earlier point than that found among the Hmong or Molokans. However, both the members of the community and the authorities have described the emerging problems in similar fashion, by focusing on the presumed "absence of law" in the old communities and the efficacy of corporal punishment, and by attempting to force the situation into a broader ethnic category (e.g., Asian American) in order to define policies and responses.

The Mexican Pattern: Persistent Identity

Explanations of youthful crime in succeeding Mexican communities were different from those given for the groups described above. The problems of youth integration, although similar, were not perceived in the same way within the Mexican immigrant communities as in the Laotian or Molokan communities. Because of the old and persistent social identity, the Mexicans drew much more on preexisting alliances and perceptions to deal with the problems of youthful crime emerging in their communities. Nevertheless, this occurred in the context of the same migration-induced stress on the social bond between parents and children.

The major difference was that Mexican immigrants did not perceive the police to be potential allies of the community. In no account was it indicated that the behavior of youth would improve "if only they would understand our ways better," as it was among the Mien and Molokan. Confrontations were not blamed on misperceptions about parenting strategies, but on racism within the Los Angeles Police Department. Such accusations were common as early as 1942 in the Mexican American community. In contrast, there have never been systematic claims made to this effect on the behalf of either of the Asian groups surveyed here or of the Molokan Russians.

Polarizing the police and parents were ethnic activists who were well aware of how to use the national media. In the 1940s, writers of national stature, such as Carey McWilliams of the The Nation, took up the cause of the Mexican American immigrants. As a new wave of immigration from Mexico has emerged during the past 25 years, this process seems to have been repeated, and the polarization between police and parents, two groups that might otherwise have a similar interest in social control, has persisted.

The Korean Pattern:
Normative Misjudgments Without Children

Koreans immigrants misinterpret U.S. laws in patterns similar to those of other immigrant groups. The absence of youthful gang activity in this group, however, as noted previously, has meant that these misinterpretations have been less likely to have serious impacts on the juvenile justice system.

Acquisition of Legal Norms and Identity Transformation

Social disorganization theory has been discredited, with good reason, because it assumes that ghetto societies are normless, at least relative to the greater society. However, there is something about this theory that is relevant, because in the process of changing from one set of legal norms to another—that is, the process of being intuitively able to ignore the taken-for-granteds of one normative system and accepting those of another—a group necessarily passes through a liminal state in which there is confusion about when, where, and what normative expectations are relevant to social action. This occurs across generations, not within individuals.

The discussion in this chapter has shown that this liminal state is not necessarily found within any particular person, but in the interactions between succeeding generations in immigrant communities (parent-child) and between the immigrant community and the legal/political bureaucracy. Thus what is being discussed is not the socioeconomic correlates of youthful crime typically generated by criminology, but an analysis of relationships. The quality of both sets of relationships changes in predictable fashions that are part of the process of migration. A focus on the nature of these relationships has at least as much explanatory power in the case of immigrant groups as the traditional socioeconomic status variables typically used by criminology.

Relationships between immigrant parents and their children shift because migration means that the culturally grounded taken-for-granteds of parents are no longer relevant to the upbringing of their own children. Or, put in the context of Figure 7.2, parents socialized into Society B have only enough knowledge and capabilities to allow them to manipulate the law of Society A to a limited extent. Children, meanwhile, are being socialized by Society A, and develop the assumptions needed to manipulate the Law/State A in a fashion not completely understood by their parents. As a consequence, the ideal-typical bonds holding together sons, fathers, grandfathers, and so forth are broken as immigrant children search for a normative structure consistent with their day-to-day interactions. This normative structure is typically found in the form of peer group interactions, whether with schoolmates, playmates, or fellow gang members.

At the same time, however, host-country institutions undergo a process in which they attempt to socialize the new immigrant group into preexisting expectations. This, too, varies according to the historical relations between the particular groups. It also varies according to what the popular discourses of the day might be. Examples range from Molokan delinquency, which was thought of in the context of the "Americanization problem," to Mexican American "zoot suit gangsters," which have been considered in the context of softball teams. Hmong are thought of as time travelers who have moved from the 16th to the 20th century, and an issue of rape was recast by "Hmong feminists" and a clever lawyer as an issue of "adultery." Post office boxes for the Mien have been compared with hamburgers for American soldiers in Saudi Arabia. In each case, there have been legitimate efforts to force unusual practices into familiar categories. This process may be awkward to an ethnographic purist, but it is also part of the interaction out of which immigrant subcultures are generated.

The point is not that such problems can be prevented, or that they are caused by naïveté or stupidity. Rather, they are the misjudgments expected in the process of migration. Good and conscientious people will make special efforts to accommodate the unfamiliar behaviors and actions of immigrants; however, they will necessarily do so only in the context of the culturally grounded explanations available to them. Many will, through their efforts, ease the transition for a great number of people. And yet these mistakes will still, even must, occur if immigrant groups are to accommodate the new interactions necessitated by a new environment. The common process underlying the negotiation of such situational definitions (be they between parents and youth or between "the system" and an immigrant group) is that there is a search for what Luhmann (1985, pp. 31-40) calls a mixture of cognitive and normative expectation. This is the structure of the law that must be negotiated and renegotiated among parents, children, the clan, the *sobranie,* and the modern state.

NOTES

1. Attorneys practicing in the American jurisprudential system have inherently adversarial roles, and have indeed institutionalized this capacity to take the role of the other. These individuals often move back and forth among the roles of judge, prosecutor, and defense attorney in the course of their careers.

2. Luhmann (1985, pp. 159-164) writes that as society becomes more functionally differentiated, law itself becomes more contingent. That is, it moves further from God-given natural law and becomes malleable according to the complex needs of the differentiated system. Typically, this malleability is mediated by parliamentarians or administrators who, with structurally circumscribed freedom, choose among alternative sets of norms when identifying what will become law and thereby order citizens' lives with respect to welfare benefits, taxes, criminal penalties, civil dispute settlement, and so on. The current move toward harshness of criminal penalties is one example of this. Writers of legislation (or initiatives) choose from among a number of possible norms for one to become "law." For example, there was no inevitability in the choice of a sentencing policy of "three strikes and you're out." The initiative drafters could have just has easily have chosen a "four-strikes" policy or a "two-strikes" policy for the law and also met the popular political demand for harsher penalties. Indeed, the only relative advantage of a three-strikes policy seems to be in the political value of the baseball metaphor. Nevertheless, "three strikes" is law, and, at least until a new metaphor comes along, will remain so. Legal systems grounded in immutable tradition of course do not have this flexibility. For an immigrant socialized in an inflexible God-given system such as the Molokan, the mutability of the modern system is particularly disconcerting.

3. In turn, the "labeled" community comes to "fill in" the description. In order to do so, the community necessarily consults anthropologists about issues of authenticity; as a consequence, anthropologists have effectively written in a role for themselves in the politics of group identity. This is why anthropologists, and not sociologists, are called as expert witnesses when a "cultural defense" is used at trial.

4. Magagnini (1994c) writes: "Many immigrants who come from countries where the police are agents of repressive regimes . . . still don't trust American authorities and are [therefore] reluctant to report crime" (p. B4). I have heard variations on this theme from many people within the subculture of law enforcement, but I have never heard it from an immigrant who was not connected with law enforcement. Rather, immigrants usually claim that their reluctance to report crime stems from the fact that they believe doing so will do no good. Typically, what they complain about are the liberal arrest and release policies embedded in constitutional guarantees concerning bail and evidence (see also Magagnini, 1994a, 1994b, 1994c; Song, 1988, pp. 62-68; Waters & Cohen, 1993).

5. John Song (1988) has written about another example of this that he observed in Monterey Park, California: "Many immigrants and refugees fail to distinguish between law and law enforcement. . . . Chinese and Vietnamese shopowners in Monterey Park, for instance, have a feeling that they have to give the police something in order to be helped. After all, this is common practice among business people at home. Few officers can resist a 'free gift' if you keep offering them the 'gift,' with no immediate strings attached. The officers in Monterey Park may be clean, but the temptations of the Asian immigrants' common practices may pose a threat to their integrity in the long run" (p. 68). In other words, an innocuous practice is the consequence of a

systematic misunderstanding of how the American system of law enforcement (in this case police protection) works.

6. The Portland Police did what they could to work around this basic problem of "hegemony" and were keenly aware of cross-cultural issues involved in law enforcement. However, they stated in a formal agreement with Hmong leaders: "We . . . pledge the honor of our respective offices and the resources of our respective organizations toward the execution of a comprehensive partnership agreement of mutual policies and practices conforming to the aspirations of the Oregon Constitution, the expectations of Federal, State, and local law, in deepest respect toward the ethno-cultural norms of the H'mong customary law (where such law is not inconsistent with the letter and interests of Oregon law)" (National Crime Prevention Council, 1994, p. 20).

7. One of Smith and Tarallo's (1993) Mien respondents offered a similar story about the conflict between Mien traditions and the U.S. juvenile justice system: "Raising children in U.S. can be difficult because the cultural conflict. When the children grow-up, they seem to reject from their parent because the language and economics and we are unable to discipline our children like we did in our country. When we discipline our children, the authorities consider that a child abuse. If we do not discipline them they will be bad and run away with others. Juvenile delinquent is a big issue for the Mien community" (p. 113).

8. These conversations took place in Lao without a tape recorder. I transcribed notes in English immediately after the meeting.

9. As in many traditional patrilineal societies, paternal uncles have a special responsibility toward their nephews. This responsibility was particularly strong in this family because the father of the two misbehaving youths had recently been murdered by another Mien man who believed he had been cuckolded. The elder son (i.e., nephew) who was at one time labeled the "number one Mien criminal in Oak Park" by law enforcement was married in a traditional Mien ceremony in January 1994. At that time, he had been out of jail for at least a year.

10. Although certainly this view of social control is an ideal and was not necessarily actual practice, the presence of it in the Mien worldview shapes Mien perceptions of the American justice system. The result is that American legal principles emphasizing individual liberty, including those having to do with bail, evidence, innocence, and trials, are not well understood, and are believed to show that the police and legal system are "soft on crime." In contrast, a persistent story I have heard in law enforcement circles is that Southeast Asians consider bail to be a "bribe" to let individuals go free illegally. There is some indication that at one time this was believed in one part of the Vietnamese community. However, I did not hear of such misconceptions among Laotians in summer 1991.

11. Such assumptions make up what Fitzpatrick (1992) calls the "mythology of modern law." In this case, there were assumptions about the nature of remorse and guilt. In order to test this response, I asked a middle-class white male neighbor how he would respond to a prowler. His response was different from that of the Mien, and reflected very different assumptions about what the

responsibilities of government and the police are. He said that he would call the police, but he would not expect a response for 2 hours or so, because "government budgets are so tight these days." Anyway, he explained, the main purpose in calling the police is not to seek protection (which is what the Mien assumed), but to establish that a report was made in case something was stolen and it became necessary to make an insurance claim. "As a homeowner, I have insurance, so a burglar breaks in and steals my TV, it means I get a new TV."

When I asked a middle-class white female neighbor what she would do, she said that she would lock herself and her kids in a room and call 911. She would expect that the police would take 15-20 minutes to arrive, and then they would search for the prowler. In this respect her expectations were similar to those of the Laotians. She did not, however, have any elaborate strategy for speeding up the response rate, as the Laotians did.

My own response when there was a prowler at our family's apartment in 1990 was first to debate with my wife for 15 minutes whether it was worth calling the police, and then to compromise by calling the apartment complex manager. The manager decided that maybe the police should be advised, although, given that the man was already gone, it was not necessary for them to come out. We ended up calling the police, who, it turned out, were only half a block away responding to a similar call. They arrived in 2 minutes.

My point in relating these stories is to illustrate how responses to victimization and expectations about the role of police vary. Admittedly, there are at least two confounding factors here, both immigrant status and social class, so it is not possible to attribute the attitudes to one factor or the other. However, the differences are still remarkable.

12. It is hard to tell whether this "we-they" construction is the product of the teacher's aide, the reporter, or both. Whichever it is, the author is reproducing what Samuel Huntington (1981) calls a very basic creed that is embedded in the "rule of law." According to Huntington, this creed is very elemental to what it means to be American.

13. Song (1988) quotes a Garden Grove police captain who described to him the "Vietnamese sense of justice" in much the same fashion: "One thing I have noticed is that when the Vietnamese person started cooperating with us, giving us information about crime, say he was robbed, and taken to a photo lineup to identify the possible suspect in that crime. If people who robbed this individual were not in the six pictures that we showed him, but he recognized another one that he knew to be a bad person he should identify him. Just based on that. That happened more than once. We tried to tell them that you couldn't do that. They said that I know he didn't rob me, but he robbed someone else, so he should be punished" (p. 131).

Smith and Tarallo (1993) also found similar acceptance in the Vietnamese community of what might otherwise be regarded as extralegal behavior in police practices. Following police sweeps of local Vietnamese restaurants and pool halls after a series of home invasion robberies, complaints were filed about unreasonable search and seizure. Smith and Tarallo quote one Vietnamese state worker who claimed: "Personally, I don't think [the raids] violated their civil

rights. Hey, compared to Vietnam, it's nothing. I feel those actions are necessary. It doesn't sound like democracy, but hell, it works" (p. 90).

14. In the Mien community, it was claimed that the woman was in fact
the second wife of the man legally described as her "uncle." Mien claimed that
her status as a niece was preserved in order that the family could be admitted
to the United States, despite laws against bigamy.

15. See also the case of *Dang Vang, Yia Moua, Yang Xiong, Maichao Vang
v. Vang Xiong S. Toyed* (1991). This is a civil case similar to the criminal case
described here. It was determined in the civil case that a Hmong social worker
had raped the defendants under color of state authority, and the plaintiffs were
awarded $300,000.

16. Even though prosecutions for opium trafficking were by and large successful, federal and local governments have discontinued aggressive enforcement
of the drug laws. By 1994, Customs Service policies limited enforcement action
to "knock and talk" visits, in which recipients of shipments were not prosecuted. Local authorities were also declining to prosecute under California laws.

17. See also Klein's (1971) discussion of gangs in Los Angeles.

18. As will become clear in the comparisons with the Molokan Russians
and early-20th-century Mexican immigration, the use of cultural relativism as
a legitimating argument is relatively new.

19. This is not to say that old-fashioned xenophobia has disappeared from
California, although for the most part it has disappeared from official sources.
It does occasionally rear its head in discussions of Laotian crime. The police
chief of Willows, a man sympathetic to the growing Hmong and Laotian
population in the town, gave me a copy of a letter to the editor of the *Willows
Journal* that had been published September 2, 1991, under the headline "Crime
Observation—and Guts to Sign It." He thought the letter illustrated well the
tensions that had emerged in some sectors of the Willows community since
the Laotian population had increased from almost zero to 500-600 people (10%
of the small town's population) in the previous 2-3 years. The text of the letter,
and the editor's reply, read as follows:

> I have just finished reading about the big drug bust in Glenn County.
>
> The names of those arrested are hispanic or anglo, and yet in reading the
> paper and listening to people, all crimes and all problems in this county are
> caused by Laotians, or Hmongs or other Orientals.
>
> They must have changed their names.
>
> Please print my name.
>
> Al Frank
>
> *Editor's Note:* How refreshing.

Sweeping generalizations about immigrant groups and racial tensions are
not unusual during the process of migration. As the discussion below of the
case of Mexican immigrants to early-20th-century Los Angeles makes clear,
arrest patterns there followed very explicit policies in which xenophobia figured
prominently as a legitimated and official response to crime within the immigrant community.

20. An inevitable "march toward assimilation" is implicit in the description of the Molokan community made by a probation officer in 1929. At the time, Molokan boys were regarded by the probation department as presenting "one of the most serious and stubborn social problems in the city" (Young, 1932, p. 197):

> Somehow every Molokan boy expects to be on probation. "Juvenile Courts," "Juvenile Hall," probation officer" seem perfectly normal events in the life of these boys. When I go to see a boy at school, there is always a flock running up to my machine, chatting most friendly. It seems that I have had contact with almost every boy there. . . . A few years ago a Molokan boy was through with his escapades when he was fifteen or sixteen years old. Now from sixteen to eighteen years is the hardest age, and some of them are transferred into the Criminal Court at the age of nineteen. Before the range of the delinquencies was narrow; now no act is too daring. . . . While in 1929 we noticed some decrease in actual numbers, we don't feel we have the situation completely in hand. We are gaining ground and also the confidence of the group. However, since they have organized the young people's church, delinquency has declined. (quoted in Young, 1932, p. 198)

Young goes on to describe the "delinquency contagion" that affected the community she was studying:

> Rarely is a "job" pulled single-handed. "C'mon let's go robbin' " is an invitation frequently arising out of sport motives, and few boys turn a deaf ear to such an invitation for adventure. Molokan parents have long since sensed what might be called a "delinquency contagion," and in many instances have forbidden their children to associate with "undesirable companions." But their children have no criteria for judging the "undesirable," particularly when their standards differ so vastly from those of their elders. Children of working parents have little or no supervisions after school hours. They soon forget "the orders" of their elders; and, free as a lark, they give themselves a "vacation," finding satisfaction in leading a precarious existence in the "city wilderness." (p. 201)

Contrast this with a view described by Sokolov (1918), who wrote some 13 years before Young about the pronounced absence of youthful crime in the Molokan community. The important thing to notice in this passage is the alarm in the neighborhood when such a thing happened:

> On the whole, it may be said that the Russians in this city are a quiet and law-abiding people. They are not given to any of the vices or crimes as a class, that are bound among other nationalities. There are records of only several cases of arrests of Russian men for drinking. Thus far there have not been any cases of arrests of women for any misconduct or vice. A number of small boys have been known to get into trouble because of petty larceny, and have been detained in the juvenile hall. If anything of this sort occurs, the entire neighborhood is generally astir. The parents are greatly alarmed and are ready to follow advice that would prevent recurrence of such trouble. (pp. 14-15)

I suspect that the discrepancy between these two accounts can be accounted for in large part by the passage of time. Sokolov studied the community some 10 years before Young, during a period when the authority of the *sobranie* was still strong. Sokolov's observation that the "entire neighborhood is generally astir" after an arrest contrasts strongly with the observation of Young's informant that virtually every boy attending a particular school expected to be on probation.

21. Fictional characters like the Cisco Kid and the Frito Bandito have been among the stereotypes generated out of this relationship. Historical figures include the Gold Rush era's Joaquin Murieta and the "California bandits" of the late 19th century. Often, too, Mexico's civil war spilled over into the safe haven of Southern California in the form of refugees during the 1910s.

22. Another celebrated example of how the Mexican American community of Los Angeles was able to mount an effective public relations effort involved the "Sleepy Lagoon case" of 1942-1944. After a gang fight in the Sleepy Lagoon area, one youth was left dead. Police quickly arrested 22 Mexican American youths, all of whom were tried for conspiracy to commit murder. In a trial that was widely regarded as biased, 3 were convicted of first-degree murder, 9 were convicted of second-degree murder, and 5 were convicted of lesser offenses. All of the convictions had been overturned on appeal by 1944.

23. McWilliams wrote a number of books dealing with farm labor conditions and racial relations in California during the 1930s and 1940s. He was also West Coast editor of *The Nation* from 1945 to 1955 and editor from 1955 to 1975.

Part IV

Conclusions

CHAPTER 8

What Can Be Said About Youthful Crime in Immigrant Communities?

*M*y point in this book has been to establish when and where rates of youthful crime in immigrant communities are high or low. As noted in Chapter 1, based on my analysis I have proposed an interactive model of how youthful crime emerges in immigrant communities (Figure 1.1). This model is dependent on the assumption that there is a "process" to migration. This process involves the becoming of a new identity at the same time that an old identity is shed. As I have stated, if a process of becoming and "disbecoming" is assumed, youthful crime in immigrant communities can be explained.

The assumption that this process underlies youthful crime in immigrant groups leads to a number of conclusions, both theoretical and policy related, which I present in this chapter. Below, I first discuss the immigrant groups examined in this book, and what their experiences mean for them and for other modern immigrant groups. I then address what this research means for migration studies. This is a new field currently dominated by the economistic "push-pull" paradigm, in which the focus is on costs and benefits of migration, rather than the socialization processes described here. I also examine what this research means for criminology. In doing so, I draw comparisons between previous assumptions about youthful crime and what I propose here, which focuses instead on structure. Finally, as this subject is topical, I address issues of policy, focusing on the difficulties involved in developing any specific policies that will deal precisely with youthful crime in immigrant communities. This conclusion emerges naturally from the model, in which crime is seen as only one of several unintended consequences of migration policies designed to maintain a democratic industrial economy.

WHY YOUTHFUL CRIME OCCURS IN IMMIGRANT GROUPS

The conclusions drawn from the materials presented in this book can be thought of in terms of an equation, in which youthful crime is the dependent variable (Table 3.4) and there are four independent variables: age and gender distribution (Table 4.4), social cohesion (Table 5.1), socioeconomic status (Table 6.1), and perceptions of law (pp. 177-182). The conclusion is that age and gender distribution forms the basis for how the other variables affect youthful crime rates. This variable underlies any rising incidence of youthful crime, and it is only in the context of large numbers of young boys that immigrant groups begin to suffer from waves of youthful crime. Put in simple terms, it is first a second-generation problem. It is not a consequence of poverty, imported subcultural values, low socioeconomic status, insensitive law enforcement, or weak social solidarity. For those familiar with regression, one way of stating this conclusion is as follows, with the variable migration having a value of 0 or 1:

Youthful Crime = (Young Males × Migration) + Group Solidarity +
    Socioeconomic Status + (Misperceptions of Norms ×
    Migration × Young Males),

where in the step-by-step analysis, the interaction between young males has a strong slope and high explanatory value, and of the others—that is, group solidarity and socioeconomic status—only group solidarity has significance on a slightly negative correlation with youthful crime. Notably, both socioeconomic status and group solidarity effect crime in any group, not just immigrant groups. Finally, "misperceptions of norms" is a constant that amplifies the incidence of youthful crime when young immigrant males are present.

What this says is that the combination of a population with a high percentage of young males and the predictable misinterpretation of legal norms found in immigrant communities is a particularly volatile mixture. In the context of youthful crime, such misinterpretation means that the police, the court system, probation services, and so on are not likely to be used strategically by either the immigrant community or the host community, with a wave of youthful crime the likely consequence. This is what happened in the case of the Molokans, Mien, ethnic Lao, and Mexican immigrants in the 1940s. The model could also probably be extended quite easily to groups such as the Vietnamese and Cambodians, who also arrived in the 1980s, and the Ukrainians/Russians who arrived in California in the early 1990s.

This theory is notably different from theories that associate outbreaks of youthful crime in immigrant communities with poverty, imported cultural traditions, social ecology, labeling, and strain. Such elements are often relevant when gangs are analyzed by themselves, without reference to the migration milieu. Migration "amplifies" the effects of a population's having a large number of young boys. In a hypothetical population that has fast growth without permanent migration, there would not necessarily be any youthful crime problem. Countries that continue to have high birthrates, urbanized populations, and little permanent immigration, such as Saudi Arabia, would perhaps meet these criteria.

But back to the United States. The interaction described here is a very specific amplification. Misinterpretation of the law, in and of itself, is not enough to trigger a youthful crime wave. For example, the widespread misunderstanding in the Korean community that *kye* is illegal is a good example of a misunderstanding that, although relevant to how the justice system is perceived, is irrelevant to youthful crime rates. The point is that misinterpretations are inevitable; however, it is in the context of a high proportion of young males in the population that such misinterpretations develop into a wave of youthful crime.

Social Structure as Variables: Demographics,
Social Cohesion, and Urban Residence

It is clear that the demographics of a population (i.e., high proportions of young native-born children of immigrant parents) correlate
with high rates of youthful crime (see Chapter 5). Youthful crime and
gang activity correlated well with high arrest rates for Molokans,
Laotians, and Mexicans. Having higher proportions of young males
seems to have an amplifier effect in such groups. Likewise, at times
when the proportion of 15- to 25-year-old native-born males (i.e.
second generation) is low, generally low rates of youthful arrest are
found. This was true for Molokan Russians, early Mexicans, and
Laotians in the time just after immigration. The predictive value of
this variable is so strong that the other variables (social cohesion and
socioeconomic status) seem trivial as primary causal factors.

However, closer inspection of the data reveals that, although the
effects of age demographics are overwhelming, there is some variation
around the edges that needs to be explained by the effects of other
causes. The Molokan Russians provide the best example of how other
variables can interact with age structure. On the basis of the age
demographics presented, it would have been expected that there
should have been a high incidence of youthful crime among Molokans
lasting from about 1917 to 1940. In fact, the high incidence lasted
from about 1923 to the mid-1930s. Contextualizing this in terms of
what else was happening in the Molokan community points to potential explanations. In 1917-1919, the Molokan community focused on
resistance to the military draft, probably with strengthened relationships between parents and sons, and experienced higher levels of social
control as a consequence. Second, the move into the suburbs, which
seems to have accelerated during the 1930s, lowered the youthful
crime rate. Both of these circumstances can be thought of in terms of
the variable "social cohesion."

Like the Molokans, the Mexicans of East Los Angeles had a high
incidence of youthful crime at a time when a large cohort of young
males began to enter the at-risk age for youthful crime. Based solely
on demographics, this wave would have been expected to last from
about 1938 to 1963, but there is little evidence that it lasted much
beyond about 1943. What is the explanation?

In the data, there are plausible answers. First, large numbers of Mexican American males enlisted in the military during World War II, and military service apparently redirected the attention of this at-risk age cohort. After the war, the G.I. Bill accelerated the movement of members of this cohort out of at-risk neighborhoods. In the context of the data on the Molokans, this is interesting, because it was the lack of control of the elders over the Mexican American youth that permitted their enlistment, with an apparent reorientation of identity the consequence. An unintended result seems to have been a reorientation of youthful relationships away from gangs and toward alternative institutions such as the military and the American G.I. Forum.

A variation on these themes is found in the Laotian groups. Unlike in the Molokan and early Mexican cases, waves of youthful crime among Laotians have been generated by youth who were themselves foreign-born. Young's (1932) original conclusion about the Molokans she studied—that is, that the critical variable is the effect schooling has on relationships between youth and parents—is relevant. The first group of Molokan youth Young describes generally did not stay in school beyond the fourth grade and, as a consequence, did not have the cultural discontinuities that could have led to a wave of youthful crime. In contrast, their younger siblings, most of whom were born in the United States, had more education, and it was among this group that the wave of youthful crime emerged. This example seems relevant to the evaluation of present-day Laotians in particular.

In the case of the Laotians, the time lag between migration and the emergence of youthful crime was only about 5-10 years—significantly shorter than in the Molokan example. In the context of the Molokan example it can be presumed that one reason this crime wave emerged so quickly is that, by the latter part of the 20th century when the Laotians arrived, compulsory education laws were more carefully enforced. The consequence was that large numbers of foreign-born children were exposed to host-country norms earlier and for a longer period. This is a plausible explanation for why a youthful crime wave emerged so quickly in the Laotian community, and why it took so much longer for waves of such crime to emerge in the Molokan and Mexican communities during the first half of the century. In other words, this difference in historical time interacts with group-specific demographics.

However, although age and gender structure is correlated with high rates of youthful crime, and it remains a necessary prerequisite of an outbreak of youthful crime in an immigrant community, I want to stress that it is not causal. Unusual age structures, such as large proportions of young males relative to adults, lead to two other clusters of conditions. First is a breakdown in parental control, as large numbers of young males reach at-risk ages for criminal activity. This too spreads throughout the ethnic and juvenile subcultures, attracting the attention of law enforcement, which accelerates arrest rates. Second is the poverty that, in modern industrial America, leads to inner-city residence and high rates of youthful crime, no matter what the immigrant status of parents.

Age and gender structure is central, however; immigrant groups that do not have large proportions of young males, for whatever reason, do not have high youthful crime rates. Indeed, judging from the evidence about Koreans, as well as that from the early history of Mexican, Laotian, and Molokan immigrants, rates of youthful crime for such groups may even be lower than for the surrounding populations.

On the other hand, in the context of the unusual demographics found in immigrant groups (i.e., a high proportion of high-risk males), there is variation in how well groups are able to manipulate their situations. The Hmong of Laos provide a good example. They have been able to mitigate some of the circumstances that could be caused by tension between parents and youth by establishing alternative institutions. In part this is the case because the Hmong leadership has maintained enough authority that it can take steps to protect the population, as it did, for example, by directing Hmong immigrants to settle in several rural Central Valley communities in California. Such exercise of authority is possible, of course, only in the context of strong leadership; in this case the Hmong leadership was strong enough to control the inertia that, under other circumstances, would have pulled the Hmong immigrants toward settlement in inner-city neighborhoods.

A final conclusion is that socioeconomic class does not have much predictive power with respect to youthful crime waves in immigrant groups. Groups with low economic status in the United States (e.g., Molokans from 1905 to 1923, Mexicans from 1920 to 1938, Hmong) have sometimes had rates of youthful crime lower than would have been expected given the number of young males in their populations. Indeed, quite often improving socioeconomic conditions have coincided with outbreaks of youthful crime. Presumably, a roundabout argument could be made about the nature of relative deprivation to explain the outbreaks of youthful crime described here. However, it is more straightforward to focus on immigrant-specific second-generation problems, including unusual age demographics amplified by the becoming and disbecoming inherent to the process of migration.

The Acceleration Effect: The Law and Its Uses in Immigrant Communities

What of the role of law, and how it affects youthful crime rates? The discussion of law in Chapter 7 shows that misunderstandings and misconceptions of legal norms are inherent to the immigrant condition, whether or not the demographics are there to trigger a youthful crime wave. In other words, like unusual demographics, "legal pluralism" is accentuated by the migration process. Such misinterpretations occur inevitably as a consequence of migration, and their effects are amplified within communication networks that are unique to the immigrant community. For example, in the case of the Molokan Russians and Laotians, both of which had trouble with youthful crime, this resulted in remarkably similar misunderstandings of child protection laws. In the case of Koreans, it resulted in misunderstandings about the nature of *kye* fraud. In this respect, the patterned misunderstanding of the law is a constant affecting social action within the immigrant community, whether or not there is a large number of young males.

However, the misinterpretation of law, although inherent to the immigrant situation, does not necessarily result in high rates of youthful crime. Obviously, in groups that do not have young males, rates of youthful crime will be low. On the other hand, having large numbers of children can cause other conditions that lead to high rates of youthful crime, including poverty, urban residence, and breakdown in internal solidarity. Groups that have a large number of children are in turn more likely to have less income per family member, and are therefore poorer and more likely to live in low-rent urban areas.

ANSWERING BROADER QUESTIONS ABOUT YOUTHFUL CRIME: APPLYING THE MODEL

My goal in this book is not simply to explain the five groups described here, but to use a model parsimoniously to assess how youthful crime emerges in immigrant communities. For example, looking back at

Table 4.1 (which shows the proportion of young boys in each population), simply on the basis of demographics, immigrant groups such as Filipinos, Chinese, Mexicans from 1920 Los Angeles, and Thai can be assumed to be at relatively low risk for youthful crime because less than 6.0% of the population between the ages of 13 and 19 is male. And with the possible exception of small population of Thai,[1] according to Table 3.1 (i.e., rates per 10,000 committed to CYA), this would be accurate.

It is also possible to make the generalization that those immigrant groups in which more than 7.5% of the population is made up of 13- to 19-year-old males would be expected to have high rates of youthful crime. This would single out the Molokan Russians, Lao, and Vietnamese—again, this is an accurate indicator.

Groups in the intermediate ranges (with 6.0% to 7.4% 13- to 19-year-old males) are of course more ambiguous, and correlate with high and low rates of youthful crime. For such groups, it would be necessary to assess more specifically the circumstances of the migration. Relative distribution within the 13-19 age range would be one criterion (i.e., controlling for unusually high proportions of 17- to 19-year-old males in the migrant stream, as with the Mexicans); other criteria would be patterns of residence, social cohesion, and so on.

Using such principles, it is possible to infer answers about the potential for youthful crime waves in some of the groups surveyed in the literature review. For example, my guess is that 13- to 19-year-old males were a fairly low proportion of the Vancouver Chinese population that Helen MacGill (1938) studied in the 1920s. Likewise, in 1920s Chicago, given that Shaw and McKay (1942) describe high rates of youthful crime for Italians and Poles, but low rates for Germans, there were probably fairly low proportions of young males in the German population as opposed to the Italian and Polish populations.

More important than why a youthful crime wave is likely to emerge, however, is how it can be mitigated. Here, understanding the "how" of the question is critical. Again, comparisons provide some answers.

First, external events can have the effect of controlling a youthful crime wave in unexpected ways. For example, the "delay" of the wave in the Molokan Russian population may have been caused by the cohesion that was generated by the attempts of the U.S. government to draft young Molokan men. The World War II draft seems to have had a similar effect on the large Los Angeles cohort of maturing Mexican American men, albeit for different reasons. Such external events are of course period specific, and not given to manipulation for the specific purposes of crime control (e.g., it would be impossible to draft all young men for military service so that they will not join gangs).

Events internal to a group are also likely to mitigate the effects of a youthful crime wave if they affect the ability of the older generation to communicate relevant goals to the young. The Hmong, in particular, were seemingly able to do this in the early 1990s, despite the lack of a major issue like the draft on which to focus, and despite the demographic pressures for youthful crime to emerge as a major issue. Likewise, the Molokans were able to do it through the *sobranie* at the time of the World War I draft. In other words, the example of the Hmong seems to indicate that an external event is not necessary for the coordination of the concerted social action needed to repair intergenerational disputes in a fashion that will control youthful crime. Here, too, such internal cohesion is, as Shaw and McKay (1942) said long ago, specific to the internal dynamics of a group, not externally generated. In other words, although it may be strategic for outside agencies to take advantage of a Molokan *sobranie*, or an agency like Lao Family Inc., it is not possible to generate such solidarity externally. Why some migrant groups have this and others do not is of course beyond the scope of this book. Nevertheless, it is important to note the significance of internal group factors in mediating the problems associated with the socialization of young boys.

THEORETICAL CONCLUSIONS

The Migration Process

This book deals with how and why a particular social problem emerges in immigrant groups with some regularity. A conclusion that has dropped out of this analysis is that waves of youthful crime are not inherent to particular cultural groups, or even to particular "types" of cultures. Rather, waves of youthful crime in immigrant groups emerge out of intergenerational conflict, which, due to the dynamics of migration, can sometimes emerge with unusual suddenness and intensity. Youthful crime emerges, in other words, not out of a particular culture group, but out of the type of parent-child relationship that tends to be created by the process of migration. There are two general

principles potentially involved, both of which are related to the relationship between parents and youth:

1. Migrant groups inherently have unusual demographics, which in
   turn pattern social reproduction independent of culture. This
   happens because migrant groups are never cross sections of the
   sending societies, but rather selected groups that emerge out of
   the dynamics between the sending and receiving countries.
   These dynamics, particularly in an industrial society like the
   United States, are also patterned by the socioeconomic situations
   in which the new social locations will develop.

2. Migration implies the shedding of one set of preexisting social
   norms in exchange for another. This is never a smooth process,
   and it inevitably involves misinterpretations and misunderstandings about the bases for normative action on the part of
   both immigrants and the receiving community.

The patterned nature of the migration process has been overlooked
in the past because scholars have typically focused not on migration as
a process in and of itself, but on the social histories of particular ethnic
groups. As a consequence, their research has lacked a comparative
context within which the unique history and culture of each group could
be controlled for. My intent in using a variety of California immigrant
groups in this study has been to separate out these issues so that the
very real process of migration can be understood.

Implications for Criminology

Previous explanations for youthful crime have emerged from the
field of criminology. Criminologists have generally analyzed immigrant populations without accounting for the unusual social circumstances under which immigrant groups are being reproduced. Thus,
although Shaw and McKay (1942) acknowledge that "intergenerational conflict" is at the root of social disorganization and they analyze
immigrant groups, they never develop a description of what it is about
immigrant groups that makes them different from nonimmigrant
groups. Thus, although they raise important issues about the crimi-
nogenic nature of immigrant neighborhoods of first settlement, they

apparently never noticed that outbreaks of youthful crime occur at some points in a group-based migration process but not others. And although they do note a correlation between the number of young males in a neighborhood and its delinquency rate, they do not mention that different immigrant groups had high proportions of young males.

The criminological strain theorists of the 1950s pointed out that social disorganization theory is applicable in only very limited circumstances, and that Shaw and McKay's school made an overgeneralization in assuming that data from Chicago's immigrant community could be applied to all groups. Strain theorists went on to describe the complex norms that existed in supposedly normless situations, including inner-city gangs in places like Chicago and Los Angeles. Significant for this research, the strain theorists highlighted the fact that not all immigrant groups simply have a second-generation problem. But it is also important to consider that some ethnic groups, including the immigrants from Mexico discussed here, deal with other preexisting normative expectations. That these expectations are there, and that they help create youthful crime patterns in the Mexican American community, is an indication that strain theories do have something to add the discussion. The problem, however, is that strain theories ignore the cultural discontinuities inevitably caused by migration. Such effects are present, whether or not there is systematic exclusion from the society.

Finally, the "gang" literature that has emerged in the 1990s focuses not on intergenerational dynamics, but on the products of gang subculture. Thus, although much has been learned about how particular gangs are or are not structured (see Huff, 1996; Klein, 1995; Shelden, Tracy, & Brown, 1997), and the inherent difficulties of defining gangs have been discussed at even greater length (Klein, 1995; Shelden et al., 1997), the negative cases—that is, those communities that do not have gangs—have been ignored.

This is a chronic problem in criminology, known in sociological shorthand as "sampling on the dependent variable." This means that criminological studies typically focus only on criminals and criminal acts, while ignoring the overall context in which deviance occurs and does *not* occur. In large part this is a consequence of the policy-driven nature of criminology: Funding is available to study areas where there is crime. The absence of crime (or gangs) is unremarkable, and therefore of little interest to funding agencies or academics intent on seeking this funding.

POLICY IMPLICATIONS

Up to this point, I have purposely avoided drawing any policy-focused conclusions about the control of youthful crime in immigrant communities, although there are a number of such conclusions that can be reached. Does this research point to any specific police practices or policies that can be adopted to prevent certain kinds of crimes, such as the home invasion robberies that plagued Sacramento's Southeast Asian community for months in 1993-1994?

Unfortunately, my conclusions are somewhat pessimistic. If youthful crime is a product of a high-birthrate immigrant community, then the possible "solutions" are limited. One would be to turn off immigration; another would be to segregate from the mainstream any immigrant populations that are deemed needed, as is done in some Middle Eastern countries. In effect, the only way to "control" youthful crime in immigrant groups is to adopt policies that are inconsistent with a modern economy or to control/segregate immigrants in a fashion inconsistent with the basic principles of civil rights. This could include limiting the immigration of spouses. Given the nature of these solutions, I must reluctantly conclude that little can be done to prevent outbreaks of youthful crime among immigrant populations.

Any nation that by design or circumstance recruits immigrant members will have problems with youthful crime in immigrant communities. The United States is, of course, an outstanding example of such a country. Indeed, except during wars and the Great Depression, an almost constant supply of cheap immigrant labor has fueled the American economy since 1840. In other words, the "breakdown in parental control" that leads to high rates of youthful crime in immigrant communities has been almost constant, and will remain so as long as other nations are a major source of U.S. labor.

However, there is another reason immigration restrictions should not be considered in a vacuum. Besides being economically impractical, "turning off the immigration spigot" ignores the numerous strengths that immigrants continue to bring to the United States, including the unusually large proportions of immigrant youth who do better than the mainstream population and raise the standards of our universities and colleges. The Southeast Asian immigrants of the past 20 years are an exemplary group. Keep in mind the anecdote that started this book. Along with the unusually high proportion of Southeast Asian youth committed to the California Youth Authority, an even larger proportion attends the University of California, Davis.

Although my conclusions are in some respects pessimistic, at least regarding youthful crime within immigrant communities I can also suggest ways to mitigate the problem. First, it should be noted that crime within immigrant communities, and specifically youthful crime, is not a general phenomenon. There is no evidence to support the xenophobic generalization that immigrant groups are inherently more criminal than any other population. There is, however, evidence that there are systematic and predictable baby booms within some immigrant populations that result in rising rates of youthful crime. This happens when immigrant parents confront the problems inherent to the socialization of young boys, typically 15-25 years after the peak of the boom. There is also evidence to indicate that this crime wave is likely to be systematically misinterpreted by immigrants and host-country law enforcement alike, again due to the process of migration. Such misinterpretations tend to exacerbate the problem, making it worse than it would have been in a stable population dealing with a similar wave of births.

During this process, there are several stages at which steps might be taken to mitigate the problems that arise. First, however, it is important to specify what parts of the process are unlikely to be affected by the public policies of a free society.

Things That Will Not Work

1. Research has shown repeatedly that the fertility rate for the first generation in an immigrant group is brought from the country of origin. Fertility rates are a product of childhood socialization, and programs aimed at birth control education and family planning are unlikely to change this basic fact. For example, birth control programs among the Hmong were aggressively implemented by the Thai government when the Hmong were still living in Thai refugee camps. Although such programs may have long-term effects, the 1990 U.S. Census data indicate that the short-term effects of such programs were negligible at best. Such programs initiated among new immigrant groups in the United States are likely to have similarly negligible effects.

2. There is a positive relationship between increases in education and the rates of youthful crime in immigrant populations, at least up to a point. In other words, in immigrant groups, some education leads

to more crime. This is because schools are the main agents socializing immigrant youth into the host-country values. Limiting education may result in lower rates of youthful crime in the short run, as it did with the Molokans in the 1910s. However, such a policy also results in a less productive workforce. Again, this is not a particularly practical "solution" to the issue of youthful crime in immigrant communities, because the majority of immigrant youth are not involved in youthful crime. In fact, as noted previously, the proportion of young people from immigrant groups enrolled at various campuses of the University of California indicates that children from immigrant populations, even those affected by high rates of youthful crime, often do quite well by the measures of conventional society.

3. Although there will probably always be a few culturally sensitive social workers, police officers, and teachers, it is unlikely that there will ever be enough to bridge the communication gaps that inevitably arise out of the process of migration. Bridging such gaps requires a large investment in time as each new immigrant group arrives. Bureaucratizing and organizing such a workforce takes years, as aggressive efforts to train bilingual teachers for the Hmong and Laotian communities has shown (see Waters & Cohen, 1993). The irony of the situation is that by the time a substantial cohort of teachers has been trained, the absolute numbers of students in need of such services will have declined significantly as early "normal" socialization into English-speaking skills improves. Again, such a succession of events is inherent to the process of migration. This does not mean that talented individuals should not be encouraged to assist members of immigrant societies in their becoming effective members of American society. However, such efforts are not a panacea.

4. Adult education classes aimed at immigrant communities can be important for affecting immigrant attitudes and for informing immigrants about host-country norms. Peripheral issues, such as the wearing of bloomers by girls playing on jungle gyms and even attitudes toward the registration of marriage in the Molokan community (see Chapter 7), can be addressed through such approaches. However, such classes are unlikely to result in the reorientation of parental attitudes toward concepts of justice, child rearing, or other fundamental issues to which they have been socialized in their home countries. Because these issues are at the heart of the second-generation problem, this leads to an irony: Every group, for better or worse, cites parenting values brought from abroad when explaining successes and failures. Thus, for

example, the successful Asian student credits her success to the values of the Asian family, and Asians describe youthful crime in their communities as a result of those same values. In other words, there is little to be gained by attempting to reorient the attitudes of immigrant parents.

Some Things That Can Work

There are several ways in which the capabilities for controlling youthful crime can be developed within the context of a modern society. These include strengthening existing resources within immigrant communities, many of which are informal, by recognizing that some immigrant populations bring with them internal mechanisms for social control that can be encouraged and developed. Most important, it needs to be recognized that youthful crime waves occur only at specific points during the process of migration—that is, when unusually large cohorts of young males enter the at-risk age for criminal activity. At other stages in the migration process, there is every indication that rates of arrest and incarceration for youthful crime are actually lower than in the general population.

The Hmong experience provides one example. As I have noted, the Hmong leadership organized the settlement of groups of Hmong in a number of small Central Valley towns (e.g., Willows, Linda, Redding). According to informants, a major reason for this decision was that the Hmong leaders wanted to restrict the young people from having contact with gangs and other negative attractions of the inner cities. Whether the lower rates of youthful crime in the Hmong population are due to their residence in such communities is unknown. However, it is worth noting that the degree of social control exercised by the Hmong leadership, whether in organizing moves to rural counties, sponsoring youth attending California's universities, or ostracizing wayward youth, has probably influenced the rate of youthful crime to some degree.

The same agencies that have provided leadership for Hmong have more recently run up against antidiscrimination laws for "favoring" Hmong over other refugee groups. Thus, in awarding contracts and enforcing laws, it is important to recognize the group-specific effectiveness of such agencies. For example, it was probably counterproductive for the federal government to insist that Lao Family Incorporated provide services also to Russian refugees, as it did in the early 1990s.

The potential for waves of youthful crime can be predicted from demographic statistics that are widely available. Planning for personnel requirements and mitigation programs can begin years in advance. Mitigation programs could include organized sports, Scouting, and the like. Likewise, the training of police officers, teachers, and others who will be dealing with such issues can begin in anticipation of a difficult situation. However, it should be borne in mind that external interventions will probably not stop the emergence of youthful crime in immigrant communities, because it is rooted in parent-child relationships unaffected by such programs.

The value of the few grassroots immigrant organizations within particular immigrant communities needs to be recognized. However, it also needs to be recognized that each such agency is legitimated primarily within a single ethnic group, and it is unlikely that the personnel or the agency as a whole can effectively address the problems of other ethnic groups.

The migrant groups described in this book have all had California as their eventual destination. During the past 150 years, immigration has helped define what California is. As long as the state remains the destination for many immigrant groups, California's leaders and citizens will have to address the strengths and weaknesses inherently associated with immigrant communities.

NOTE

1. As noted previously, there is some question about whether young Lao and Thai in the California Youth Authority are using the same criteria for self-identification as were used in the 1990 census (see Chapter 5, note 7).

The Case of the Migrating Bushtit

*I*n August 1989, I was called to Willows, California, to act as a Lao/English interpreter in the local justice court. A Laotian man had been arrested for shooting a bird in the local park with a pellet gun. In order to make a point to the local Lao community that birds were not to be shot in the park, the game officer had written out a ticket for the infraction. The case was called to court, and I was the interpreter for a short, quizzical Lao man whose name I forget. This doesn't matter, however, as this anecdote is about the difference between American law as it is written in the lawbooks and as it is administered in the courtroom. As you will see, the identity of the Lao man is tangential to this basic issue.

Under normal circumstances, the Lao man would have been urged to plead guilty by his court-appointed attorney, who would then have asked the judge to issue a warning and a suspended sentence. The district attorney would have insisted on a fine, maybe $30.00 or $40.00, and been done with the case. All would have been negotiated in a courthouse hallway or even side alley, which is how most of American justice is dispensed.

Willows, however, is a quiet place, and the defense attorney was an energetic fellow who was tired of pleading off a succession of methamphetamine, petty theft, and burglary charges out in the hallway. For that matter, the district attorney, a tall man who cultivated a good-ol'-boy drawl and wore a cowboy hat and elaborate belt buckle to court, was also probably bored. To make a long story short, standing outside a side door on one of Willows's thoroughfares, the public defender asked the Lao man to plead not guilty and give the prosecution a chance to prove its case. He brushed aside the district attorney's efforts to negotiate a more standard settlement. The confused Lao man was ready to accommodate any authority figure, and apparently assumed that a public defender in a hallway was such an august personage.

Upon arriving in the courtroom, the Lao man began to have doubts, and quizzed me (the only person he actually talked to—he probably thought I had some power too) about what the point of all this was, and whether it should just be pushed aside. He pointed out that he was just trying out his gun, and had had no intention of eating the bird, as some Willows residents believed. Dutifully, I translated his questions for his attorney, in order to avoid the ultimate interpreter's sin of practicing law without a license. The public defender had more in mind, however, and brushed the questions aside. Certainly he didn't care that his client had never intended to eat the bird; such intent has nothing to do with the law.

The case was called, and the three of us were pushed forward. The Lao man dutifully pled not guilty. The state was required to make its case.

The first (and only) witness was the game warden who had issued the ticket. A young blond man in uniform with movie-star good looks, he was uncomfortable in his role as witness. Indeed, it was well-known in Willows that he had worked carefully with the Lao community to ensure that they observed California's legal codes dealing with fishing, hunting, gathering snails, and other things Laotians were wont to do. (I also served as interpreter for a Lao woman who had received a ticket for snail poaching in Willows. She pled guilty for a public defender who had no sense of humor—but that is another story.) The warden told the district attorney how he had observed the man shooting the bushtit. Very solemnly, he produced a freezer box, from which he took a small plastic bag. In the bag was the bushtit itself. The bird was entered into evidence.

Then it was the defense's turn. Very solemnly, the public defender read the relevant code section having to do with the hunting of native birds. He then cross-examined the game warden on his credentials (a master's degree in wildlife biology), and asked him to identify and describe the bushtit. The bushtit was slate gray, 2.5 inches long, and had a number of other distinguishing characteristics. It had been shot with a pellet at a distance of 20 feet. This created some confusion for me, because I did not know the Lao or Thai (or the English) words for various parts of the bird's anatomy. I even became flustered over the word for gray. The issue was then broached: How do we know that this bushtit was a native of California? How could the game warden tell where the bird came from?

By this time everyone in the courtroom was red-faced with suppressed laughter. Nevertheless, the judge pushed the case along, as did the public defender and district attorney. Fortunately for me, no one could check my Lao translation, which at this point was becoming garbled. In search of a respite, I reached for my dictionary in order to look up "slate gray." The judge said that "gray" would do.

Finally the judge pronounced, "Guilty!!" and fined the poor man $30.00. The man, relieved, agreed to pay immediately. The judge dismissed court after this case, and left for his chambers; I never did hear what he thought of the case. I shuffled toward the back door with the attorneys and the defendant, and the game warden rushed toward the poor Lao man to shake his hand and to apologize for the inconvenience of the proceedings. I ambled into the hallway with the two adversarial attorneys, who, once outside the courtroom, burst into laughter—not at the case itself, but in utter amazement that the Lao man had managed to shoot a 2.5-inch bird with a pellet gun at all.

Modern Bureaucratized Man Abroad: The Legal Epistemology of Stung Ducks

*I*n the West we assume that the rule of law is rational and reasonable, and, according to our own epistemological assumptions, it is. However, as the following example shows, what is actually rational and reasonable is a social construction in which are embedded, among other things, jurisprudential assumptions about what are legitimate items for dispute. An immigrant, of course, has not necessarily been socialized to understand what items are appropriate for legal adjudication and what are not. I will illustrate the tenuous hold the law has over an immigrant through a story of my own encounter with unwritten but potent traditional laws in rural Tanzania. This encounter created confusion within me about my rights and responsibilities vis-à-vis another man. I still have doubts about whether I ever fulfilled the moral obligations I may have had under Tanzanian traditional law. More important, this story shows why individuals who are in unfamiliar legal situations tend to shrink from any confrontation.

In 1986, I was involved in purchasing oxen for an ox-training program in Kigoma, Western Tanzania. On the particular trip during which my legal dispute arose, I was assigned the task of purchasing 12 oxen in an open-air field, putting them in a covered truck, and returning to Kigoma. By the second day of the trip, we had purchased enough oxen that we needed to rent a tree under which we could graze our oxen while completing our purchases. After paying a nominal sum to the owner of the tree to do this, we returned to purchase the rest of our oxen. At midmorning, however, I was approached by the truck driver and told that there was something of a crisis back at the tree. Our oxen had excited a beehive in the tree above them, and the bees had in turn created some havoc among the tree owner's flock of ducks. The driver

209

agreed with my initial assessment that the claim itself was probably based in the farmer's interest in squeezing money out of a "rich" foreigner. The driver agreed also that the bees probably had swarmed spontaneously, without reference to our oxen, and that the victimization of the ducks was not really our fault. Nevertheless, he also pointed out that if it was in fact our oxen that had excited the bees, we would in fact be liable for any damage incurred by the farmer. On a more practical level, the driver also pointed out that under traditional law, we would not be able to reclaim our oxen from underneath the tree until the claim was settled. This led to an immediate parley near the tree, because all present agreed that I was potentially liable for the ducks' suffering.

The parley quickly turned into a paralegal affair conducted near our still-content oxen. The "trial" was conducted in the Kisukuma language by a "judge" who I was told was a local elder of some authority. Our "defense lawyer" immediately turned to the ox trainer in our group, who was the only one who spoke that language, and he in turn translated the proceedings into Kiswahili, the national language of Tanzania, for the benefit of the truck driver and myself. The first order of business was to determine that yes, I was liable for any damages that my oxen might have caused by exciting the bees who in turn stung the ducks. I am not sure how my "guilt" was determined, but it was impressed on me that I had lost the case in very quick order. All that remained was to assess the amount of damages, which it was agreed should follow the local market's price. This turned out to be problematic, given that no ducks had actually died and it was not clear whether the duck meat had actually been damaged by the bee stings; no real market value could be set on the ducks' pain and suffering.

After this impasse had been reached, our Kisukuma-speaking defender pointed out that the farmer had failed to obtain a government permit for a beehive in the first place, and therefore our cattle were not liable for exciting the bees. This legalism depended on a law that, as far as I could determine, was generally unenforced. But then I was the only one present who had never heard of this licensing law, and as it helped my case, I agreed to take it very seriously. Anyway, this whole process took place over a period of about 6 hours, and it was finally concluded that I was not responsible for the ducks' pain and suffering. Or so I was told.

A Long Hot Summer in the Polk Street Apartments

(adapted from Waters & Cohen, 1993, pp. 59-61)

*T*he Polk Street and Behringer Court Apartments are home to one of the two concentrations of Mien in North Highlands, California, in Sacramento County. For local citizens, the complex is sometimes portrayed as being an idyllic throwback to a rural Laotian village.

Laotian village or not, the new reputation for the Polk Street Apartments among Mien is one of violence and an atmosphere of fear—and with good reason. At the time this project began (in June 1991), the complex was known for housing the quieter and less volatile of the two Mien populations. Indeed, in our June 1991 notes, we speculate about why the Polk Street Mien population of North Highlands was so much better than the Oak Park (a poor downtown area of Sacramento) Mien, who had been subject to the raids of the Sacramento Bad Boys gang during 1989-1990.

A chronology of the summer's events illustrates how quickly a once "model" society can turn into a place of fear and violence.

May 1991: A federal sting operation results in the arrest of two individuals for opium trafficking.

June 1991: The landlord begins evictions, apparently with the aim of controlling gang activity. In retaliation, the windows of the manager's apartment are shot out. No one is hurt or arrested.

June 1991: As a result of a gang-related dispute over a girl, a 39-year-old Mien man is stabbed to death across the street from the Polk Street Apartments.

June 1991: A Hmong man and four Mien juveniles are arrested for possession of a pipe bomb and an assault rifle in the complex. It turns out that the Hmong man had been ostracized from the Hmong community some time ago. Authorities have no idea why these boys would have use for a pipe bomb.

July 1991: A security company is hired by the management and posts a young Caucasian guard at the complex. On his second night, the man is hit on the head with a baseball bat. Three Mien and one Lao youth from another area are arrested. The crime was reported in progress by two Mien families, who called 911 and said that four youths were involved. These families were contacted by the police, who have their apartment numbers, but they refuse to talk. Police arrest four young men who are seen hanging around together, and find a broken and bloodied baseball bat in the bushes. After the victim recovers, he indicates that he saw one of the four arrested men shortly before being hit on the head. Otherwise, he remembers nothing. About this time, we begin to approach people to ask them if they would be willing to talk to us for this project. Oak Park Mien warn us away, saying that Polk Street has become a "bad place." Our sources also express satisfaction about the four who have been arrested and express the hope that they will all be put in jail for a "long, long time." We are also told that one of the perpetrators remains free.

July 1991: One Lao juvenile is arrested for the June murder. Lack of willing witnesses does not permit the investigation to go further.

August 1991: Charges are dismissed against three of the four defendants in the baseball bat case due to lack of evidence (see Appendix D). The fourth is released on $3,000 bail after the pretrial hearing. The defense attorney tells me that he will drag out the case on the remaining defendant as long as possible, and points out that the only actual legally admissible evidence against his client is the testimony of the victim, whose memory is questionable in the first place, due to the fact that he was subsequently hit on the head with a baseball bat. The victim did not see the defendant with the baseball bat, or with the others with whom he was arrested. The people who made the report in the first place refuse to testify.

August 1991: After a neighborhood watch program is conducted by the Sacramento County Sheriff's Department and a new security agency is hired—Freedom Security, which is owned and operated by ethnic Lao—the complex calms down. A representative of the Sheriff's Department expresses to us the belief that this security agency has better control over the complex than the previous agency. For the month of August, the complex is "quiet."

September 1991: After getting an introduction, I visit the Polk Street Apartments. PSB (Polk Street Boys) graffiti are present in one corner of the complex. However, when I talk to one of the elderly leaders, he indicates that the complex is calm. He and a friend of his credit Freedom Security, which they say is more effective because the company uses older men as guards, and not "children," like the 19-year-old man who was beaten with the baseball bat. Otherwise, they speak only in generalities. At the second house, the Lao youth we had been told to contact is away at school, but his sister gives us the phone number.

September 1991: A 39-year-old Caucasian woman is shot in the shoulder while sitting in her car after a dispute involving Mien members of the Polk Street Boys. We finally contact the Lao youth. He refuses to talk to us because "I don't know nothing about that stuff. . . . I just want to go to school. . . . When they [the gangs] ask me to come join them, I just tell them that I want to go to school."

The Baseball Bat Case

An Overzealous Prosecution or the Yankees at Bat?

*T*he case of *People v. Saephan et al.* (August 6, 1991) dominated relations between the Mien community and law enforcement in the summer of 1991. Within the Mien community, it cemented the perception that the police are "soft on crime," because three of the four suspects had the charges against them dropped and the fourth was released on bail. In effect, the defendants had already been tried and convicted in the court of Mien opinion before any court trial could take place.

The case also focused the law enforcement community's frustration with the Mien community. Two calls had been made to 911 to report the incident, but neither of the callers would agree to testify about the identity of the attackers in what was a particularly brutal case. As a consequence of their frustration, the prosecuting attorney and others involved in the case made a number of rather cynical references to the defendants being just a "poor baseball team" during court recesses.

The defense attorneys were able to take advantage of the mutual frustration between the potential Mien witnesses and the prosecution that in fact there was no evidence at all connecting the defendants to what they agreed was a brutal crime.

The following observations are based on my notes from the pretrial hearing, after which three of the four defendants were released for lack of evidence.

Account of Officer Parker, witness, sheriff's deputy for 13 years (July 12, 1991, early morning):

> 4930 Polk Street—two calls. Apartment 84 anonymous call to 911. Complainant says that Asian youths are beating up a security guard. Parker found the security guard about 12:45 a.m. The security guard (Zanotti) said that he had had a verbal confrontation with four Asians who had damaged a car. When Parker found Zanotti, the security guard was there leaning against car.

213

The officer asked Zanotti if the defendant Soumeng Saephan was involved. Zanotti said no, but Parker patted Saephan down anyway because of where his hands were being held.

Because of concern with gangs at Polk Street, Parker told Zanotti to stay near office the office of the building. Parker left at 1:00 a.m.

Parker returned at 2:07 a.m.. in response to another anonymous call, this one from Apartment 86. The caller said that a security guard was being beaten up.

The guard was found on Lenore Street about two blocks away from the complex by another sheriff's deputy. SSI, the security officer company that had employed Zanotti, actually found him. Zanotti had screamed for help over radio. SSI had responded and found him. The sheriff's deputy actually found Zanotti on a living room table. Zanotti told Parker that "guy you patted down earlier is the guy who did this." According to Parker, the only guy patted down earlier was Saephan.

All anonymous calls say that four Asian youths beat Zanotti with baseball bat and kicked him.

Zanotti—Saephan motioned for attack by tilting head? Belief of Zanotti. After motion of the head, was hit. Then lost consciousness momentarily. Woke up and saw Saephan kicking him.

Parker knew Saephan from numerous other calls to Apartment 104. For this reason, he parked by the telephone pole near 104. From there, he saw four Asian males standing in front of Apartment 104. When they saw Parker, they went inside of 104. Parker went and knocked on door, then went inside and saw four Asian youths sitting and watching TV. Made arrest. Broken bat found in complex. Only half found, and had blood stains.

Cross-examination of Parker and Zanotti for defense by Clinkenbeard:

Defendant (Saephan) had on New York Yankees shirt, blue. Blue baseball hat. Mr. Zanotti said that he didn't know who had the bat.

100% sure that Mr. Saephan kicked him. But that night, didn't mention about "nodding head." Nodding head only came up after discussion in office yesterday. Mr. Rodrigues, resident in Apartment 104, also in apartment during arrest.

Zanotti not sure of number of youths. Thought that there were four, maybe five guys in the gang.

References

Acuña, R. F. (1972). *Occupied America: The Chicano's struggle toward liberation.* San Francisco: Canfield.

Acuña, R. F. (1984). *A community under siege: A chronicle of Chicanos east of the Los Angeles River 1945-75* (Monograph No. 11). Los Angeles: Chicano Studies Research Center.

Allsup, C. (1982). *The American G.I. Forum: Origins and evolution.* Austin: University of Texas, Center for Mexican American Studies.

Arthurs, H. W. (1985). *Without the law: Administrative justice and legal pluralism in nineteenth century England.* Toronto: University of Toronto Press.

Balderrama, F. E. (1982). *In defense of La Raza: The Los Angeles Mexican consulate and the Mexican community, 1929 to 1936.* Tucson: University of Arizona Press.

Beach, W. G. (1932). *Oriental crime in California.* Stanford, CA: Stanford University Press.

Bean, Frank, & Swicegood, G. (1985). *Mexican-American fertility patterns.* Austin: University of Texas Press.

Bean, F., & Tienda, M. (1987). *The Hispanic population in the United States.* Newbury Park, CA: Sage.

Beers, D. (1993, July). The crash of blue sky California: The aerospace industry is dying and with it a way of life. *Harper's, 287,* 68-77.

Benda-Beckmann, F. von. (1988). Comment on Merry. *Law and Society Review, 22,* 897-900.

Bernstein, D. (1991, October 29). Prison for importing Thai drug: Only followed orders of elder, woman says. *Sacramento Bee,* p. B1.

Bogardus, E. S. (1934). *The Mexican in the United States.* Los Angeles: University of Southern California Press.

California State Attorney General. (1990). *Organized crime in California, 1989* (Annual Report to the California Legislature). Sacramento: California Department of Justice.

Caplan, N., Choy, M. H., & Whitmore, J. K. (1992, February). Indochinese refugee families and academic achievement. *Scientific American, 266,* 36-42.

Caplan, N., Whitmore, J. K., & Choy, M. H. (1989). *The boat people and achievement in America.* Ann Arbor: University of Michigan Press.

Carpenter, N. (1927). *Immigrants and their children 1920: A study based on census statistics relative to the foreign born and the native white of foreign or mixed parentage* (Monograph No. 7). Washington, DC: Government Printing Office.

Chin, K.-L. (1990). *Chinese subculture and criminality.* Westport, CT: Greenwood.

Chin, K.-L. (1996). *Chinatown gangs: Extortion, enterprise, and ethnicity.* New York: Oxford University Press.

Cohen, A. (1955). *Delinquent boys.* Glencoe, IL: Free Press.

Cohen, L. E., & Land, K. C. (1987). Age structure and crime. *American Sociological Review, 52,* 170-183.

Cummins, J. (1981). The role of primary language development in promoting educational success for language minority students. In C. F. Leyba (Ed.), *Schooling and language minority students: A theoretical framework* (pp. 3-50). Sacramento: California State Department of Education.

Dang Vang, Yia Moua, Yang Xiong, Maichao Vang v. Vang Xiong S. Toyed, No. 90-35354 CV-87-691-JLQ (U.S. Ct. App., 9th Cir., filed September 5, 1991).

Delbert, J., & Robinson, N. (1989). Chinatown's immigrant gangs: The new young warrior class. In H. M. Launer & J. E. Palenski (Eds.), *Crime and the new immigrants.* Springfield, IL: Charles C Thomas.

Dunn, E. (1976). American Molokans and Canadian Dukhobors: Economic position and ethnic identity. In F. Henry (Ed.), *Ethnicity in the Americas* (pp. 97-114). Paris: Mouton.

Dunn, S. P., & Dunn, E. (1978). Molokans in America. *Dialectical Anthropology, 3,* 349-360.

Easterlin, R. (1980). *Birth and fortune: The impact of numbers of personal welfare.* New York: Basic Books.

Eisenstadt, S. N. (1959). Delinquent group-formation among immigrant youth. In S. Glueck (Ed.), *The problem of delinquency* (pp. 201-208). Boston: Houghton Mifflin.

Empey, L. T. (1982). *American delinquency: Its meaning and construction.* Homewood, IL: Dorsey.

English, T. J. (1996). *Born to kill: America's most notorious Vietnamese gang and the changing face of organized crime.* New York: William Morrow.

Espinosa, K. E., & Massey, D. S. (1997). Determinants of English proficiency among Mexican migrants to the United States. *International Migration Review, 31,* 28-50.

Falk Moore, S. (1978). *Law as process: An anthropological approach.* London: Routledge & Kegan Paul.

Fitzpatrick, P. (1992). *The mythology of modern law.* London: Routledge.

Francis, R. D. (1981). *Migrant crime in Australia*. St. Lucia: University of Queensland Press.

Frazier, E. F. (1966). *The Negro family in the United States* (Rev. and abr. ed.). Chicago: University of Chicago Press.

Freed, D., & Jones, C. (1992, May 26). Blacks, Koreans seek conciliation. *Los Angeles Times*, pp. A1, A12.

Gamio, M. (1969a). *The lifestory of the Mexican*. New York: Dover. (Original work published 1931)

Gamio, M. (1969b). *Mexicans in the United States*. New York: Dover. (Original work published 1930)

Geertz, C. (1983). Local knowledge: Fact and law in comparative perspective. In C. Geertz, *Local knowledge: Further essays in interpretive anthropology*. New York: Basic Books.

Goffman, E. (1986). *Stigma: Notes on the management of spoiled identity*. New York: Simon & Schuster. (Original work published 1963)

Goldstone, J. (1991). *Revolution and rebellion in the early modern world*. Berkeley: University of California Press.

Gomez-Quiñones, J. (1994). *Roots of Chicano politics*. Albuquerque: University of New Mexico Press.

Gordon, L. (1990). The missing children: Mortality and fertility in a Southeast Asian refugee population. *International Migration Review, 23*, 219-237.

Gottfredson, M. R., & Hirschi, T. (1990). *A general theory of crime*. Stanford, CA: Stanford University Press.

Griffiths, B. (1948). *American me*. Boston: Houghton Mifflin.

Griffiths, J. (1986). What is legal pluralism? *Journal of Legal Pluralism, 24*, 1-57.

Gross, G. (1989). Crime and the new immigrants. In H. M. Launer & J. E. Palenski (Eds.), *Crime and the new immigrants*. Springfield, IL: Charles C Thomas.

Guttentag, M., & Secord, P. F. (1983). *Too many women? The sex ratio question*. Beverly Hills, CA: Sage.

Habarad, J. (1987). *Spirit and social order: The responsiveness of Lao Iu Mien history, religion and organization*. Unpublished doctoral dissertation, University of California, Berkeley.

Hamilton, G. G., & Waters, T. (1995). Economic organization and Chinese business networks in Thailand. In E. K. Y. Chen & P. Drysdale (Eds.), *Corporate links and direct foreign investment in Asia and Pacific* (pp. 87-111). Pymble, Australia: Harper Education.

Hamilton, G. G., & Waters, T. (1997). Ethnicity and capitalist development: The changing role of the Chinese in Thailand. In D. Chirot & A. Reid (Eds.), *Essential outsiders: Chinese and Jews in the modern transformation of Southeast Asia and Central Europe* (pp. 258-284). Seattle: University of Washington Press.

Hammond, R. (1991, April 2). Some call it rape. *Twin Cities Reader*.

Hardwick, S. W. (1993). *Russian refuge: Religion, migration, and settlement on the North Pacific rim*. Chicago: University of Chicago Press.

Hayner, N. (1942). Five cities of the Pacific Northwest. In C. R. Shaw & H. D. McKay, *Juvenile delinquency and urban areas: A study of rates of delinquents in relation to differential characteristics of local communities in American cities* (pp. 354-395). Chicago: University of Chicago Press.

Helzer, J. (1993). *Maintenance of ethnic identity: Hmong and Mien settlement and survival in Northern California.* Unpublished master's thesis, California State University, Chico.

Hirschi, T., & Gottfredson, M. R. (1994). *The generality of deviance.* New Brunswick, NJ: Transaction.

Horowitz, R. (1983). *Honor and the American dream: Culture and identity in a Chicano community.* New Brunswick, NJ: Rutgers University Press.

Huff, C. R. (1996). *Gangs in America* (2nd ed.). Thousand Oaks, CA: Sage.

Huntington, S. P. (1981). *American politics: The promise of disharmony.* Cambridge, MA: Belknap.

Hurh, W. M., & Kim, K. C. (1984). *Korean immigrants in America: A structural analysis of ethnic confinement and adhesive adaptation.* Rutherford, NJ: Fairleigh Dickinson University Press.

Hurh, W. M., & Kim, K. C. (1990). Religious participation of Korean immigrants in the United States. *Journal for the Scientific Study of Religion, 29,* 19-34.

Inciardi, J. A., Block, A. A., & Hallowell, L. A. (1977). *Historical approaches to crime: Research strategies and issues.* Beverly Hills, CA: Sage.

Jankowski, M. S. (1991). *Islands in the street: Gangs and American urban society.* Berkeley: University of California Press.

Johnson, J. (1997a, May 25). Surviving where a gang rules. *Los Angeles Times.*

Johnson, J. (1997b, May 28). Mistrust stymies efforts to battle blight. *Los Angeles Times.*

Johnson, J., & Cardenas, J. (1997, May 26). Orion Avenue's apartments become both refuge and jail. *Los Angeles Times.*

Johnson, J., & Cole, C. (1997, May 27). Gang life's grip proves hard to escape. *Los Angeles Times.*

Katz, J. (1988). *Seductions of crime: Moral and sensual attractions in doing evil.* New York: Basic Books.

Keefe, S., & Padilla, A. (1987). *Chicano ethnicity.* Albuquerque: University of New Mexico Press.

Kim, K. C., Hurh, W. M., & Kim, S. (1993). Generation differences in Korean immigrants' life conditions in the United States. *Sociological Perspectives, 36,* 257-270.

Klein, M. (1971). *Street gangs and street workers.* Englewood Cliffs, NJ: Prentice Hall.

Klein, M. (1995). *The American street gang: Its nature, prevalence, and control.* New York: Oxford University Press.

Launer, H. M., & Palenski, J. E. (Eds.). (1989). *Crime and the new immigrants.* Springfield, IL: Charles C Thomas.

Lee, P., & McMillan, P. (1992, May 27). Skepticism greets meeting between blacks, Koreans. *Los Angeles Times,* pp. A1, A13.

Light, I. (1974). From vice district to tourist attraction: The moral career of American Chinatowns 1880-1940. *Pacific Historical Review, 43,* 367-394.

Light, I. (1977). The ethnic vice industry 1880-1944, *American Sociological Review, 42,* 464-479.

Light, I., & Bonacich, E. (1988). *Immigrant entrepreneurs.* Berkeley: University of California Press.

Long, L. D. (1993). *Ban Vinai: The refugee camp.* New York: Columbia University Press.

Long, P. Du Phuoc, & Ricard, L. (1996). *The dream shattered: Vietnamese gangs in America.* Boston: Northeastern University Press.

Low, J. (1992). *Tiles of the mosaic: The ethnic, social and family backgrounds of freshmen entering UC Davis in fall 1991.* Davis: University of California, Student Affairs Research and Information.

Luhmann, N. (1985). *A sociological theory of law.* London: Routledge & Kegan Paul.

MacGill, H. G. (1938). The Oriental delinquent in Vancouver. *Sociology and Social Research, 22,* 428-438.

Magagnini, S. (1994a, February 6). Laotian Immigrants try to hold on to vanishing culture. *Sacramento Bee,* pp. B1, B4.

Magagnini, S. (1994b, February 1). Reign of terror hits more refugees: Home invaders rob, beat Mien family. *Sacramento Bee,* pp. A1, A12.

Magagnini, S. (1994c, January 24). Tips for Hmong to avert home invasions. *Sacramento Bee,* p. B4.

Marquez, B. (1993). *LULAC: The evolution of a Mexican American political organization.* Austin: University of Texas Press.

Massey, D., Alarcon, R., Durand, J., & Gonzales, H. (1985). *Return to Aztlan: The social process of international migration from western Mexico.* Berkeley: University of California Press.

McGrath, D. (1993, September 29). An oasis of hope in Meadowview's blight. *Sacramento Bee,* p. A2.

McGrath, R. D. (1984). *Gunfighters, highwaymen and vigilantes: Violence on the frontier.* Berkeley: University of California Press.

McWilliams, C. (1948). *North from Mexico: Spanish-speaking people in the United States.* Philadelphia: J. B. Lippincott.

Merry, S. E. (1986). Everyday understandings of the law in working-class America. *American Ethnologist, 13,* 253-270.

Merry, S. E. (1988). Legal pluralism. *Law and Society Review, 22,* 869-896.

Mertz, E. (Ed.). (1994). Community and identity in sociolegal studies [Special issue]. *Law and Society Review, 28*(5).

Mexican Fact-Finding Committee, State of California. (1930). *Mexicans in California.* San Francisco: Author.

Moore, J. (1975). *Final report: Community variations in Chicano ex-convict adaptations.* Los Angeles: University of California, Chicano Pinto Research Project.

Moore, J. (1991). *Going down to the barrio: Homeboys and homegirls in change.* Philadelphia: Temple University Press.

Moore-Howard, P. (1987). *The Hmong yesterday and today.* Unpublished manuscript, Sacramento City Unified School District.

Morawska, E. (1985). *For bread with butter: The lifeworlds of East Central Europeans in Johnstown, Pennsylvania.* New York: Cambridge University Press.

Morgan, P. A. (1990). The making of a public problem: Mexican labor in California and the marijuana law of 1937. In R. Glick & J. Moore (Eds.), *Drugs in Hispanic communities* (pp. 233-252). New Brunswick, NJ: Rutgers University Press.

National Crime Prevention Council. (1994). *Building and crossing bridges: Refugees and law enforcement working together.* Washington, DC: Author.

Nettler, G. (1984). *Explaining crime* (3rd ed.). New York: McGraw-Hill.

Padilla, F. M. (1992). *The gang as an American enterprise.* New Brunswick, NJ: Rutgers University Press.

Panunzio, C. (1942). Intermarriage in Los Angeles, 1924-33. *American Journal of Sociology, 47,* 690-701.

Pedraza, S., & Rumbaut, R. (Eds.). (1996). *Origins and destinies: Immigration, race and ethnicity in America.* Belmont, CA: Wadsworth.

Pospisil, L. (1971). *The anthropology of law: A comparative theory of law.* New York: Harper & Row.

Portes, A. (1995). Children of immigration: Segmented assimilation and its determinants. In A. Portes (Ed.), *The economic sociology of immigration: Essays on networks, ethnicity, and entrepreneurship* (pp. 248-280). New York: Russell Sage Foundation.

Portes, A., & Rumbaut, R. G. (1990). *Immigrant America: A portrait.* Berkeley: University of California Press.

Ragin, C. (1987). *The comparative method: Moving beyond quantitative and qualitative methods.* Berkeley: University of California Press.

Raspberry, W. (1993, July 15). Middlemen merchants, almost by definition, must be "foreign" to their customers. *Los Angeles Times,* p. B7.

Rios-Bustamente, A., & Castillo, P. (1986). *An illustrated history of Mexican Los Angeles 1781-1985.* Los Angeles: Chicano Studies Research Center.

Robison, S. M. (1958). A study of delinquency among Jewish children in New York City. In M. Sklare (Ed.), *The Jews: Social patterns of an American group* (pp. 535-541). Glencoe, IL: Free Press.

Rodriguez, L. (1993). *Always running: La vida loca.* Willimanitic, CT: Curbstone.

Romo, R. (1983). *East Los Angeles: History of a barrio.* Austin: University of Texas Press.

Rumbaut, R. G., & Weeks, J. R. (1986). Fertility and adaptation: Indochinese refugees in the United States. *International Migration Review, 20,* 428-466.

Sample, H. A. (1994, January 12). U.S. aid for state—dicey: Wilson plans need immigration funds. *Sacramento Bee,* p. A1.

Sanderson, J. P. (1856). *Republican landmarks: The views and opinions of American statesmen on foreign immigration, being a collection of statistics of population, crime, pauperism, etc.* Philadelphia: J. B. Lippincott.

Savitz, L. D. (1975). *Delinquency and migration.* San Francisco: R. & E. Research Associates.

Schneider, J. C. (1980). *Detroit and the problem of order, 1830-1880.* Lincoln: University of Nebraska Press.

Shaw, C. R., & McKay, H. D. (1942). *Juvenile delinquency and urban areas: A study of rates of delinquents in relation to differential characteristics of local communities in American cities.* Chicago: University of Chicago Press.

Shelden, R. G., Tracy, S. K., & Brown, W. B. (1997). *Youth gangs in American society.* Belmont, CA: Wadsworth.

Sherman, G. (1943, June 2). Youth gangs leading cause of delinquencies. *Los Angeles Times*, sec. I, p. 10.

Sherman, S. (1985, September 15). Lost tribes of the Central Valley. *San Francisco Chronicle-Examiner*, World section, p. 13.

Smith, M. P., & Tarallo, B. (1993). *California's changing faces.* Berkeley: University of California, California Policy Seminar.

Sokolov, L. (1918). *The Russians in Los Angeles* (Sociological Monograph No. 11). Los Angeles: University of Southern California Press.

Song, J. (1988). *No white feathered crows: Chinese immigrants and Vietnamese refugees' adaptation to American legal institutions.* Unpublished doctoral Dissertation, University of California, Irvine.

Sung, B. (1977). *Gangs in New York's Chinatown.* New York: City College of New York, Department of Asian Studies.

Sutherland, E. H., & Cressey, D. R. (1974). *Criminology* (9th ed.). Philadelphia: J. B. Lippincott.

Taft, D. R. (1936). Nationality and crime. *American Sociological Review, 1*, 724-736.

Tapp, N. (1988). *Sovereignty and rebellion: The white Hmong of northern Thailand.* Singapore: Oxford University Press.

Taylor, P. (1931). Mexicans. In Wickersham Commission (National Commission on Law Observance and Enforcement), *Report on crime and the foreign born.* Washington, DC: Government Printing Office.

Thomas, W. I., & Znaniecki, F. (1995). *The Polish peasant in Europe and America* (E. Zaretsky, Ed.). Champaign: University of Illinois Press. (Original work published 1920)

Thrasher, F. (1927). *The gang: A study of 1,313 gangs in Chicago.* Chicago: University of Chicago Press.

Thrasher, F. (1963). *The gang: A study of 1,313 gangs in Chicago* (Abr. ed.). Chicago: University of Chicago Press.

Time for sanity. (1943, June 11). *Los Angeles Times*, p. 1.

Tönnies, F. (1971). The place of birth of criminals in Schleswig-Holstein. In F. Tönnies, *On sociology: Pure, applied and empirical* (W. Cahnman &

R. Heberle, Eds.) (pp. 241-250). Chicago: University of Chicago Press. (Original work published 1929)

Toy, C. (1991). *Coming out and running with the boys: An analysis of Chinese gang participation.* Davis: University of California, Department of Sociology.

Tripp, M. W. (1980). *Russian routes: Origins and development of an ethnic community in San Francisco.* Unpublished master's thesis, San Francisco State University.

Truesdell, L. E. (1933). *Special report on foreign-born white families by country of birth of head, with an appendix giving statistics for Mexican, Indian, Chinese and Japanese Families (1930 Census).* Washington, DC: U.S. Department of Commerce, Bureau of the Census.

Truesdell, L. E. (1943). *Sixteenth census of the United States: 1940. Population, nativity and parentage of the white population, general characteristics, age, marital status, and education for states and large cities.* Washington, DC: Government Printing Office.

Vansina, J. (1991). *Paths in the rainforest.* Madison: University of Wisconsin Press.

Van Vechten, C. C. (1942). The criminality of the foreign born. *Journal of Criminal Law and Criminology, 32,* 139-147.

Vernez, G. (1993). Mexican labor in California's economy: From rapid growth to likely stability. In A. F. Lowenthal & K. Burgess (Eds.), *The California-Mexico connection.* Stanford, CA: Stanford University Press.

Vigil, J. D. (1989). *Barrio gangs: Street life and identity in Southern California.* Austin: University of Texas Press.

Visher, C., Lattimore, P. K., & Linster, R. L. (1991). Predicting the recidivism of serious youthful offenders using survival models. *Criminology, 29,* 329-366.

Vold, G. B., & Bernard, T. J. (1986). *Theoretical criminology* (3rd ed.). New York: Oxford University Press.

Voss, H. L. (1966). Socio-economic status and reported delinquent behavior. *Social Problems, 13,* 314-324.

Waters, M. (1990). *Ethnic options.* Berkeley: University of California Press.

Waters, T. (1990). Adaptation and migration among the Mien peoples of Southeast Asia. *Ethnic Groups, 8,* 127-141.

Waters, T. [A. E. Waters]. (1995a). *Crimes of passage: The socialization of youth in immigrant communities.* Unpublished doctoral dissertation, University of California, Davis, Department of Sociology.

Waters, T. (1995b). Towards a theory of ethnic enclave formation: The case of ethnic Germans in Russia and North America. *International Migration Review, 29,* 515-544.

Waters, T. (1996). The demographics of the Rwanda crisis, or why current voluntary repatriation policies will not solve Tanzania's (or Zaire's) refugee crisis. *Journal of Humanitarian Affairs* [On-line]. Available: http://131.111.106.147/Articles/A019.Htm

Waters, T., & Cohen, L. E. (1993). *Laotians in the criminal justice system* (Working paper). Berkeley: University of California, California Policy Seminar.

Whyte, W. F. (1943). *Street corner society: The social structure of an Italian slum.* Chicago: University of Chicago Press.

Whyte, W. F. (1993). *Street corner society: The social structure of an Italian slum* (4th ed.). Chicago: University of Chicago Press.

Wickersham Commission (National Commission on Law Observance and Enforcement). (1931). *Report on crime and the foreign born.* Washington, DC: Government Printing Office.

Williams, R. (1964). *Strangers next door: Ethnic relations in American communities.* Englewood Cliffs, NJ: Prentice Hall.

Young, P. (1932). *The pilgrims of Russian-Town.* Chicago: University of Chicago Press.

Zoot suit war. (1943, June 21). *Time,* pp. 18-19.

Index

About the Author

Tony Waters is Assistant Professor at California State University, Chico. He earned his PhD in sociology at the University of California, Davis, in 1995. From 1980 to 1983, he was a Peace Corps volunteer and refugee camp worker in Thailand, where he learned to speak Thai and Lao. Since then, he has remained in contact on a social level with Laotian refugees living in Northern California; some of the data collected for this book are a result of these continuing contacts. He has published articles about Southeast Asian refugees in Thailand and the United States in *Ethnic Groups* and *Disasters*, and is coauthor (with Lawrence E. Cohen) of a California Policy Seminar working paper titled *Laotians in the Criminal Justice System*. His recent publications have focused on issues of refugees and development in Tanzania, where he worked on the Burundi and Rwanda borders in 1984-1987 and 1994-1996. His articles about development and refugees in Tanzania have appeared in *African Studies Review*, *Journal of Modern African Studies*, *Disasters*, and other journals. His current scholarly interests are focused on developing undergraduate courses at CSU Chico in criminology, macro-sociology, and sociology of Southeast Asia. He is also writing a book about the sociology of refugee relief operations based on his experiences in Tanzania.